EDUCATION, POLITICS, AND PUBLIC LIFE

Series Editors:
Henry A. Giroux, McMaster University
Susan Searls Giroux, McMaster University

Within the last three decades, education as a political, moral, and ideological practice has become central to rethinking not only the role of public and higher education, but also the emergence of pedagogical sites outside of the schools—which include but are not limited to the Internet, television, film, magazines, and the media of print culture. Education as both a form of schooling and public pedagogy reaches into every aspect of political, economic, and social life. What is particularly important in this highly interdisciplinary and politically nuanced view of education are a number of issues that now connect learning to social change, the operations of democratic public life, and the formation of critically engaged individual and social agents. At the center of this series will be questions regarding what young people, adults, academics, artists, and cultural workers need to know to be able to live in an inclusive and just democracy and what it would mean to develop institutional capacities to reintroduce politics and public commitment into everyday life. Books in this series aim to play a vital role in rethinking the entire project of the related themes of politics, democratic struggles, and critical education within the global public sphere.

SERIES EDITORS:

HENRY A. GIROUX holds the Global TV Network Chair in English and Cultural Studies at McMaster University in Canada. He is on the editorial and advisory boards of numerous national and international scholarly journals.

Professor Giroux was selected as a Kappa Delta Pi Laureate in 1998 and was the recipient of a Getty Research Institute Visiting Scholar Award in 1999. He was the recipient of the Hooker Distinguished Professor Award for 2001. He received an Honorary Doctorate of Letters from Memorial University of Newfoundland in 2005. His most recent books include Take Back Higher Education (coauthored with Susan Searls Giroux, 2006), America on the Edge (2006), Beyond the Spectacle of Terrorism (2006), Stormy Weather: Katrina and the Politics of Disposability (2006), The University in Chains: Confronting the Military-Industrial-Academic Complex (2007), and Against the Terror of Neoliberalism: Politics Beyond the Age of Greed (2008).

SUSAN SEARLS GIROUX is associate professor of English and Cultural Studies at McMaster University. Her most recent books include The Theory Toolbox (coauthored with Jeff Nealon, 2004), Take Back Higher Education (coauthored with Henry A. Giroux, 2006), and Between Race and Reason: Violence, Intellectual Responsibility, and the University to Come (2010). Professor Giroux is also the managing editor of The Review of Education, Pedagogy, and Cultural Studies.

Critical Pedagogy in Uncertain Times: Hope and Possibilities
Edited by Sheila L. Macrine

The Gift of Education: Public Education and Venture Philanthropy
Kenneth J. Saltman

Feminist Theory in Pursuit of the Public: Women and the "Re-Privatization" of Labor
Robin Truth Goodman

Hollywood's Exploited: Public Pedagogy, Corporate Movies, and Cultural Crisis
Edited by Benjamin Frymer, Tony Kashani, Anthony J. Nocella, II, and Richard Van Heertum; Foreword by Lawrence Grossberg

Education Out of Bounds: Reimagining Cultural Studies for a Posthuman Age
Tyson E. Lewis and Richard Kahn

Academic Freedom in the Post-9/11 Era
Edited by Edward J. Carvalho and David B. Downing

Educating Youth for a World beyond Violence: A Pedagogy for Peace
H. Svi Shapiro

Rituals and Student Identity in Education: Ritual Critique for a New Pedagogy
Richard A. Quantz with Terry O'Connor and Peter Magolda

Citizen Youth: Culture, Activism, and Agency in a Neoliberal Era
Jacqueline Kennelly

Conflicts in Curriculum Theory: Challenging Hegemonic Epistemologies
João M. Paraskeva; Foreword by Donaldo Macedo

Sport, Spectacle, and NASCAR Nation: Consumption and the Cultural Politics of Neoliberalism
Joshua I. Newman and Michael D. Giardina

America According to Colbert: Satire as Public Pedagogy
Sophia A. McClennen

Immigration and the Challenge of Education: A Social Drama Analysis in South Central Los Angeles
Nathalia E. Jaramillo

Education as Civic Engagement: Toward a More Democratic Society
Edited by Gary A. Olson and Lynn Worsham

Why Higher Education Should Have a Leftist Bias
Donald Lazere

Corporate Humanities in Higher Education: Moving Beyond the Neoliberal Academy
Jeffrey R. Di Leo

Corporate Humanities in Higher Education

Moving Beyond the Neoliberal Academy

Jeffrey R. Di Leo

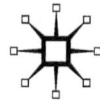

CORPORATE HUMANITIES IN HIGHER EDUCATION
Copyright © Jeffrey R. Di Leo, 2013.

All rights reserved.

First published in 2013 by
PALGRAVE MACMILLAN®
in the United States—a division of St. Martin's Press LLC,
175 Fifth Avenue, New York, NY 10010.

Where this book is distributed in the UK, Europe and the rest of the world, this is by Palgrave Macmillan, a division of Macmillan Publishers Limited, registered in England, company number 785998, of Houndmills, Basingstoke, Hampshire RG21 6XS.

Palgrave Macmillan is the global academic imprint of the above companies and has companies and representatives throughout the world.

Palgrave® and Macmillan® are registered trademarks in the United States, the United Kingdom, Europe and other countries.

ISBN: 978–1–137–36461–6

Library of Congress Cataloging-in-Publication Data

Di Leo, Jeffrey R.
  Corporate humanities in higher education : moving beyond the neoliberal academy / Jeffrey R. Di Leo.
    pages cm.—(Education, politics, and public life)
  Includes bibliographical references and index.
  ISBN 978–1–137–36461–6 (hardback)
  1. Education, Humanistic—United States. 2. Universities and colleges—United States. I. Title.

LC1023.D55 2013
370.11′2—dc23   2013027034

A catalogue record of the book is available from the British Library.

Design by Newgen Knowledge Works (P) Ltd., Chennai, India

First edition: December 2013

10 9 8 7 6 5 4 3 2 1

Contents

Acknowledgments		vii
Introduction		ix
1	Corporate Literature	1
2	Humanities, Inc.	13
3	Paralogical Inquiry	27
4	Apocalyptic Fear	45
5	Critical Affiliations	57
6	Wrangling with Rank	71
7	Authorial Prestige	89
8	The Publishing Market	105
9	The Junkyard of Ideas	121
Coda		133
Notes		137
Bibliography		165
About the Author		175
Index		177

Acknowledgments

My primary debt of gratitude goes out to Henry Giroux whose work on the politics of higher education is a model of engaged and committed scholarship. I have benefited greatly from the many books and essays that he has shared with me over the years—and deeply admire the unflinching power of his writing. I am honored and proud to be contributing to the series that he and Susan Searls-Giroux edit for Palgrave Macmillan.

I would also like to single out a number of colleagues whose timely suggestions and insightful conversations have challenged and inspired me in various ways: R. M. Berry, Michael Bérubé, Ron Bogue, Terry Caesar, Bud Fairlamb, William Germano, Dagoberto Gilb, Evan R. Goldstein, Robin Truth Goodman, Scott Jaschik, Charles Johnson, Vincent Leitch, Sophia McClennen, Ethelbert Miller, Paul Allen Miller, Christian Moraru, Jeffrey Nealon, Sharon O'Dair, Brian O'Keefe, Marjorie Perloff, Danny Postel, Kyle Schlesinger, Nicole Simek, James Sosnoski, Steve Tomasula, Joseph Urgo, Tom Williams, Jeffrey J. Williams, and Zahi Zalloua.

A special note of appreciation also goes out to Keri Farnsworth for her editorial assistance and to David Felts for his work on the index.

And finally, as always, I would like to thank my wife, Nina, for her unfailing encouragement, support, and patience.

Introduction

Neoliberalism is recalibrating academic identity. The paradigmatic neoliberal academic is a docile one. He is the product of an academic culture dominated by the recording and measurement of performance, rather than the pursuit of academic freedom or critical exchange—an academic climate that renders him risk averse and compliant.[1] Neoliberal managerialism constructs and functions through manageable and accommodating subjects. These docile neoliberal subjects excel when they "follow the rules" regarding say "outcomes-based curricula" and the "culture of continuous improvement," but risk failure when they begin to question the neoliberal academic practices to which they are subjected.

The freedom to question and to explore subjects wherever they may lead is the heart of a healthy academy—and the soul of academic freedom. The reinforcement of faculty and student subjectivities that are passive, docile, compliant, and submissive may be suitable for vocational training centers—which seem to be the telos of neoliberal academe—but are not acceptable in a vision of higher education wherein dialogue and critique are championed. The ability to challenge authority and to think critically about all aspects of society and culture, including academic culture, is absolutely necessary for higher education to flourish—without this ability, higher education flounders.

The docile academic subjects privileged by neoliberal academic culture are the products an authoritarian ideology that is an anathema to both the liberal arts in particular and academe in general. The active or engaged academic is necessary not only for progressive education to occur, but also for the academy to engage in democratic education, that is, education that supports critical citizenship and progressive values. Nevertheless, in spite of its centrality to the performance of neoliberal academe, this docile academic subject was not its formative subject. Rather, the formative subject of neoliberal academe was a far more active one.

The promise (or illusion) of neoliberalism was that it would allow everyone the opportunity to be a shareholder, an owner, and an entrepreneur.[2] The rise of the information and knowledge society over the past 40 years afforded academe an unprecedented vantage point within this new economy—an economy derived in large measure through neoliberal policies. As knowledge production and information dissemination is an integral part of academe, it emerged as a major stakeholder in this new economy. However, this new economy is quickly fading away and being replaced by a much more vicious one: the debt economy.

Like its predecessor, the knowledge economy, the debt economy is a derivation of neoliberal policies, and, as such, is very difficult to both avoid and fight. "Neo-liberal discourse is not like others," warns the French sociologist and philosopher Pierre Bourdieu. "Like psychiatric discourse in the asylum, as described by Erving Goffman," comments Bourdieu, "it is a 'strong discourse' which is so strong and so hard to fight because it has behind it all the powers of a world of power relations which it helps to make as it is, in particular by orienting the economic choices of those who dominate economic relations and so adding its own specifically symbolic-force to those power relations."[3] But just as the neoliberal economy is not absolute, so too are the identities and relations associated with it not absolute.

The "indebted man"[4] that emerges out of the intensification of neoliberalism is the docile subject of academe. However, the earlier illusions of neoliberalism led us previously to believe that the neoliberal man was an entrepreneurial one. Recall the images of the entrepreneurial man as a creative visionary and an independent worker who was proud of being his own boss and aggressively leading academe through the marketplace of ideas. This illusion ended when the dot-com bubble burst in 2000, and officially gave way to the debt economy with the financial collapse of 2008. But old habits are hard to break.

We still see colleges and universities partaking of neoliberalism's entrepreneurial apple in their frequent calls for management that are "entrepreneurial" in spite of the association of these identities with neoliberal managerialism. What makes the emergence of the "indebted man" out of the grave of the "entrepreneurial man" so scary though is that while the latter at least held promise—even if it turned out to be snake oil—the former is completely bereft of hope.

Neoliberalism's indebted man only brings despair. He is the return of the existential man who was both responsible for his freedom and—in turn—guilty for his fate.⁵ All of his actions are carefully monitored, measured, and assessed so that he knows exactly the limits of his freedom and the scope of his guilt—or, more appropriately, the limits of his credit and the range of his debt. However, unlike the existential man whose "hell" was other people, the indebted man's hell are his creditors, or more precisely, his debt. In fact, his entire social existence is defined by it.

Unlike his predecessor, the entrepreneurial man, whose social existence was defined by economic and/or social exchange, the indebted man's social existence is demarcated by debt, or, alternately, credit. For neoliberalism's entrepreneurial man, equality of exchange was the groundwork of his identity. Economic and symbolic exchange for him was predicated on some notion of equality. Such, however, is not the case for the indebted man—a type of existence wherein equality (and symmetry) of exchange has given way to the inequalities (and asymmetries) of the debt–credit relationship.

If one is concerned with the infection of academe by neoliberalism, then it will be difficult to avoid consideration of how the concept of neoliberalism's indebted man refigures academic identity and the relationship among members of the academy both with each other and with the emergent debt economy. It would certainly be helpful if there were some clear and distinct theoretical tools and vocabulary both for the economy of debt and its resultant ethics, but unfortunately there are none. This makes the task of identifying the emergent "indebted academic," the newest and latest modulation of neoliberalism in academe, all the more challenging. So, what can we expect from academe in the age of debt? And, more particularly, what is the identity of the indebted academic—and how will he critically function—within academe's emergent debt economy?

Critical Debt

At the manifest level, deepening student debt is one of the principal results of neoliberal policies in academe. Since the mid-1970s, neoliberal policies have transformed the financing structure of welfare state spending. Instead of central banks coining money to ease public debt, neoliberal policies promote appeal to financial markets to deal with increasing debt. This means that in practice debtors such as our students now find it necessary to rely on private creditors and to "submit to the conditions dictated by shareholders, bondholders, and the other owners of securities."⁶ These students form the groundwork of indebted academe—and are its most repulsive consequence.

The indebted condition of students compels increasing numbers of them to see higher education as a means of getting out of debt—and not as a means to getting an education. The circle here is vicious: by going to college, students get themselves into debt. This, in turn, leads them to see education only as a way to get themselves out of debt. Given the vicious circle of student debt, it is not surprising that many of them choose to use their "credit" hours toward more vocationally based majors where it is believed that the odds of being able to repay their student debt more quickly are higher.

All of this student debt then comes to roost on the house of higher education. It has produced an academic environment wherein higher education is viewed as having an economically driven, or, more specifically, debt-driven, rather than an educationally driven mission, an environment wherein decisions about higher education and its practices, policies, and mission are determined by the debt–credit relationship, and not by the production of knowledge and reproduction of democratic values.

The neoliberal academy in the age of debt literally views students as "credit hours," that is, potential sources of debt from which the academy may profit by being "lenders" or extending these students "credit." It recognizes that these students are faced with choices in the marketplace for education and encourages institutions of higher education to compete with each other for their debt. In this environment, measurement and ranking of things like reputation, student satisfaction, and graduation rates come to have a major role in educational practices and policies. Moreover, they have become directly related to the allocation of resources and acquisition of funding.

Completely lost in this vision of higher education as driven by debt and market mechanisms is the notion of education as a public good that is supported by the state. This has led to a decrease in state support for public education and its increased privatization. In this "post welfare-state" environment,[7] student debt has reached epidemic proportions, and higher education has been compelled to forge closer ties with industry—and anything else that can bring in revenue. "Under neoliberalism," writes Henry Giroux, "everything either is for sale or is plundered for profit."[8] This includes, of course, higher education, upon whose house neoliberalism has become a scourge[9]—and the rise of the debt economy is only aggravating the situation.

Caught in the crosshairs of a situation not of our choosing or making are those of us who work in higher education and who do not see it as fundamentally driven by finance. Nonetheless, the debt economy has now become our economy. We participate in it by working for institutions that sustain it and teaching students that suffer from it. So what do we do?

In this debt climate, a major part of our job is to make this economy clearly and distinctly visible, and to wrest it from power. Debt is at the center of neoliberal politics, and consequently, central to understanding and combating neoliberalism. Critically engaging debt in our scholarship and classroom praxis is vital for wresting the stranglehold of neoliberalism from our universities. However, this task is complicated because, as noted earlier, the subjectivities privileged in neoliberal academe are docile and risk averse—and these will not be the characteristics of those who work to undermine neoliberalism in academe.[10]

Critically engaging the performance paradigms of neoliberal academe is not for the fainthearted—or perhaps even the nontenured. Protecting our students—and ourselves—as much as possible from the negative consequences of participating in neoliberal academe is found in both acts of resistance—*and* acts of *vision*. One of our specific tasks is to help our students understand the lure of the entrepreneurial man and his connections with neoliberalism; to help them understand the double meanings of "interest" and "credit," namely, how they allow debt interest to determine intellectual interest, and how academic "credit" is linked to sustaining a debt–credit economy.

In this vicious climate, the indebted academic should not be blamed for losing all hope. It has been said that credit is "one of the most effective instruments of exploitation man has managed to create, since certain people, by producing credit, are able to appropriate the labor and wealth of others."[11] Whereas neoliberalism's entrepreneurial man held out the promise of profit, the indebted man only offers the perils of debt—entrepreneurial vision has morphed into indebted blindness. The labor and wealth of academe has been squandered—and we are now left to pick up the pieces with what little time and resources neoliberal academe affords us.

However, we know that "neo-liberalism is a very smart and very modern repackaging of the oldest ideas of the oldest capitalist."[12] We also know that it is very dangerous too. It has been called "an ideology and politic buoyed by the spirit of a market fundamentalism that subordinates the art of democratic politics to the rapacious laws of a market economy that expands its reach to include all aspects of social life within the dictates and values of a market driven society."[13] But how do we make visible something like the debt economy when theoretically we barely have a conceptual hold on it? I think that this can be done by going back to the larger frame of the consequences of neoliberalism in academe, and asking what these have contributed to the educational mission of the university—asking whether the emergence of the debt economy is something that has benefited or harmed students, faculty, and society. Few will be surprised to learn from this exercise that the consequences of neoliberalism in academe have primarily been harmful to those who are supposed to be the primary beneficiaries of higher education, namely, students, faculty, and society.

Looking back now with students and others at the plundering of higher education by neoliberalism's entrepreneurial man becomes an object lesson in the terror of neoliberalism. Where the entrepreneurial academic saw profit and sales, the indebted academic now sees only credit and debt. Gone too is the notion that higher education still trades on equalities of exchange and is fundamentally fair to all. The debt economy is one of continuous economic inequality and asymmetry. All profits gained by the entrepreneurial man are now seen by the indebted man as merely loans generated through credit. The myth of exchange is replaced by the existence of debt.

The debt economy now becomes an excuse to prolong and intensify the neoliberal agenda. In many states, this amounts to reclaiming state education through accountability and austerity measures. In many others, it means expanding the privatization of higher education by passing along the cost and debt of education to students. For the indebted man, these actions come with a specific type of moral psychology, namely, one wherein the indebted is always already guilty or at fault for their debt.

The power of debt is that it frees one to honor their debt. Like Socrates who on his final day felt the need to settle his debts, we too absorb the freedom to repay our debts, which may in fact occupy the entirety of our adult life,[14] or better yet, our existence.[15] Just like the cars and homes we buy on credit, so too is our education—acquired on credit—and in debt. One of the many tragedies of credit-card education is the erosion of the humanities and critical thinking.

As the neoliberal academy grows in power and influence, the humanities decrease by the same measure. Unlike Socrates whose humanities left him enough to repay his debts upon his death, the humanities of the university in the age of debt do not. Moving beyond the neoliberal academy though may not be as easy as simply paying our debts or returning to its predecessor—but it certainly will not be as difficult as trying to function as an academic committed to critical inquiry, social justice, and democratic education in the age of neoliberalism.

Critical inquiry, social justice, and democratic education are antithetical to neoliberal academe. Pursuit of them is a form of debt accumulation for each moves counter to the performative telos of neoliberal education and against the grain of neoliberal academic identity. However, to acquire and function through debt in this way is not the same as a student owing monetary capital to a financial institution, but it is no less reprehensible as the loss of critical and intellectual capital cuts to the heart of academic freedom—"the right to teach what one believes, to espouse unpopular academic and non-academic causes, to act upon knowledge and ideas as one perceives them without fear of retribution from anyone."[16] Pursuit of critical thinking, social justice, and democratic education are only possible by functioning outside of the parameters of neoliberal academe as pursuit of each works against the ends of neoliberalism.

The indebted academic is in large part characterized by the limits placed on his critical freedom in neoliberal academe. These limits are determined by the performance measures and outcomes assessments that determine and delimit his existence in academe. The difference between his critical aspirations and what is expected of him in neoliberal academe might be regarded as his "critical debt." In a pre-neoliberal version of academe, critical debt might have been thought of as a type of moral obligation, that is, what is owed to others for one's critical contributions. However, in neoliberal academe, critical debt is about intellectual shortcoming, that is, what critically is lost through our participation in neoliberal academe. This is, of course, an ethical problem too as it cuts against our ability to pursue our critical vision or academic freedom wherever it may lead. Debt as the basis of academe recalibrates academic identity such that even one of our most basic functions, critical thinking, becomes an exercise in debt accumulation—and a fundamentally punitive activity. Question is, how much critical debt must we acquire before we deem academe itself bankrupt?

Reveal, Resist, Remove

In the spirit of two inspiring books, Bourdieu's *Acts of Resistance: Against the New Myths of Our Time* (1998), a book that aims to "provide useful weapons to all those who are striving to resist" neoliberalism, and Henry Giroux's *The Terror of Neoliberalism: Authoritarianism and the Eclipse of Democracy* (2004), a book that aims to makes it visible, critically engage it, and remove it from power, this book aims to reveal and critically engage its presence in the humanities with the ultimate aim of providing strategies for resistance and removal. There is no more urgent task currently facing the humanities in particular and higher education in general than dealing with the consequences of neoliberalism in academe.

However, it is important to remember that neoliberalism is not *only* a problem in academe, but also for many other aspects of society and the world. "Public lands are looted by logging companies and corporate ranchers; politicians willingly hand the public's airwaves over to broadcasters and large corporate interests without a dime going into the public trust; Halliburton gives war profiteering a new meaning as it is granted corporate contracts without any competitive bidding and then bilks the US government for millions; the environment is polluted and despoiled in the name of profit making just as the government passes legislation to make it easier for corporations to do so; public services are gutted in order to lower the taxes of major corporations; schools increasingly resemble malls or jails, and teachers, forced to raise revenue for classroom materials, increasingly function as circus barkers hawking everything from hamburgers to pizza parties," laments Giroux, "—that is, when they are not reduced to prepping students to get higher test scores."[17] As such, the problems brought about in academe as a result of neoliberal practices are but a slice of a much larger set of problems caused worldwide by it.[18] Still, regardless of this fact, these problems are no less significant: for those of us in academe who do not believe in teaching for the test or viewing students as customers, the corporate environment of higher education has become a threat to our academic identities and the very culture that sustains them.

Corporate Humanities in Higher Education puts forth the following questions: How do we *critically* function as academics in an environment where extreme free market capitalism has become the driving force of higher education? How do the humanities crumble under the knife of neoliberalism and vocational training? How do we speak with our colleagues and students in this environment? How do we write about each other in this environment? How do we value what we write as academics in this environment? How should we regard the aim of the humanities in general in the age of neoliberalism? Responses to these questions and related ones get at the core of how we function as academics within the neoliberal academy. They reveal key aspects of the character of academic identity in an educational culture dominated by market mechanisms and managerial control. Responses to these questions also lends support to a few fundamental theses about neoliberalism in academe.

Thesis One—Neoliberalism in Higher Education Is a Bad Thing

Overall, this claim is fairly straightforward until one qualifies it with "—even though the marketplace for ideas is not." As much as it would be easier to avoid this qualifier, it would not be true. As I have pointed out elsewhere, academe is often characterized as an *oasis* from the market-driven forces of the public–private sector.[19] Within the academy, ideas are many times said to be pursued without regard to their market value by individuals dedicated to the life of the mind, and students and teachers often enjoy in academe a reprieve from the pressure to conform their practices to the requirements of "cash value" or "public sentiment." While this "market-free" vision of the academy may be its ideal, it has never really existed. Academe is and has always been a type of marketplace or site where knowledge is disseminated, discovered, and debated, and academic values are directly linked to these knowledge-driven practices within this marketplace. While it may bother some to regard academe as a marketplace of ideas, particularly when one sees the damaging effects of academe through the lens of an extreme free market philosophy, there is a difference between the two—and it is not trivial or unsubstantial. *Extreme* free market capitalism as the determinate of higher educational policy, practice, and values *is* a bad thing, but not all uses of the market in academic decision making.

Thesis Two—Neoliberalism Threatens to Turn Academics into Docile Subjects

This damaging dimension of neoliberal academic culture is an important one even if it is one that is not widely acknowledged or discussed. One of the few to recognize this is Joëlle Fanghanel in her recent study, *Being an Academic* (2012), where she notes that compliance with neoliberal academic culture can be seen as "reinforcing the notion that the neoliberal agenda renders academics risk averse or "docile neoliberal subject[s]."[20] Again, as noted earlier, instead of pursuing academic freedom or teaching to transgress, the paradigmatic neoliberal subject is caught up in an academic culture that revolves around the measurement and assessment of performance, that is, academic accounting rather than intellectual agency. It is interesting to note that at the macro-level of institutions, neoliberalism creates an environment of competition, whereas at the micro-level of individuals within those competitive institutions, neoliberalism constructs and functions through manageable and compliant subjects. Rule-following behavior, particularly in the pursuit of predetermined curricular learning outcomes within a culture of measurement and assessment, affords the docile neoliberal subject many opportunities for achievement and success. However, scrutiny and failure are the consequences of academic behavior that goes against the norms of neoliberal practice.

Thesis Three—Docile Academic Subjects Are a Bad Thing

At its very best, the academy is a place where any and all topics may be pursued by individuals vested with the freedom to take this inquiry wherever it may lead. Knowledge production and intellectual inquiry require faculty and student subjectivities that are active, forceful, resistant, and assertive. The passive, docile, compliant, and submissive characteristics favored by neoliberal academic culture are more suited to vocational training and information dissemination, rather than intellectual inquiry and academic agency. The freedom to think critically about all aspects of society and culture, including the academic culture within which one participates, is vital to a progressive vision of higher education. The capacity to challenge authority comes from academic subjects who are active and engaged. The docility of the neoliberal academic subject has at its source an authoritarian ideology that is the scourge of both the liberal arts in particular and the academy in general. Progressive and democratic education requires academic subjects that are active and engaged—without them it flounders.

Whether or not one agrees with all three theses, it is important to foreground them at the outset as they provide a stage for the various interventions in this book. Roughly speaking, the first two chapters, "Corporate Literature" and "Humanities, Inc.," take up Thesis One; the third and fourth chapters, "Paralogical Inquiry" and "Apocalyptic Fear," take up Thesis Two; and the fifth chapter, "Critical Affiliations," takes up Thesis Three. The final four chapters return to the first thesis, but with a twist as each deals with a different negative aspect of neoliberalism in scholarly practice in the humanities. Chapter 6 ("Wrangling with Rank") looks at the shortcomings of neoliberalism's emphasis on rank as applied to academic journals; chapter 7 ("Authorial Prestige") examines how the neoliberal value of prestige undermines poststructuralism's "death of the author"; chapter 8 ("The Publishing Market) discusses how neoliberalism—in spite of its emphasis on the market—has, in fact, shrunken the publishing market; and chapter 9 ("The Junkyard of Ideas") considers how the neoliberal value of productivity in academe increases the quantity of academic publications—while at the same time establishes their "obsolescence" or "disposability."

The reason the final four chapters deal with neoliberalism in scholarly publishing in the humanities is that this is one of the more publicly accessible faces of academic culture. Academic journals circulate and are produced both inside and outside of academe; books published by academics are also part of a production and distribution industry that extends from within academe (e.g., university presses) to outside of it (e.g., multinational publishing corporations and independent small presses); and, finally, the products of our academic labors—be they reviews, articles, essays, books, and so on—are academic culture's most lasting and public aspect. Whereas the first five chapters deal more with internal dimensions of academic culture (e.g., how we talk to each other within the academy), the latter four chapters take up some of the more external dimensions of academic culture.

Be that as it may, the circuit of culture does not lend itself well to an internal/external distinction—even when applied to the academe's supposed "ivory tower." Following the work of the former directors of the Birmingham Center for Contemporary Cultural Studies, Richard Johnson and Stuart Hall, the circuit of culture involves how the cultural artifact is articulated (representation), what social identities are associated with it (identity), how it is produced (production), how it is consumed (consumption), and what mechanisms regulate its distribution and use (regulation). On this model of cultural studies, the beginnings of an explanation of the meaning of cultural artifacts are found in the articulation of these processes and none of the processes are privileged. In order to explain adequately the meaning an artifact comes to possess, the various combinations of these processes must be explored. To be sure, the articulation of these processes can and does lead to variable and contingent outcomes.[21] It is for this reason that any consideration of academic culture is a slippery and messy business.

The title of this book, *Corporate Humanities in Higher Education*, alludes to the Janus-faced nature of academe today: one face is that of the corporate university with its increasingly extreme emphasis on a neoliberal management philosophy coupled with vocational training; the other face is that of a humanities with roots in the philosophy, literature, and history of Greek antiquity. As the neoliberal academy grows in power and influence, the humanities seem to decrease by the same measure. This presents a serious problem for humanists, namely, how does one function in an academy that values critical inquiry into the humanities less and less? And what does this mean for the future of the humanities in the neoliberal academy? How does one speak for and from the humanities in this academic environment?

Corporate Humanities in Higher Education proposes that working in the humanities in a neoliberal age requires us to be even better at what we do best, namely, providing critical insight on each others' work and valuing our contributions for the ways in which they advance critical dialogue within the academy, rather than stifle it. It is in this spirit that the works of a number of prominent humanists writing in America today—people such as Martha Nussbaum, Louis Menand, Frank Donoghue, and others—are engaged in this book.

On the one hand, their contributions should be valued for their efforts to identify and respond to the challenges facing the humanities today. These efforts should also be as widely disseminated and discussed as possible—and it for this reason that care is taken to review and represent their arguments as fully as possible. They are the stars and public faces of our profession, and what they have to say about the humanities is well worth our time and attention. Their arguments also represent major branches of response to the crisis in the humanities. And while for some it may be preferable to disguise their positions in generalities or hide them in footnotes, it is not so here.

On the other hand, valuing these contributions does not necessary entail agreeing with them. This gets to the heart of the healthy academy—and the soul of academic freedom. If we are not critically dialoguing with the work of our colleagues, then we are not engaging in that aspect of academe that makes it special. In a similar vein, the position may be advanced that the more dominant an idea and more prominent a critic, the bigger the demand for a more strenuous response. Rather than regard the work of prominent critics in our field as precious and beyond reproach, the healthiest response to them is a thoroughgoing critical engagement—wherever this engagement may lead. To respect our colleagues and their ideas does not necessarily mean that we need to agree with them. For some, following this principle can be very difficult. The resolution to the problems facing the humanities in the age of neoliberalism will not be achieved through mere consent with the positions of any and all advocates of the humanities. Even the positions of the most public advocates of the humanities must be met with a spirit of critical engagement.

One of the unique features of *Corporate Humanities in Higher Education* is that it is written by an upper-level university administrator who is also the editor of two major humanities journals. For nearly a decade, I have been a dean of Arts and Sciences at a state university, and for over two decades, a humanities journal editor. Moreover, based on the comments and reports of others, I have been highly successful in both endeavors. Regardless, however, of the quality of my administrative and editorial experience, it must be noted at the outset that my approach in this book is tempered by a pragmatism grounded in these real-life, academic-world experiences. I am not speaking from the position of someone who is theoretically espousing a critique of mainstream ("neoliberal") administrative policies, but as someone who lives with and administrates in the context of these policies and practices every day. Administrating—and editing—in dark times not only gives one a different sense of the perils of higher education today—but also provides one the opportunity to resist pernicious and destructive higher educational practices from within.

The other unique feature of *Corporate Humanities in Higher Education* is that it is written by someone who has strong affiliations with a number of distinct disciplines within the humanities. My doctoral work is in both philosophy and comparative literature, and I have published widely in both areas. However, by professional title, I am a professor of English and philosophy. Thus, by my count, I have professional footprints in three distinct disciplines: English, philosophy, and comparative literature. Add to this an undergraduate degree in economics—in addition to philosophy—and you have someone with a fairly robust perspective on the liberal arts. Thus, my point of view on the problems facing the humanities today—steeped as it is in a combination of interdisciplinary education and administrative experience—both provides me with not only a great vantage point to identify and assess these problems, but also to work toward alleviating them.

Corporate Humanities in Higher Education does not aim to provide all of the answers to the questions facing the humanities. Nor does it presume that its own critical interventions and conclusions are beyond reproach. Rather, it strives to advance at least one fundamental idea: that is, moving beyond the neoliberal academy may not be as easy as returning to its predecessor—but it certainly will not be as difficult as trying to function as an academic committed to critical inquiry and democratic education in the age of neoliberalism. Shaping the academy of the future is our most urgent task. One that we must approach with a sense of openness and dialogue tempered by feelings of hope and optimism—even though the academy, and the humanities in particular, are going through dark times.

1

Corporate Literature

The rise of neoliberalism is fundamentally changing the face of higher education in America. Many within the academy fear that they are changes for the worse—and that the vision of the academy they believe in is on the brink of complete destruction. This disappearing academy was more democratic and less hierarchical than the emergent one; more collegial and less autocratic; and more personal and less managerial. Academic autonomy too is becoming a thing of the past in the emergent academy. Whereas twentieth-century American professors enjoyed a high degree of control over university curriculum and the fundamental right to critically inquire into any subject without fear of losing their position within the university, academics in the new millennium are facing increasing degrees of curricular scrutiny, as well as department closures, unreasonable expectations, and job insecurity. This coupled with the possibility of academic life without academic freedom and shared governance is radically changing the manner in which many approach—or at least should approach—academic life.

One of the major causes of these changes in the academy is the escalating trend to see higher education as a type of business or corporation. In the business world, products are marketed and produced with the aim of growing market share, and values and processes are determined by their ability to raise sales and profitability. The application of increasingly severe versions of this operational philosophy to the academy has in large part contributed to the move toward contingent faculty appointments, a vocationally based curriculum, and the curtailing of critical freedoms. If this situation is not reversed, there is a strong possibility that the university of the future will be more like a vocational training center staffed by part-time instructors than a nexus of critical inquiry facilitated by full-time faculty.

But the changes do not end here. Students too are getting into the corporate spirit. In their recent book, *Higher Education? How Colleges Are Wasting Our Money and Failing Our Kids—And What We Can Do about It*, Queens College political science professor Andrew

Hacker and *New York Times* journalist Claudia Dreifus report that "over half of all undergraduates now enroll in vocational *training* programs, which range from standbys like nursing and engineering to new arrivals like resort management and fashion merchandising."[1] With numbers like these, it is not surprising that liberal arts faculty are finding it increasingly difficult to compete with their vocational, technical, and professional colleagues for resources—particularly, during times of economic crisis.

It is within these conditions, namely, the rising dominance of vocational majors and the well-documented ascent of the corporate university that I would like to propose that if we do not change the way we approach literature, philosophy, and other areas within the humanities, the corporate university will not only continue to attract larger numbers of majors, and marginalize and remove large chunks of the humanities curriculum, it may also put the humanities on the path to extinction. Moreover, we should also be careful in the way we discuss the crisis in the humanities both with fellow humanists as well as with our colleagues outside of the humanities. No one is better qualified to make the case for the humanities amidst the remonstrations of the corporate university than we humanists. But with this qualification comes responsibility—a responsibility to not just reveal the nature of the crisis, but also to strive for solutions to it. As such, this chapter is concerned with both literature *on* the corporate university as well as how we approach literature *within* the corporate university.

Corporate Scholarship

If humanities scholars were not interested in the future of their disciplines, and simply allowed the forces of the neoliberal university to determine their fate, then there is every reason to believe that these disciplines would eventually disappear into academe's vocational haze. However, many humanities faculty are concerned with the future of their disciplines—and have chosen to devote some of their professional and scholarly attention to it.

Every week, new articles appear in periodicals such as *The Chronicle of Higher Education* and *Inside Higher Ed* concerning the economic and political dimensions of universities. While many are written by professional journalists, a significant number are written by academics—some gainfully employed, but others not. These articles written by our colleagues often provide valuable insight into the trials and tribulations of academics working under the yoke of neoliberal policies. Collectively, they amount to an important set of notes from the field about higher education today—and are often amplified by comments on them collected as online appendices or supplements. In fact, in my opinion, the commentary on these articles is often more stimulating and richer than the articles themselves. Together, the article and its commentary give a face to some of the unseen yet damaging effects of neoliberalism in higher education today.

But commentary on and concern for the future of the humanities is not solely the province of academic journalism or the blogosphere. It is something that has recently invigorated and given a whole new dimension and meaning to academic conferences and meetings. In fact, discussions of the academic condition of the humanities has become one of the—if not the—hottest and most contested topics of late within scholarly organizations affiliated with the humanities. It is not uncommon now to find, for example, standing room only audiences at the Modern Language Association (MLA) or American Comparative Literature Association (ACLA) for presentations about the job market or the fate of tenure, while sessions devoted to subjects such as comparative arts or Chaucer have more empty seats than full ones. The degree to which these professional organizations have allowed issues concerning academic working conditions to be scheduled as sessions at their annual meetings might be regarded as directly proportional to the degree to which these professional organizations perceive these issues to be urgent problems for their disciplines. In addition, their popularity among conference participants only further attests to the seriousness of the situation.

Discussion of the problems facing the humanities, in particular, and higher education, in general, by academics both in publications and at professional conferences is one of the more encouraging aspects of academe today. It reveals our willingness to not just sit idle and be docile subjects for an academy that increasingly seems to favor passivity over activism. In addition, the willingness of academics to write about and discuss the problems facing the humanities is augmented by the rise of cultural studies in our profession—one of the major contributions of which is the normalization of this metaprofessional scholarship, particularly among committed humanities professors. While the profession of literary studies has by far been the loudest and most articulate voice in this discussion (bolstered in part by Cary Nelson, an English professor, who recently served as president of the American Association of University Professors), other humanities disciplines such as philosophy and history have not been far behind.[2]

What is important to recall is that prior to the rise of cultural studies in the late 1980s and 1990s, discussion of the metaprofessional dimensions of the university were nowhere as dominant as they are today. Philosophy professors used to research and write about philosophy, and English professors about literature. These were the hot topics at scholarly meetings, while metaprofessional subjects such as the job market, academic publishing, and tenure were primarily discussed in the lounge over coffee. While students and professors definitely had strong opinions on these subjects and shared many of the same concerns that are in vogue today about the job market, salaries, job security, and publishing, they were not things that were widely regarded as fair game for conference presentation, let alone scholarly publication or professional writing.

We've come a long way though over the past 20 years—and this is one of the reasons to be hopeful that the humanities can weather education's corporate hurricane. The publication of books like Bruce Wilshire's *The Moral Collapse of the University: Professionalism, Purity, and Alienation* (1990), David Damrosch's *We Scholars: Changing the Culture of the University* (1995), and Stanley Fish's *Professional Correctness: Literary Studies and Political Change* (1996) opened the door for taking these discussions out of the coffee lounge and into the scholarly forum. If major scholars in our field, for example, Wilshire in philosophy, Fish in English, and Damrosch in comparative literature, were publishing scholarly works on the economic and political life of the academy, then the rest of us could—and should—too. The book, however, which kicked the door down—and radically altered the nature of metaprofessional discourse in the humanities—was one by a relatively unknown associate professor of comparative literature at the Université de Montréal.

Bill Readings's *The University in Ruins*, which came out in 1996, turned the discussion of the academy by humanists decidedly more political and economic. And his book, more than any other from this period, established the role of the market in the administration of universities as a central topos in our metaprofessional deliberations. Soon the phrase "corporate university" came to be the central signifier for everything that is wrong with universities in America. Excellent books such as Derek Bok's *Universities in the Marketplace* (2003) and David Kirp's *Shakespeare, Einstein, and the Bottom Line* (2003) continued to hammer home this point over the next 15 years. These and other studies inform us that universities in America have been and continue to be run more like businesses or corporations than—well—universities.[3]

However, in spite of their collective insights on the corporatization of the university, there has not been much consensus within corporate university literature on either how to get out from under this administrative model nor how the humanities is going to survive—if not thrive—under this model. Moreover, the majority of the studies published in the past ten or so years continue this trend. In addition (and somewhat unsurprisingly), most recent studies of university conditions do not even discuss the attacks of September 11, 2001, or the repressive, neoliberal, educational policies established in the wake of these events, both of which play a large role in the challenges currently facing the humanities. A good example is the much discussed and very popular recent study by an Ohio State University English professor.

In *The Last Professors: The Corporate University and the Fate of the University* (2008), Frank Donoghue predicts that while "professors have only been around for the last eighty years,"[4] don't count on them being around for the next 80. In the process, though, he makes no pretense about having a solution to this situation, and clearly states, "I offer nothing in the way of uplifting solutions to the problems that I describe."[5] Rather, Donoghue simply aims to show both how we got into this situation, and why we are not going to be able to get out of it. The future of the faculty and disciplines caught in this downward spiral is not his concern.

While his honesty about this is commendable, the fact that he does not propose any solution begs the question as to the purpose of the book, particularly when so much had already been written about this subject. The bibliography to Donoghue's book has almost 200 entries, most of which confirm his point that corporate logic and values provided the foundational and continuing conditions of the university in America. While it is interesting to read, for example, about the ways in which business interests have historically tempered and contained the humanities, it is disappointing to find not even a glimmer of a *defense* of the humanities against corporate interests or an attempt to help affected faculty resolve this situation. What does one say, for example, to a business person, university regent, or a state legislator who asks why *should* we support the humanities in higher education rather than say provide students with skills to succeed in business? What does one say to a distraught colleague whose work in the humanities is deemed unimportant or inessential? Studies without such insight are in times of well-known academic crisis of limited value.

Moreover, and perhaps more problematic, there is no effort to argue that corporate values such as efficiency, productivity, and usefulness are in themselves the wrong values for the academy (even though Donoghue finds them to be "oppressive"[6]). Statements such as "the very corporate values from which we humanists wish to distance ourselves"[7] pepper the book though it is never demonstrated that values such as "usefulness" are ones which *we humanists* need to distance ourselves from—after all, isn't, for example, "usefulness" the cornerstone of American pragmatism, which is itself a paradigmatic example of American humanism? And what is so wrong about striving to be productive, for example, in one's scholarship, or efficient, for example, in preparing for one's classes?

As such, Donoghue's book is not a defense of the values that the academy should have, and not an argument against the values that it does have. Nor does it make any effort to contend with the devastating effect of the corporate university on the humanities. In this respect, Donoghue's book is not that different from most of the other recent studies of the corporate university: lots of description of problems with faculty salaries, tenure, adjunct hiring, loss of research support, decrease in publishing opportunities, vocationalization of the curriculum, and so on, though little insight how to get out of this situation or how to at least cope with it.[8]

Unfortunately, studies like Donoghue's are far too common. Though their doom and gloom snapshots of academe may sell well and make for good summer reading, they must be regarded as missed opportunities to work toward a revaluation of the academy—and the demise of the corporate university. Instead of simply bemoaning long-standing oppressive values underlying academic culture, scholars like Donoghue need to build a case for their revaluation, particularly if these values are participating in the demise of the humanities.

Nonetheless, arguments in support of the humanities in the face of the growing corporatization of the university are not easy to make—particularly when so many undergraduates are now enrolled in vocationally grounded education (and particularly if one refuses to instrumentalize the humanities). After all, student demand is a large part of the corporate university's modus operandi. And though Hacker and Dreifus might find some joy in ranting that these programs do not qualify for inclusion in an institution of higher learning, and take some pleasure in saying things like "While we're sure something is imparted in these classes, we're not comfortable calling it *education*"—responsible, collegial scholars do not do this.[9] Denigrating and insulting our colleagues and our students is not the way to ensure the future of the humanities. Nor do making trite comments like this one (also by Hacker and Dreifus) help very much: "College should be a cultural journey, an intellectual expedition, a voyage of confronting new ideas and information, together expanding and deepening our understanding of ourselves and the world."[10] Statements like this only make it more difficult for the liberal arts to differentiate their aims from those of say a Carnival cruise ship—with books. Instead of repeating shopworn assessments of the problems facing higher education (à la Donoghue) or insulting our colleagues and students (à la Hacker and Dreifus), we need to look for ways out of the neoliberal abyss.

Corporate Pedagogy

In many ways, the problems facing the humanities have only intensified since the events of September 11, 2001. Not only has there been an increase in military funding of university research, but there has also been a rise in support for academic programs that support the militarization of higher education.[11] Moreover, during this same period, there has been a decrease in funding for humanities scholarship and research aimed at fundamental social and environmental issues, as well as cutbacks in liberal arts coursework and programs. In this context, the liberal arts and critical studies in American higher education are better labeled the *neo*liberal arts and *un*critical studies. What is even worse is the way in which neoliberal ways of viewing higher education and the liberal arts have trickled down into the views of American youth.

The future of the liberal arts hinges in large part on the ability of people who have a passion for the liberal arts to be able to share their emotional force and communicate their intellectual power with others. Seeing and hearing people who are fully committed to their art is often believed the best way of supporting the arts. The poet who intensely and emphatically reads his poetry reveals his commitment to his art; the philosopher who cleverly turns every statement into a question and undermines beliefs demonstrates the perennial and complex nature of philosophy; the novelist who convinces others to believe in her characters and care for their well-being shows the power of mimesis.

However, part of the current problem of the humanities is that these traditional ways of drawing people into the humanities are no longer working. Students facing the prospect of going into debt to attend college are less interested today in studying things that might be good for the mind, but are potentially hard on their wallets—and career aspirations. A generation or two ago, students were more passionate about things like poetry and history. The current generation though is more committed to pursuing lucrative vocational careers than enjoying the critical and creative wonders of the liberal arts; more devoted to relieving their massive student debt than pursuing majors that they believe will only exacerbate their economic woes.[12]

Pollster Daniel Yankelovich has noted that "75 percent of high school seniors and 85 percent of their parents said college is important because it 'prepares students to get a better job and/or increases their earning potential.'"[13] In itself, the situation would not be so dire for the liberal arts if these students and their parents had some knowledge of—if not appreciation for—the liberal arts. After all, corporate employment aspirations (and success) are not mutually exclusive with an appreciation for the liberal arts. However, according to Yankelovich, "44 percent of students and 19 percent of their parents could not answer the question, What does a liberal arts education mean?"[14] In addition, Yankelovich's polling indicated that "[t]he overall impression of liberal arts education among 68 percent of the students and 59 percent of the parents was negative or neutral."[15]

These beliefs about higher education and its value would be challenges for the humanities even in good economic times. However, since the economic meltdown of 2008, they have made the situation in the humanities even worse. The rising cost of higher education and the shrinking job market coupled with prevailing perceptions about the value of a college education have had a decidedly negative impact on the liberal arts.

Some of the more disturbing numbers associated with this negative impact are the decreasing numbers of humanities majors. For example, 40 years ago, 64,286 students received bachelor's degrees in English. However, in 2007, it was reported that the number of bachelor's degrees awarded in English had shrunk to 53,040. This drop would not be so significant if one did not also consider that during this period, the total number of bachelor's degrees almost doubled. Taking this into account, the 64,286 majors in 1971 equates to approximately 128,500 in 2007, thus bringing the weighted decrease in English majors over this span to around 60 percent.[16]

Perhaps a better gauge of the state of the liberal arts though is the number of students who attended liberal arts colleges, but did not receive degrees in the liberal arts. In 1987, just over 10 percent of all students attending the 225 liberal arts colleges in the United States received degrees in vocational fields. Whereas by 2008, that percentage rose to nearly 30 percent. At the lowest tier (or ranked) liberal arts colleges, the percentage is well over 50 percent.[17]

Can liberal arts get a bigger slap in the face than this? Is there a clearer indicator of the decreasing value of a liberal arts education than students attending liberal arts colleges but in increasing numbers *not* majoring in the liberal arts? In the same way that a drastic increase of business majors at colleges dedicated to the arts would not be a good sign for the arts, so too are increasing numbers of vocational majors at colleges dedicated to the liberal arts a bad sign for the liberal arts. One goes to Julliard to study opera—not operations management; one goes to Williams College to study philosophy—not finance.

Vocational aspirations and careerism among students are radically altering liberal arts education in America. The liberal arts curriculum is slowly giving way to vocational—or, if you will, *corporate*—instruction. If something is not done about this soon by critically engaged academics, there is every reason to believe that the move toward more vocational courses and majors will accelerate—and that the liberal arts curriculum that remains will more and more be tailored to serve the needs of an increasingly vocationally and corporately minded student base. How then do we, as educators, meet the demands of vocationally motivated undergraduate students while, at the same time, resist pulling our liberal arts courses from their historical, political, and critical roots? How do we protect the distinctiveness of the liberal arts, while at the same time persuade students of their difference from vocationally grounded courses and majors? Pursuit of answers to pedagogically complex questions like these will go a longer way toward resolving the problems facing the humanities in the corporate university than merely continuing to heap scorn upon our vocationally minded colleagues and students.

It is my belief that we should not ignore the desires of our vocationally minded students nor denigrate them, but rather engage them in a progressive form of dialogue with and through the liberal arts courses that we offer. We need to view the humanities courses that continue to be offered as opportunities to demonstrate to our students—and the advocates of vocationally based curriculum—their multifaceted educational value. Not just *say* what we are teaching is important, but *show* it. At a time when the humanities is struggling within the corporate university for funding, respect, and its future, we need to view each course that we offer as though the fate of the humanities hinged on its success. While this defensive posture may seem unfair, particularly when courses in "resort management" and "fashion merchandizing" do not have the same pressures put upon them, we must realize that it is not vocationally based education that is under siege within the corporate university. Rather, it is areas of the curriculum such as literature and philosophy that are struggling to prove their value to a growing vocationally, technically, and professionally minded student base.

All of this is of course no easy task. In many ways, every course and major within the corporate university curriculum should be regarded as a "corporate" course or major—or thought of as implicitly containing the adjective "corporate." That is to say, "Introduction to Literature" is actually "Introduction to *Corporate* Literature" within the corporate university. Why? Because this signifies the way in which the corporate university continuously puts its intellectual value under erasure; makes the course a continual site of contestation and defense; demands that the course always consider itself from the perspective of the neoliberal values that threaten its future. This implicit adjective demarcates the conditions of possibility of this course within a model of university organization that allows vocational, technical, and professional values to determine curriculum rather than academic freedom, disciplinary constraint, and intellectual history. Academic interests are contingent upon market interests in the neoliberal university—and the implicit adjective "corporate" serves as a grave reminder of this.

Nevertheless, "corporatizing" humanities courses does not mean that we ignore the historical and political dimensions of the works that we are teaching; nor does it mean that we avoid topics that challenge the values of our vocationally, technically, and professionally minded students. Rather it means that we need to be careful not to assume that our students *prima facie* care about the critical foundations of the texts and topics that we are exploring with them. On the one hand, this situation is not unique to humanities instruction under the shadow of neoliberalism; on the other hand, the corporate university only makes it more difficult to engage in critical pedagogy and progressive education. The neoliberal managerial end of teaching to "measurable learning outcomes" does not square well at all with the critical pedagogical aims of democratic education, critical citizenship, and teaching to transgress—all aims that defiantly resist the kind of measurement espoused by neoliberal academe.

Critical humanities, that is, studying the humanities through the lens of race, class, gender, sexuality, and so on, amplified by a commitment to social justice and democratic education has never been an easy task. It is a form of humanities education that is challenging for both instructors and students as it demands high levels of critical attention, rather than mere accumulation of information; a form of humanities education where students are active producers of knowledge, rather than passive or docile receivers. However, it is the right way especially when shared with students through a pedagogical style grounded in a sense of equal partnership in the educational process. Critical pedagogy is premised on students and instructors being collaborators in an educational process that is enriching and empowering for both sets of participants. Furthermore, critical pedagogy encourages us to open the classroom up into the world—and to welcome the messiness and complexity that is life and knowledge outside of the confines of "measured learning outcomes."

One of the best ways to encourage students who are reticent to critically inquire into issues in the humanities is to bring these issues to them in forms with which they are more comfortable. In the philosophy classroom, for example, this can be achieved to great effect by introducing philosophical topics through films or current events—and much the same holds for the literature classroom. Whereas reading and discussion, for example, of Simone de Beauvoir's *The Second Sex* (1949) is often met with disinterest and glazed eyes, introducing it through say a film like director Ridley Scott's *Thelma and Louise* (1991) provides the students with a philosophy lesson that is both entertaining and enlightening. In addition—and more importantly—pedagogical approaches like this gets students engaged with and interested in topics in the humanities. Whereas a generation or two ago such pedagogical methods were sneered at by mainstream academic philosophers as "watering down" the philosophy curriculum, today they are regarded by many as a necessity in classrooms where there is resistance among students to the humanities curriculum. Moreover, the future of the humanities may in fact hinge on our ability as teachers to demonstrate the value and significance of key texts and topics through a multitude of venues and modes, that is, it may hinge on our ability to be pedagogically progressive and intellectually inventive.[18]

Teaching "corporatized" literature or philosophy courses requires a more complex dialogue between teacher and students in order to respect mutual desires. This dialogue can start with instructors recognizing that many of the students who are taking their humanities classes do not see the value of them and do not understand how they connect with their "vocational" aspirations. By adjusting the entry point of our classes slightly to break down this resistance and to show how the texts and topics discussed connect with wider discussions—and can even be drawn into a dialogue with what the students formerly thought of as "merely" entertainment (e.g., film and television)—the humanities within the corporate university can get a renewed lease on life.

Nevertheless, all of this requires a balancing act between our sense of what committed humanities instruction demands—and what our students need. Our ability to juggle competing desires, for example, our desires for disciplinary rigor and textual fidelity against our student's desires to only pursue courses that will "get them a job," may in fact play a larger role in determining the fate of the humanities than we think. In the end, strange as it may seem, this respect of different desires may be one of the only ways to prevent the eventual extinction of large swaths of the liberal arts curriculum—especially if our corporate liberal arts courses bring about a greater knowledge of and appreciation for the liberal arts.

Academics need to continue to show concern with the crisis in the humanities, but not by simply writing off its problems as intransigent or longstanding. Also, we need to recognize that while we are busy worrying about things like tenure and academic freedom, the very disciplines through which we exercise that tenure and freedom are eroding away beneath us. Tenure and academic freedom are not worth very much to the philosopher whose philosophy department has been closed, or to the foreign languages professor whose language is being phased out of the curriculum. Odd as it may sound, it may be our capacity as teachers and advocates of the humanities that is our best defense against extinction—it surely though is not pedagogical apathy or intellectual arrogance.

While scholarly attention to perennial metaprofessional topics like tenure and academic freedom is important, attention to the demise of the liberal arts curriculum by vocational, technical, and professional pursuits seems more urgent, particularly for effected scholars. However, rather than writing about the erosion of the humanities curriculum by the hand of the corporate university, we need to use our pedagogical prowess to act against it. With micro-level and creative adjustments in pedagogy such as the corporatization of liberal arts courses, academics can work toward altering negative neoliberal perceptions of the value of the liberal arts. While most would probably rather teach their courses as "pure" liberal arts courses, this academic freedom is currently not widely available in the age of the neoliberal arts. So, until the neoliberal arts revert back to being the liberal arts, curricular and pedagogical compromises are an effective way to protect the liberal arts from immediate demise.

2

HUMANITIES, INC.

It is old news that the humanities are in peril. It is also well known that their crisis is not just going to go away on its own—even though some humanists seem to act as though this were the case. In fact, there is every reason to believe that neoliberal educational practices and the growth of the corporate university are only going to deepen the problems facing the humanities.[1] Declining numbers of majors, reductions in financial support, and a general lack of understanding of the nature and value of the humanities are opening the door to a more vocationally centered vision of higher education. In a political economy and academic environment wherein educational values are determined by market share, majors and courses that cannot be directly connected to marketable skills and job attainment are regarded as expendable. As a result, the humanities are losing students and energy at an alarming rate—and are in need of reprieve, if not renewal.

So what is going to provide the reprieve? Where will the renewal come from? What is going to end the decline? One source of reprieve are the micro-level adjustments in pedagogy presented in chapter 1. However, the corporatization of liberal arts courses is only a temporary reprieve. The hegemony of the humanities by the neoliberal university only allows them to persist under its own terms. Once they cease to serve the ends of the neoliberal agenda—or start to get in the way of pursuit of these ends—the humanities as we have known them will disappear. Nevertheless, what emerges from the ashes of this hostile takeover (or makeover) of the humanities in large part will be determined by how the humanities itself reacts to its future within the neoliberal university.

Humanities scholars have been very good at pointing fingers at others for their woes, but have been hard pressed to provide convincing arguments in support of humanities education within the neoliberal university. In particular, humanities scholars—even the most highly regarded—have had difficulty making a case for the humanities that is convincing not only to those inside the humanities, but also to those *outside* of the humanities; credible to those informed about the humanities as well as to those *uninformed* about them; persuasive to those sympathetic to the humanities as well as to those *hostile* to them. Martha Nussbaum's recent efforts to defend the place of the humanities within the neoliberal university exemplify the problems well.

Not for Profit

In *Not for Profit: Why Democracy Needs the Humanities* (2010), Nussbaum argues that assaults on the humanities are also assaults on democratic education. "Thirsty for national profit, nations, and their systems of education," writes Martha Nussbaum, "are heedlessly discarding skills that are needed to keep democracies alive."[2] "If this trend continues, nations all over the world will soon be producing generations of useful machines, rather than complete citizens who can think for themselves, criticize tradition, and understand the significance of another person's sufferings and achievements," continues Nussbaum. "The future of world's democracies hangs in the balance."[3]

Not for Profit presents a passionate case for systems of education that result in "a more inclusive type of citizenship"—rather than ones solely focused on profit making.[4] For Nussbaum, the humanities and the arts are the place where students acquire the "skills" necessary to keep democracies alive and become complete citizens—rather than "useful machines." If we continue to "ask our schools to turn out useful profit-makers rather than thoughtful citizens,"[5] our world will become one comprised of "technically trained people who do not know how to criticize authority, useful profit-makers with obtuse imaginations."[6] According to Nussbaum, "greedy obtuseness" and "technically trained docility"[7] "threaten the very life of democracy itself" and "impede the creation of a decent world culture."[8]

From the point of view of someone in the humanities, Nussbaum presents a compelling case for the importance of the humanities to the development of democratic culture. Critical thinking and reflection provide citizens with the capacity to see beyond local problems and loyalties and "imagine sympathetically the predicament of another person."[9] Imagination and thought enriches our relationships with others and "makes us human."[10] However, the single-minded quest for economic growth and financial profit tends to abandon these democratic values, particularly in times of severe economic crisis. As a result, democratic education gives way to education for profit in times of financial crisis.

"Distracted by the pursuit of wealth," comments Nussbaum, "we increasingly ask our schools to turn out useful profit-makers rather than thoughtful citizens."[11] Economic strains only exacerbate this situation and put pressure on institutions to abandon the liberal arts model of university education. This model, which flourishes in the United States and is unlike that of just about every other nation in the world, gives students the freedom to study a wide range of courses during the first two years of their university education. Rather than focusing on studying a single subject, students educated in the liberal arts model of education take an array of courses spanning the arts and sciences. The liberal arts model challenges "the mind to become active, competent, and thoughtfully critical in a complex world"[12] rather than encouraging students to passively assimilate "facts and cultural traditions." The result is a model of education that produces "informed, independent, and sympathetic democratic citizens."[13]

To this point, Nussbaum's argument for the importance of the humanities to democratic citizenship is relatively uncontroversial to someone inside the humanities. Nussbaum draws heavily on the educational philosophies of John Dewey and Rabindranath Tagore to make her case, and in the process demonstrates many of the similarities between their positions. For admirers of Dewey's educational philosophy unfamiliar with the work of Tagore, her comparisons show the potential of comparative global humanities. In addition, comparing highly influential Indian and American educational philosophies in support of liberal arts education gives her general argument a more global feel, and makes her sub-arguments such as those against educational practices that merely "teach to the test" and those that advocate passive memorization (over active learning) even more compelling. Nonetheless, Nussbaum's case against education for profit somehow still takes a wrong turn.

Instead of simply arguing that active learning in the humanities is necessary to democratic education, Nussbaum also adds that it leads to economic growth—and financial profit. A "flourishing economy," writes Nussbaum, "requires the same skills that support citizenship."[14] In her opinion, those who believe that passive pedagogies, technical training, and the elimination of the humanities curriculum lead to economic growth are mistaken. While it may not look like programs in the arts and humanities lead to economic growth, argues Nussbaum, they do. So how?

Education in the arts and humanities cultivates and develops sympathy. For Nussbaum, sympathy is necessary for economic development that values equality.[15] Comments Nussbaum, "a cultivated and developed sympathy is a particularly dangerous enemy of obtuseness, and moral obtuseness is necessary to carry out programs of economic development that ignore inequality."[16] Paraphrasing Tagore, Nussbaum writes "aggressive nationalism needs to blunt the moral conscience, so it needs people who do not recognize the individual, who speak group-speak, who behave, and see the world, like docile bureaucrats."[17] Nussbaum's point here is that if equality and concern for the lives of others are important, then we will favor a form of economic development that promotes them.

For Nussbaum, the arts and humanities are where we gain the ability to not only "think well about political issues affecting the nation," but also "to recognize fellow citizens as people with equal rights, even though they may be different in race, religion, gender, and sexuality: to look at them with respect, as ends, not just as tools to be manipulated for one's own profit."[18] As such, those who promote educational models based on the acquisition of highly applied skills as the optimal means toward profit making and economic growth "have adopted an impoverished conception of what is required to meet their own goal."[19] For Nussbaum, critical thinking and global awareness are just as important to the future of democracies—as they are to the promotion of education for profit.

For many, though, bridging an education for democracy with one for profit is an exercise in futility. The former leads to the advocacy of public goods such as health, education, equality, and liberty; the latter though, which in its neoliberal form, promotes the unfettered flow of the global market and economic growth as the source of value, decimates public goods such as health, education, equality, and liberty. In fact, Nussbaum even notes that empirical studies have shown these public goods are "very poorly correlated with economic growth." [20] For example, old South Africa under apartheid used to be at the top of the economic development indices even though it featured "staggering distributional inequalities, the brutal apartheid regime, and the health and educational deficiencies that went with it."[21] In addition, contemporary China may be enjoying economic growth, but you would not be able to predict this from its record on political liberty. "So," remarks Nussbaum, "producing economic growth does not mean producing democracy."[22]

One way to describe the blind spot in Nussbaum's position is its omission of any discussion of how *neoliberalism* has decimated higher education and democratic values. In fact, not only is the term not mentioned in her study, there is very little acknowledgment as to the role of the market in determining value and reshaping educational practice. While it may be true that liberal arts education can produce both a democratic culture and economic development, students now tend to look to higher education as a means to increase their profit-making capacities rather than their social and political ones. And universities that are focused on promoting democratic culture rather than profitable jobs for their graduates are becoming more the exception than the norm.

If Nussbaum's argument is the best that liberal humanism can give to the neoliberal onslaught, then liberal education in America should be worried. The days of arguing that the arts and the humanities should be supported because they produce "good citizens" and provide "the ability to think critically"[23] have been swept away by the tsunami of global capital. While Nussbaum presents a compelling case why *democracy* needs the humanities, she does not present a convincing case why *neoliberalism* needs the humanities. Nor does she address how public goods such as health, education, equality, and liberty can be protected in an age of neoliberalism. Furthermore, by trying to argue that the humanities are good both for democracy *and* the bottom line, Nussbaum fails to address the major challenge of the day—namely, why be a liberal humanist when neoliberalism appears to have a much more profitable upside? Nussbaum opens the door for this criticism by trying to argue *for profit* in a book titled *Not for Profit*.

THE TWO HUMANITIES

Nussbaum's arguments are typical of a liberal humanist response to the crisis in the humanities. Essentially, her position is that the critical thinking and reflection acquired through the study of the humanities provides citizens with the capacity to see beyond local problems and loyalties and "imagine sympathetically the predicament of another person."[24] Imagination and thought enriches our relationships with others and "make[s] us human."[25] However, the single-minded quest for economic growth and financial profit that is the centerpiece of the extreme market fundamentalism of neoliberal educational practice tends to abandon these democratic values, particularly in times of severe economic crisis. As a result, democratic education gives way to education for profit in times of financial crisis.

Arguments in support of humanities education like Nussbaum's are well intended and noble. They take the high road through the history of ideas to support a beloved vision of liberal humanism. As arguments by humanists, for humanists they are extremely persuasive. Phrases like "the faculties of thought and imagination" and "make us human"[26] are hard for most humanists to resist in defense of the humanities. Nevertheless, they are still extremely vulnerable to the neoliberal attack. How then does one get around the problems that beset liberal humanist responses to the crisis in the humanities? Well, if the high road does not work, then what about the low road? The best recent example of this approach is by Toby Miller.

In many ways, Nussbaum's study is the perfect foil for Miller's intervention into the crisis in the humanities debate. If Nussbaum's project can be described as a taking the high road in defending the humanities, then Miller's *Blow Up the Humanities* (2012) might be described as taking the *low road*. Miller begins his book by claiming that the humanities in the United States are not what most think they are—namely, a unified, monological entity. Rather, for Miller, the humanities are radically divided.

On the one hand, there is "the humanities of fancy private universities, where the bourgeoisie and its favored subalterns are tutored in finishing school";[27] on the other hand, there "is the humanities of everyday state schools, which focus more on job prospects."[28] The former he terms "Humanities One," and the latter "Humanities Two." His aim is both to establish the "two humanities" distinction—one that is, by the way, directly inspired by C. P. Snow's famous "two cultures" distinction—and then to blow it up.[29] In its place, Miller seeks the reunification of the humanities, that is, a type of merger between Humanities One and Humanities Two. But before we turn to what a reunified humanities looks like, let's dwell a bit on how and why Miller thinks the humanities today are radically divided.

For some, it might have been enough to leave the division between the two humanities as one relative to institutional prestige. For example, it is not difficult to imagine that studying social and political philosophy with John Rawls at Harvard University or Martha Nussbaum at the University of Chicago would be a greatly different educational experience than studying it with an overworked and underpaid philosopher at a state school. Or, that studying the humanities at a "fancy private university" would be more academically oriented (e.g., aimed at pursuing an academic career in the humanities) and that studying them at an "everyday state school" would be more vocationally oriented (e.g., aimed at using the humanities to acquire job skills). But this is *not* what Miller does.[30]

Rather, after dividing the humanities into "Humanities One" and "Humanities Two," he then distributes the disciplines in the humanities between them. Humanities One is assigned "literature, history, and philosophy" and Humanities Two is assigned "communication and media studies."[31] Fittingly, Humanities One is the humanities of Nussbaum, the Ernst Freund Distinguished Service Professor of Law and Ethics in the Philosophy Department, Law School, and Divinity School at the University of Chicago, and Humanities Two is the humanities of Miller, the distinguished professor of Media and Cultural Studies at the University of California, Riverside. The former, a fancy private university; the latter, an everyday state school.[32]

Though Miller concedes that the disciplinary assignments of Humanities One and Humanities Two are "far from absolute," he contends that they are "heuristically and statistically persuasive."[33] His evidence here comes from two different statistical streams: the first shows that "[t]he vast growth in higher education from the 1970s has taken place among the lower middle and working classes," which tend to "enroll in state schools that are more vocational than private ones";[34] the second shows that whereas English, foreign language, philosophy, and history majors have declined since the 1970s, communication and media studies majors have increased.[35] Regarding the latter, one of the more surprising statistics cited by Miller is that "[b]etween 1970 and 2005, business enrollments increased by 176 percent," whereas during the same period communication and media studies increased by a jaw-dropping 616 percent.[36]

While it is possible to pick holes in Miller's distinctions and evidence, they still provide an intriguing point of entry into current debates concerning the humanities. Namely, Miller's "two humanities" distinction calls for us now to ask in humanities crisis discourse *which* or *whose* "humanities" is being referred to. Moreover, if nothing else, Miller has shown that at least a subsection of the disciplines in the humanities are *not* in peril in neoliberal academe. As such, by pointing out that students are attracted to communication and media studies in rapidly growing numbers, Miller in effect gives the humanities in a time of crisis a new base upon which to build support. The problem with this though—as Miller rightly points out—is that students are not attracted to communication and media studies because these majors will make them "human" but rather because they will make them "money."

Miller recognizes well both what is gained by focusing attention on Humanities Two as well as what is lost. What is gained is a way to articulate the nature and value of the humanities to larger segments of the population. While undergraduate eyes may glaze during philosophical lectures on democracy and citizenship, they perk up when the topic turns to television, film, and video games—even if there is a philosophical subtext.[37] What is often lost in pursuit of Humanities Two though is a sense of the larger context of communication and media. While students may become adept at new media production or video game design, without concurrent understanding of their social, political, cultural, and economic dimensions, they risk becoming by vocation cogs in the wheels of creative industries that often run over people and despoil the environment.

Miller discusses this at length in a chapter intriguingly titled "Creative Industries—Credible Alternative?" It is an important chapter given the amount of national attention afforded the most visible advocate of the creative industries approach, Richard Florida, who wrote the widely cited book, *The Rise of the Creative Class: And How It's Transforming Work, Leisure, Community, and Everyday Life* (2002). Florida's basic argument is that successful economic development can be had by supporting the growth of a technologically savvy "creative class." This argument has made him a high-demand figure on the lecture circuit and an oft-cited economic development authority. Miller points out that Florida even "trademarked" the phrase "creative class."[38]

Miller's opening discussion of this topic is full of promise for the humanities. "Creative-industries discourse," writes Miller, "represents the most interesting and productive response/riposte to the crisis of the humanities I have seen."[39] Not only does a creative-industries approach have "the potential to merge Humanities One and Two,"[40] it also holds promise for productive collaboration between the humanities and the sciences. In its idealized form, creative industries might amount to "Humanities 2.0," that is, places where "[n]ew humanists apply technology to stories, and new scientists apply stories to technologies."[41] Nevertheless, the creative industries response is not all sweetness and light.

"Today's discourse on the creative industries," comments Miller, "ignores such critical issues as the cognitariat, high-tech pollution, and cultural imperialism, not to mention the need to *understand* industries rather than celebrate them."[42] For example, while digital technologies are often presented as ecologically friendly, the truth of the matter is that "[w]aste from discarded electronics is one of the biggest sources of heavy metals and toxic pollutants in the world's trash piles."[43] And the list of horrors that follow from creative industries practice goes on. Utilizing examples from the game industry, Miller traces the dark side of creative industries by revealing its connections to labor exploitation, military research, and the promotion of martial masculinity and youth violence.[44] His conclusion is that the creative industries approach is deeply flawed with little or no potential to successfully merge Humanities One and Humanities Two.

Humanities Three

So where does this humanities which is no longer one go from here? What alternative is there to "the banal Arnoldian training of Humanities One and the supine vocational training of Humanities Two and the creative industries"?[45] Miller's response here is simple (and somewhat obvious given his distinguished status in this area): the answer is "media and cultural studies." "The push for the study of media texts that reflect issues of consequence to the broad population," claims Miller, "can be central to renewing the humanities."[46] A third way of looking at the humanities "must come from a blend of political economy, textual analysis, ethnography, and environmental studies such that students learn the materiality of how meaning is made, conveyed, and discarded."[47] Rather than viewing the humanities as a group of disciplines, a cultural studies approach to renewing the humanities would encourage looking "across disciplines"—and promote the idea that "cultural studies" itself is not a discipline.[48]

"Understanding culture requires studying it up, down, and sideways," writes Miller.[49] This "means knowing which companies make texts, physical processes of production and distribution, systems of cross-subsidy and monopoly profit making, the complicity of educational canons with multinational corporations' business plans, and press coverage, inter alia."[50] According to Miller, "a desirable cultural studies" is "a mixture of economics, politics, textual analysis, gender theory, ethnography, history, postcolonial theory, material objects, and policy, animated by a desire to reveal and transform those who control the means of communication and culture and undertaken with constant vigilance over one's raison d'être and modus operandi."[51] Moreover, Miller's "desirable cultural studies" "takes its agenda and mode of analysis from economics, politics, media and communication studies, sociology, literature, education, the law, science and technology studies, environmentalism, anthropology, and history"—and he adds that its "focus is gender, race, class, and sexuality in everyday life, under the sign of a commitment to progressive social change."[52]

The low road to meaning through the model of cultural studies advocated by Miller is not an easy one. There is no disciplinarity or interdisciplinary to lean on, and there are no shortcuts to understanding. Nevertheless, Miller's suggestions for renewal in the humanities not only have the potential to reenergize the humanities, but also to offer a way out of the crisis in the humanities.[53] Still, they require "blowing up" the two extant versions of the humanities: one that is described by Miller as "venerable and powerful and tends to determine how the sector is discussed in public"[54]; and another that "is the humanities of state schools, which focus more on job prospects."[55] How feasible is this? That is, how reasonable is it to expect respective proponents of Humanities One and Humanities Two to cede ground for the "new humanities," Humanities Three? Not very, I fear—and here's why.

For one, the birth of Humanities Three requires that the "venerable and powerful" Humanities One step aside or be cast aside as "King of the Humanities." And just how is this going to happen? Are the universities and endowed advocates of Humanities One like Nussbaum at the University of Chicago going to step down? Or does it mean that when they retire they are replaced by "new humanists" like Miller? Also, how likely is it for an institution such as Harvard to close its philosophy department or Yale to shutter its English department in order to make way for the new cultural-studies-driven Humanities Three? Not very, for as Harvard English professor Louis Menand has astutely noted: "trying to reform the contemporary university is like trying to get on the Internet with a typewriter, or like trying to ride a horse to the mall"—or like trying to close Yale's English department and Harvard's philosophy department.[56]

Second, how do you wean students from "the other" humanities (Humanities Two) now that they can connect it with job prospects? Do the professors in these areas simply stop teaching "creative industries friendly" communication and media studies—and adopt instead Miller's "Humanities Three"? How likely is it that the state universities that employ them will allow them to offer this more progressive curriculum? Again, not very. Nevertheless, reform realities aside, there is a lot to be said in favor of Miller's approach to and proposal for resolving the crisis in the humanities.

Miller looks at the crisis in the humanities in a new and intriguing way. For him, the crisis is that today there are two humanities and neither is the right one. Moreover, rather than just describing the crisis and then walking away from it, Miller faces up to it with a fresh proposal for reform and renewal in the humanities. And even though Humanities Three may only come to fruition in our distant future (as university reform *is* slow), Miller's proposal lends support to the notion that at least one aspect of renewal in the humanities can be institutionalized now. Namely, we can encourage proponents of both Humanities One and Humanities Two to take every opportunity that they can to help their students *understand how the university and the humanities work*; to encourage their students to examine the mutual and respective economics, politics, history, and policies of the university and the humanities; to ask how the university and the humanities produce, distribute, and dispose of knowledge; to learn how identities are formed within and by the university and the humanities; and to help their students to imagine a world where both the university and the humanities work better—a world where the university is not always sovereign to the whims of the market, and the humanities are understood and valued.

In the end, while Miller's proposals may not end the crisis in the humanities, discussions of their value inspired by his work may at least provide them with a reprieve. In this way, they are similar to the proposals given in chapter 1 as to how to deal with corporate encroachment at the course level. However, on another level, their attempt to differentiate fundamentally different approaches to the humanities is radically different from the proposals in chapter 1. So, how useful to relieving the problems facing the humanities in the neoliberal age is distinction making? How helpful is it to think of the humanities as not one, but rather two—or even three? Just as useful as it is to think of the professions in this way.

The idea that there are two humanities—one which is more academic and elite, and one which is more vocational and populist—is an exercise that helps the humanities to create an account of its value that speaks both to its academic and its vocational dimensions—and their implications. However, in the end, it is no more or less useful than thinking of the professions in this way. Why shouldn't we think of the more philosophical, historical, and political approaches to professional fields such as education, business, and nursing in a similar way to Humanities One? And the applied, practical, and vocational dimensions of these professional fields as akin to Humanities Two? Would it be surprising to learn, for example, that the University of Chicago's School of Education and the Harvard Business School's approach to their professions is more academic and elitist and that say the Cal State system's approach to business and education is more career-oriented? Why not then also build a case for "Professions One" and "Professions Two," particularly if you have already established one for the Humanities? Because we do not have to: the professions by and large are thriving (except for maybe education) and clearly not under as much fire today as the humanities. Nevertheless, they most likely have a disciplinary bifurcation similar to that of the humanities.

Conclusion

Nussbaum and Miller provide two extremes for the defense of the humanities in light of corporate interests. In a way, rather than trying to side with one view of the humanities over the other—and in spite of their respective shortcomings—it might make more sense to just keep one in each pocket when asked by a business person, university regent, or a state legislator why we should support the humanities in higher education. Both are excellent arguments for the continuing value of the humanities, and both attempt to grapple with changing perceptions of the humanities.

Nussbaum's high road allows for a classic liberal defense of the humanities albeit with a clear eye for profit, and Miller's low road affords a contemporary defense of the humanities via their creative industry potential albeit with a warning as to the potentially disturbing political and ecological consequences. Both should be seen as versions of what might be called, "corporate humanities" or "Humanities, Inc.," that is, pragmatic efforts to situate the humanities vis à vis neoliberal agendas both inside and outside the academy.

Corporate humanities always already assumes that the humanities are situated in an economic and political world dominated by extreme market-based decision making. The adjective "corporate" used to qualify "humanities" needs to be viewed as a designator of *hope* for the humanities, rather than ruin. Accepting it lends the humanities reprieve, if not puts it on the road to renewal; rejecting it places the humanities on the remainder shelf next to philological studies and boy bands. The good news is that there is a choice; bad news is that it may involve a change in the way the humanities are viewed and approached.

There is no doubt that the humanities are in crisis and that thinking of the humanities as insulated from market-based decision making is akin to putting them on the remainder shelf. Let the terms "corporate" and "Inc." be used interchangeably in conjunction with "humanities." These terms serve as reminders that the humanities is not a "remainder" from an academy that no longer exists, but rather is an active agent in a changing educational world. And while approaches like Nussbaum and Miller's have their limitations, they reveal—as do similar efforts—that in the world of neoliberal academe, there *is* only *one* humanities: "Humanities, Inc."

3

PARALOGICAL INQUIRY

Major studies of the academic condition can become good benchmarks—and some can even change the way we see higher education. Many times they help us to identify broad changes in view or even establish new perspectives. Though the change or perspective usually predates the study, it nonetheless makes the change visible—and attaches to it a concept or even gives it a name. Moreover, these studies can establish and set the tone of a conversation for generations to come—a tone from which it is many times difficult to break. Such was the case with the pioneering study of the neoliberal university.

Recognition of its emergence might be traced back to the mid-1990s, when Bill Readings caused an uproar by publishing a book that showed how colleges and universities are run more like businesses or corporations than educational institutions. Widely read and cited, its title, *The University in Ruins* (1996), says it all—and was a shot across the bow of academe. It announced that business values were supplanting academic values in the administration of universities—and laid the groundwork for a chorus of ever more dystopic political and economic accounts of the state of higher education.

Readings's book was highly influential and convinced a lot of folks whose primary area of research was not higher education to start thinking and writing about the corporate conditions of academe. Over the course of the next dozen years (1996–2008), many other fine accounts of the corporate logic of the contemporary university and its implications came out including CUNY sociologist Stanley Aronowitz's *The Knowledge Factory: Dismantling the Corporate University and Creating True Higher Learning* (2001), former Harvard President Derek Bok's *Universities in the Marketplace: The Commercialization of Higher Education* (2003), freelance journalist and New America Foundation fellow Jennifer Washburn's *University, Inc.: The Corporate Corruption of Higher Education* (2005), and more recently, Frank Donoghue's *The Last Professors: The Corporate*

University and the Fate of the Humanities (2008)—a book already noted in chapter 1. From Bok reporting how he received year after year "one proposition after another to exchange some piece or product of Harvard for money—often, quite substantial sums of money"[1] to Donoghue boldly predicting that while "professors have only been around for the last eighty years," don't count on them being around for the next 80,[2] each of these studies provided a slightly different voice to the growing chorus that the economic base of higher education in America has in fundamental ways changed.

For the most part, the consensus has been that the financial changes within the university have been for the worse—and are not reversible. However, of late, there seems to be a change in tone in discussions about the fate of the university. Whereas just five years ago, Frank Donoghue could proclaim "I offer nothing in the way of uplifting solutions to the problems that I describe,"[3] after the collapse of the economy (which occurred after the publication of Donoghue's book), this no longer seems possible—or at least responsible. With so many academics underemployed and unemployed, and so many students strapped with debt that will take most of their working lives to pay off and fewer real employment opportunities, academics now seem ready to get down to problem solving—rather than merely bemoaning changes in academic culture. Though the financial hurricane of 2008 may not have destroyed the corporate practices of universities, as a number of more recent studies show, the house of higher education is still tenuously standing—though desperately in need of reform.

In this chapter, I argue that what is needed in conversations about higher education in America are not more accounts about the growing corporatization of the university, increasing focus on research and specialization, diminishing faculty academic freedom, and rising costs and student debt. By now, most will agree that these and other changes have occurred in the American higher educational system. Rather, what is needed is more inquiry on the university from the point of view that there *may* be no going back to the way things were; that what we might call the "modern" university (that is, the model used at least since 1915, the founding year of the American Association of University Professors) is dying—if not dead—and that the new university that is emerging out of the ashes of the modern university will be fundamentally different.

If nothing is done by engaged academics, then the neoliberal university that has emerged from the shadows of the modern university will be the university of the future. Academic identity in the neoliberal university will be characterized by docility, consent, and acquiescence. However, if academics try to stave off the entrenchment of the neoliberal university by calling for a return to the modern university, the result will be the same as doing nothing. There can be no returning to this model which was forged under considerably different technological, economic, and political conditions.

The new university that is not doomed to repeat the past (viz., the modern university) and not committed to making the mistakes of the present (viz., the neoliberal university), might be called, for lack of a better term, the "postmodern" university. It requires not only a reconsideration of the economic, academic, and professional model of the modern educational system, but also must be approached with a different *vision*—one which, I argue, should be grounded more on a "negative dialogics" (viz., one which encourages systemic dissent and foregrounds epistemological instabilities and heterogeneous identities) than a "positive dialogics" (viz., one which encourages systemic consensus, and foregrounds epistemological stabilities and homogeneous identities). In the end, this *paralogical* vision will not only help the academy to get beyond the hegemonic and repressive order of the neoliberal university, but also will hasten the formation of the nonhegemonic, progressive *dis*order of the postmodern university.

I'll begin by briefly discussing one particular notion of what I am calling "negative dialogics," namely, what French philosopher and literary theorist Jean-François Lyotard (who is coincidentally also one of the fathers of postmodernism) calls *paralogy*, and then deploy this notion to gain a better understanding of what is at stake in some recent and relatively well-known discussions of the university by Cary Nelson, Ellen Schrecker, Andrew Hacker and Claudia Dreifus, Louis Menand, and Mark Taylor.[4] My claim is that in spite of the noble intentions of a number of these contemporary thinkers, their discussions of the fate of the university are ultimately empty dialogues on the modern university—a system of higher education that they fail to recognize as outdated. What is needed for the academy to break out of its neoliberal chains is dialogue on the university that disorders its development in an outdated system, and works to allow the emergence of its future, the postmodern university.

To Speak Is to Fight

In *The Postmodern Condition: A Report on Knowledge* (1984), Jean-François Lyotard argues against the notion that the goal of dialogue is consensus—a notion that he attributes to the German sociologist and philosopher, Jürgen Habermas. For Lyotard, "consensus is only a particular state of discussion, not its end."[5] Consensus requires "that it is possible for all speakers to come to agreement on which rules or metaprescriptions are universally valid for language games"—something which Lyotard contends he has shown is not possible through his analysis of the pragmatics of science.[6] For him, "it is clear that language games are heteromorphous, subject to heterogeneous sets of pragmatic rules."[7]

Nonetheless, in spite of his difficulties with consensus as the aim of dialogue, Lyotard is no enemy of dialogue as such. For him, rather than viewing the aim of dialogue as consensus and stability, he would rather that we view its aim as dissent and instability, that is to say, *paralogy*. Writes Lyotard, "This double observation (the heterogeneity of the rules and the search for dissent) destroys a belief that...humanity as a collective (universal) subject seeks its common emancipation through the regularization of the 'moves' permitted in all language games and that the legitimacy of any statement resides in its contributing to that emancipation."[8]

While Lyotard's comments about dialogue and consensus are primarily directed toward Habermas, they seem to be equally appropriate when directed toward current dialogue concerning the university, particularly when it assumes that its goal with regard to the "education game" is consensus. Why not assume in university dialogue (following Lyotard) that "consensus has become an outmoded and suspect value," and put in its place another value—one that is "neither outmoded nor suspect," namely *justice*? Imagine now conversing about the fate of the university not with the aim of reaching consensus about the homogeneity of its rules, but rather with the aim of doing justice to its instability and heterogeneity. After all, who would care about consensus, if justice replaced it as the goal of dialogue?

For Lyotard, two of the benefits of paralogical inquiry are that it eliminates "terror" and it allows terms to be defined locally. "By terror," writes Lyotard, "I mean the efficiency gained by eliminating, or threatening to eliminate, a player from the language game one shares with him."[9] "He is silenced or consents, not because he has been refuted, but because his ability to participate has been threatened (there are many ways to prevent someone from playing)."[10] However, when one eliminates the regularization of moves, one allows for the possibility of everyone participating in the game. In terms of the education game, this means that the "terror" of being silenced because of say one's rank or the prestige of one's university is possible only if the rules of the game are locally constructed to produce this result. Lyotard's "permissiveness toward the various games" shields the players of education games from acts of terror. "The decision maker's arrogance," writes Lyotard, "consists in the exercise of terror."[11] Continues Lyotard, "It says: 'Adapt your aspirations to our ends—or else."[12] Thus, for Lyotard, terroristic behavior in the education game results not from playing by ones own rules, but rather by adapting ones aspirations to the rules of the game—though such thinking would be cold comfort to the professor denied tenure for not playing by the rules.[13]

The second benefit of paralogy is the "principle that any consensus on the rules defining the game and the 'moves' playable with it *must* be local, in other words, agreed on by its present players and subject to eventual cancellation."[14] "The orientation then favors," writes Lyotard, "a multiplicity of finite meta-arguments, by which I mean argumentation that concerns metaprescriptives and is limited in space and time."[15] In terms of universities, this implies that "temporary" features may be favored over "permanent" ones—and that the notion of universal consensus on how universities should be run is "neither possible, nor even prudent"—to borrow Lyotard's comment about Habermas's search for universal consensus.[16]

In language that foreshadows contemporary discussions of the academy, Lyotard says that the paralogical "orientation corresponds to the course that the evolution of social interaction is currently taking; the temporary contract is in practice supplanting permanent institutions in the professional, emotional, sexual, cultural, family, and international domains, as well as in political affairs."[17] One could easily add the "educational" domain to Lyotard's sentence without a significant change in meaning. "This evolution," adds Lyotard, "is of course ambiguous: the temporary contract is favored by the system due to its greater flexibility, lower cost, and the creative turmoil of its accompanying motivations—all of these factors contribute to increased operativity."[18] In the case of the educational system, one might posit, following Lyotard, that its evolution too has become ambiguous. As to the question of whether to try to repair the "old" system or to simply replace it with a "new" system, Lyotard's response is quite clear: "there is no question here of proposing a 'pure' alternative to the system" as any "attempt at an alternative...would end up resembling the system it was meant to replace."[19]

Lyotard's paralogism is not one of calm, dispassionate dialogue. Rather it is an *agonistic* one. Writes Lyotard, "the first principle underlying our method as a whole: to speak is to fight, in the sense of playing, and speech acts fall within the domain of general agonistics."[20] Fredric Jameson, commenting on Lyotard's paralogism, writes that its "rhetoric" is "one of struggle, conflict, the agonic in a quasi-heroic sense," and reminds us not to "forget Lyotard's related vision of nonhegemonic Greek philosophy (the Stoics, the Cynics, the Sophists), as the guerrilla war of the marginals, the foreigners, the non-Greeks, against the massive and repressive Order of Aristotle and his successors."[21] In this light, one might regard Lyotard's paralogism as a kind of "negative dialogics," that is, dialogue aimed at disrupting the system, rather than bringing it into equilibrium. In terms of university dialogue, paralogism encourages the renouncement of the notion that, in Cary Nelson's words, "all university dialogue needs to be conducted in a calm, dispassionate, unvaryingly respectful way."[22] While Nelson rejects this kind of dialogue because it "makes the university less useful as a social model," Lyotard would reject it because it allows the university system to become more powerful as a hegemonic force and homogeneous game.[23]

How We Talk

A number of studies have been published of late that attempt to deal with the systemic problems facing higher education in America. The tendency of these studies is to treat the problems facing the university *dialogically*. In other words, they assume that the educational game has a homogeneous set of rules, and that the problems in higher education come from alterations in the common rules of the game. These studies share a similar vision of the educational system, and tend to believe that by talking among each other and sharing our problems, academics can adjust the system to meet their consensual demands. Take, for example, two recent studies: one by Cary Nelson and the other by Ellen Schrecker.

Schrecker, the former editor of the *Academe*, the official magazine of the American Association of University Professors (AAUP), and professor of history at Yeshiva University, and Nelson, past national president of the AAUP and Jubilee Professor of Liberal Arts and Sciences at the University of Illinois at Urbana-Champaign, both contend that the major problem facing the university today is that academic freedom is under assault, even if they are not of one voice as to how to rectify this.

Nelson's *No University Is an Island: Saving Academic Freedom* (2010) reminds us that academic freedom has been and is continuously under assault. "The need to clarify academic freedom anew, to elaborate on its implications, and to respond to its critics," writes Nelson, "is never ending."[24] His book, which developed out of conversations with academics all over the country, is a rich and comprehensive set of field notes on the challenges to academic freedom. For Nelson, academic freedom is but one leg of a "three-legged stool," which also includes "shared governance" and "tenure" legs—a view echoing the long-held position of the AAUP. Through numerous examples, Nelson passionately and articulately defends these tenets. He is appalled by the treatment of hundreds of thousands of contingent faculty (adjunct and nontenure track faculty), by the way research agendas are being determined by corporate interests, by administrators who autocratically rule universities and ignore faculty input, by "unbridled faculty careerism" and "unionization that has been stripped of its social agendas."[25] However, in every individual struggle and workplace injustice he observes, Nelson sees an opportunity for faculty to engage in "principled activism on behalf of their peers."[26]

What is interesting about Nelson's approach is that he never questions the system: in fact, his aim is to bring the system back into equilibrium by making sure that the fundamental rules of its game regarding tenure, shared governance, and academic freedom are preserved. In many ways, his quest for wider unionization of faculty is the workforce equivalent of the Habermasian dialogical ideal of universal consensus. In spite of its angry tone regarding the actions of some administrators, there is little paralogism in Nelson's treatment of the university, and never a questioning of the continuing relevance of the homogenous precepts regarding the three-legged stool.

Ellen Schrecker, however, while covering ground similar to Nelson, is more pessimistic regarding the future of academic freedom in *The Lost Soul of Higher Education: Corporatization, the Assault on Academic Freedom, and the End of the American University* (2010). Warns Schrecker, "unless the nation's college and university teachers get their communal act together, academic freedom may well disappear from their campuses and the academic profession as we know it could vanish from the face of the earth."[27] She also believes that "there are so many divisions within the academic community at every level that there is no guarantee the crisis will unify rather than further polarize America's campuses."[28] Though both Schrecker and Nelson share an affinity for the aim of dialogue, namely consensus, Schrecker is a bit more sober about the ability to pull this off. Nonetheless, instead of adapting her way of conversing about the university in accordance with its differential and ambiguous status ("there are so many divisions within the academic community at every level"), Schrecker holds out hope that dialogue will drive us back to universal consensus concerning academic freedom and restore the education system back to equilibrium.

Another recent study, *Higher Education? How Colleges Are Wasting Our Money and Failing Our Kids—And What We Can Do About It* (2010), by Andrew Hacker and Claudia Dreifus, takes a completely different approach to the problems facing higher education than Schrecker and Nelson. What Hacker and Dreifus want to know is whether students are getting what they pay for when they attend college. Their conclusion is that for the most part they are not. In effect, their book is a serious assault on both the corporate university *and* academic freedom: on the corporate university in the sense of its relentless attacks on vocationalism and the pursuit of increased research funding; on academic freedom in the sense of denying the value of tenure and placing the center of higher education in the hands of students—not faculty.

"Our point throughout this book," assert Hacker and Dreifus, "has been that every non-educational appendage should be made to defend its existence, from the ground up and without the benefit of doubt."[29] This puts everything from administrative overload and faculty sabbaticals to athletics and meal plans in their crosshairs. The result is that there are no sacred educational cows in this book, and doubt is cast on even some of the hallmarks of higher education such as tenure. Quip Hacker and Dreifus in response to a political science professor at Arizona State University who allegedly said to his students on the first day of class, "I have tenure, so I can teach you or not teach you, you're the ones who have to take the tests," "we suspect that he would have invested more of himself in his classes and students" "if he had a contract—renewable, say every six years," rather than tenure.[30]

While it is easy to dismiss this book as merely a neoconservative screed (and it is one), what is interesting about it for our purposes is its *irreverence* to the educational system—particularly in comparison to Schrecker and Nelson's extreme *reverence*. Hacker and Dreyfus have no reservations about tossing out most of today's curriculum (because it is vocational), nor do they seem to be very concerned with protecting shared governance, tenure, or academic freedom. In this sense, because its dialogue is aimed at *disrupting* the current education system, rather than bringing it into equilibrium, it is arguably—in spite of its conservatism—more paralogical than dialogical. That is to say, its method is more in line with the kind of method that will aid the emergence of the postmodern university than work to bring about the return of the modern university.

While it pains me somewhat to side with the methodology of neoconservatives such as Hacker and Dreyfus as opposed to radical liberals such as Nelson and Schrecker, it shows something about what is and is not at stake in conversations about the university; namely, that it is more important *how* we talk about the university, rather than *what* we specifically say. Furthermore, it suggests that the politics of university discourse may be determined more by our methodological affiliation than by our union card or our tweed jacket. Negative dialogics is blind to content and party affiliation in the deployment of its method—a method aimed at dissent and justice, rather than stability and consensus.

Riding a Horse to the Mall

The practice of paralogy in university discourse complicates the politics of the university. It calls for all discussions premised on consensus and stability (or restabilization) to be questioned; it also shows how discussions of university change and reform premised on dialogism are essentially empty conversations, particularly if the system in question is in ruins. There is perhaps no better place to see the limits of dialogism in action than Louis Menand's recent book, *The Marketplace of Ideas: Reform and Resistance in the American University* (2010).

"Knowledge is our most important business," writes Harvard professor Menand in the opening line.[31] "Knowledge is a form of capital that is always unevenly distributed," he continues, "and people who have more knowledge, or greater access to knowledge, enjoy advantages over people who have less."[32] Yet, despite this provocative opening line and the book jacket's claim that *"The Marketplace of Ideas* is certain to spark a long-overdue debate about the condition of American higher education," little space is given to exploring how the modern university can survive under the pressures of the marketplace in an increasingly corporatized university system. Rather, Menand, who is also a staff writer for *The New Yorker* and winner of the 2002 Pulitzer Prize in history for *The Metaphysical Club*, is content to limit his book to answering four questions: (1) Why is a general education curriculum so difficult to institute?; (2) What is the source of the "legitimation crisis" in the humanities?; (3) Why do some people think that interdisciplinarity is so important?; and (4) Why do most professors tend to share similar political beliefs? Nonetheless, in pursuing these questions, his frustration with the pace of change and reform within the university is obvious. Says Menand, as noted earlier, "trying to reform the contemporary university is like trying to get on the Internet with a typewriter, or like trying to ride a horse to the mall."[33]

As a thinker in the dialogical tradition, Menand envisions change and reform in higher education as a search for *consensus within the system*. For example, most of the material from the first essay, "The Problem of General Education," is drawn from a 2006 document, "Curricular Renewal in Harvard College," which Menand co-wrote with "a number of colleagues and administrators" at Harvard.[34] The moral of the story of curricular change at Harvard and other places is that it is very difficult—if not impossible—to change the educational system, especially if the aim is consensus. Writes Menand, "I am in favor of reform when it shakes the system and not when it breaks the system."[35] By self-imposing this limit on his thinking about the university, Menand is essentially committing himself to sustaining the educational system through consensual reform. This approach, in turn, leads him to neglect major *instabilities* within the system including issues of elitism, concentration of resources within the system, and the flawed logic of prestige and affiliation—as well as to offer little in the way of disruptions to the problems currently facing our higher education system.

For Menand, the fact that we face today some of the same dangers faced 100 years ago (for example, the marginalization of liberal arts majors and curricula by non-liberal alternatives) should sound an alarm about the limits of his approach to the challenges facing higher education. So invested is Menand in not breaking an educational system where vocational education dominates over the liberal arts, that when he turns to making a case for the value of the liberal arts, he is simply content to remind us that "Almost any liberal arts field can be made non-liberal by turning it in the direction of some practical skill with which it is already associated."[36] "English departments can become writing programs, even publishing programs," says Menand, "pure mathematics can become applied mathematics, even engineering."[37] Menand argues that this application of "disinterested" liberal arts knowledge to the workplace "pays off in the marketplace," which "gives us a clue to the value-added potential of liberal education."[38] Is this dialogical response really better than Hacker and Dreifus's paralogical response calling for the *reduction* of vocational, non-liberal alternatives in the university? Is Menand's dialogical concession to the power of the marketplace really desirable to Hacker and Dreifus's paralogical disruption of our educational system by reducing its vocational dimension?

Nonetheless, the latter parts of Menand's book, particularly when he discusses the changes that occurred in the humanities after 1975, provide enough material to break away from his "shake but don't break" the system attitude. He notes that while the size of the university system increased dramatically from 1945 to 1975, its curricula and disciplines remained *homogeneous*. However, despite growing at a much more modest pace post-1975, "the composition of the system—who is being taught, who does the teaching, and what they teach" was transformed.[39] In other words, the post-1975 period is notable for its *heterogeneity*.

The gender and ethnic diversity of students and faculty in the post-1975 period, claims Menand, played a large role in bringing about a curricular and disciplinary transformation. Whereas in the Golden Age of the university (1945–1975) "borders were respected and methodologies were codified," and "discipline reigned in the disciplines,"[40] the present period is "fundamentally a backlash against the excessive respect for disciplinarity of the Golden Age university."[41] Why Menand does not use this systemic backlash to engender a more paralogical view of the university is puzzling. Rather, he tries to push the backlash against disciplinarity into a dialogically stabilizing form.

For Menand, the revolution in the humanities after 1975 came in two stages. First a sense of "anti-disciplinarity" arose in nondepartmental areas of study and research such as "[w]omen's studies, cultural studies, science studies, gay and lesbian studies, postcolonial studies, and so on."[42] In the 1990s, this trend developed into a "movement in two only partly related directions: toward interdisciplinarity, and toward what might be called postdisciplinarity."[43] However, rather than developing a paralogical vision from all of this anti-, post-, and interdisciplinary behavior, Menand tries to explain it all away as forms of disciplinary behavior.

True interdisciplinarity, contends Menand, has never existed in the academy, and he is not even certain "what true interdisciplinarity might look like."[44] "Interdisciplinarity is simply disciplinarity raised to a higher power," comments Menand. "It is not an escape from disciplinarity," writes Menand, "it is the scholarly and pedagogical ratification of disciplinarity."[45] In short, "Interdisciplinarity is not something different from disciplinarity."[46] For Menand, the future of the humanities is not interdisciplinarity or postdisciplinarity; rather, "[e]clecticism seems to be the fate of the academic humanities."[47]

Menand's discussions about the impossibility of true interdisciplinarity ring hollow because they are trying to put paralogical behavior into a dialogical box. He asserts that because all PhDs are professionalized in a specific discipline—even if that discipline is "interdisciplinary" like cultural or women's studies—the promise of a true "interdisciplinarity" is never fulfilled. Menand argues that since "disciplinarity" involves the adoption or formalization of methods, paradigms, and vocabularies, and that "interdisciplinary" doctoral fields like cultural studies and women's studies also adopt methods, paradigms, and vocabularies, interdisciplinarity is just "disciplinarity raised to a higher power."

Missing from Menand's account of interdisciplinary is a discussion of the scholar who has completed studies in two or more different fields. Menand seems to believe that "interdisciplinarity" is merely "an administrative name" for disciplinary anxiety. However, contra Menand, interdisciplinarity remains not only possible but *natural* for those able to master two or more disciplines as a point of contact for academic inquiry, and it is here that higher education in America has a good chance for paralogical change. Radical interdisciplinarity is, for example, one of the ways that the academy can escape the disconnect between "pure" academic inquiry and inquiry that is responsive to problems emerging in the world.

Menand concludes his book with a powerful argument: "Professors tend increasingly to think alike because the profession is increasingly self-selecting." "The university may not explicitly require conformity on more than scholarly matters," continues Menand, "but the existing system implicitly demands and constructs it."[48] And while Menand shows how cycles of accountability and reliance on internal standards perpetuated a closed system, it is still disappointing that he makes far too little effort at showing how resistance to change in higher education might be softened.

Menand does, however, show some glimmers of paralogism at the very end of his study when he asks what would happen "if every graduate student were required to publish a single peer-reviewed article instead of writing a thesis"[49] or "if it were easier and cheaper to get in and out of the doctoral motel"?[50] Still, for a public intellectual of his stature, his paralogical moments are far too few.

Nails Across the Chalkboard

In *Crisis on Campus: A Bold Plan for Reforming our Colleges and Universities* (2010), Mark C. Taylor takes a radically different approach to the problems facing higher education today than the thinkers discussed above. For Taylor—who is chair of the department of religion at Columbia University and professor of philosophy of religion at Union Theological Seminary though taught humanities for the majority of his career at Williams College—the university needs to be completely recreated. "Just as the modern university was created at the moment of transition from an agricultural economy, so what might be called the postmodern university must be created to negotiate the shift from industrial and consumer capitalism to financial capitalism and consumer capitalism."[51] His work in this book is, to date, the best example of a paralogical approach to the postmodern university. Fittingly, it is also the most controversial.

"Parochial interests must be set aside," says Taylor, "to create global educational networks that will facilitate the production of new knowledge and cultural capital."[52] If Hacker and Dreifus see a return to the liberal arts as the only way to save the university, and Nelson and Schrecker believe that faculty solidarity is the answer, and Menand's is to simply enjoy the ecclectism, then Taylor's position is that the university as it stands now is not worth saving. The university as we have known it for the past century was particular to a certain set of cultural, political, and economic circumstances that are not available—or at least not feasible—under the current economic conditions. As a consequence, Taylor's intervention in higher education is wildly different than those of Hacker and Dreifus, Nelson, Schrecker, and Menand.

Unlike Hacker and Dreifus who sneer at the work done by professional and vocational programs, and Schrecker who fears increased vocationalism, Taylor does not seem to be bothered by vocational training in the university—though ironically he *does* have a problem with work done in his own area of expertise, the liberal arts. "While many professional schools and vocational programs are doing a good job preparing students for viable professions and careers," comments Taylor, "most graduate schools in the arts, humanities and many of the social sciences are far less successful."[53] Furthermore, like Menand, he bemoans the "process of self-replication" where professors are "afraid of experimentation and change and fall back on the familiar past,"[54] but unlike him, Taylor says that we need to get rid of the system that perpetuates this. For Taylor, the process of self-replication has resulted in an academy where scholars are more interested in "policing their disciplinary borders and punishing those who crossed them" than embracing "new methods" that open "new lines of inquiry."[55]

According to Taylor, the continued reliance on eighteenth-century German philosopher Immanuel Kant's vision of the university is a large part of the problem with the modern university. In his 1798 treatise titled *The Conflict of the Faculties*, Kant writes:

> Whoever it was that first hit on the notion of a university and proposed that a public institution of this kind be established, it was not a bad idea to handle the entire content of learning (really, the thinkers devoted to it) by *mass production*, so to speak—by a division of labor, so that for every branch of the sciences there would be a public teacher or *professor* appointed as its trustee, and all of these together would form a kind of learned community called a *university* (or higher school).

As such, for Kant, the university is founded upon three principles: autonomy, the mechanical logic of industrialism (or, mass consumption), and the distinction between usefulness and uselessness. According to Taylor, all three of Kant's principles "must be changed."[56] Moreover, he contends that the view that "higher education should not be corrupted by money and therefore should not be involved with for-profit ventures" "is as outdated as the patronage system on which it relied."[57] "Academics have yet to admit what artists learned over two hundred years ago," says Taylor, "it is possible to pursue art for art's sake or knowledge for knowledge's sake only if someone else is paying the bills."[58]

Like Hacker and Dreifus, Taylor bemoans the fact that "too many courses represent what the professor wants to teach rather than what the students need to learn"[59] and notes that the rising cost of education will result in "more and more students" being "forced to trade down by attending cheaper schools, and a growing number of young people will be unable to afford to attend any school."[60] He also shares their view that tenure should be abolished.

"The single most important factor preventing change in higher education is tenure," writes Taylor. "The only way for American higher education to remain competitive," he continues, "is to abolish tenure and impose mandatory retirement at the age of seventy."[61] In response to the charge that tenure allows faculty "to express controversial ideas...without the fear of dismissal," he says that "in forty years of teaching, I cannot think of a single person who was more willing to express his or her views after tenure than before."[62] In one of the best lines in the book, Taylor writes, "Proponents of tenure never explain why the freedom of speech protected by the First Amendment, which is good enough for everybody else, is not good enough for them."[63] One can only imagine the tone of a debate between Nelson and Taylor on this point.

For most academics, Taylor's approach to the problems facing higher education will sound like an antagonistic student dragging his nails across the blackboard. Nonetheless, this is the sound of effective paralogical thinking. Among his many suggestions, he recommends salary increases for productive faculty, and salary decreases for unproductive ones;[64] creation of a National Teaching Academy in Chicago to support teaching excellence around the country;[65] and adding a fourth division for schools of arts and science called "Emerging Zones" in addition to the more traditional tripartite division of the natural sciences, the social sciences, and arts and humanities.[66] Taylor's proposals are innovative, visionary, controversial, and dangerous. No existing university practice is sacred to him, and all elements of the educational system should be put on the table for consideration. The modern university as we know it is outdated and broken, and the only way to respond to it is through the creation of a postmodern one.

Conclusion

Tough times call for tough measures—and paralogism is definitely one of them. As a model for dialogue about the university in a time of crisis, it encourages views that destabilize and disrupt a system of education that from most accounts is beyond repair. Its agonistic dimension facilitates speech about the university that is passionate and even frenzied. It calls for academics to become emotionally involved in university dialogue and encourages tough metaprofessional criticism. Playing on Jameson's comments on Lyotard's agonism, and Taylor's comments on the modern university, it is a rhetoric of "struggle" and "conflict" against the massive and repressive Order of the Kantian vision of the university—a guerrilla war of the marginals.

Rejecting the master narrative of the university dating arguably as far back as Kant—or perhaps as recently as the formation of the AAUP in 1915—will not be easy because many of its features benefit those who currently control the system. Administrators caught in the corporate web; tenured professors who benefit from guaranteed employment for life; governmental agencies who benefit from the outcomes of university research; and so on. But the guerrillas on the margins are not to be underestimated. As Taylor reports, "One of the dirty secrets of higher education is that only 35 percent of college and university positions are tenure or tenure-track."[67] This means that 65 percent of college and university educators sit on the margins of tenure: these teaching assistants and part-time adjuncts, with their formidable numbers, are a major threat to the status quo of the system. Also, the shrinking gap between the lifetime income of college graduates as compared to high school graduates can increase the marginal support as well: it was recently reported that the lifetime earning difference for college graduates in comparison to high school graduates is only $279,893 after one subtracts the cost of higher education.[68]

In short, a dialogical approach to the university that aims at consensus and stability within the existing system is not going to solve its problems—or bring about the downfall of the neoliberal university. As Menand ably demonstrates, reform and change in higher education moves at a glacial pace—a pace at which one cannot reasonably hope to solve the educational systems' problems before the system as a whole collapses. This is why a paralogical approach is preferable in this time of systemic crisis. Still, not every paralogically generated proposition is a good one: for example, Hacker and Dreifus's suggestion that vocational, professional, and technical education be totally erased from the university is irresponsible and regressive, and their notion that the liberal arts can and should replace it is simply not feasible. Plato's academy might have fit the needs of the students of fifth-century Athens—but it does not meet the needs of students today.

But good paralogical inquiry is not without its risks. Derided by many for his views about reform in the university, Taylor is the most progressively paralogical thinker of the group discussed. He is also the most controversial—a controversy that goes back to the publication of an essay in the spring of 2009. "End of the University as We Know It," published in *The New York Times* (which also became the basis of his book), made Taylor a lightning rod for public remonstration because of his attacks on things like tenure and traditional disciplinary structures. For example, one Barnard philosopher accused Taylor in the *Times* of "crass anti-intellectualism," while, more recently, another critic in *The New Republic* called his book "unbelievably misguided," and part of the growing "syndrome" of intellectuals turning incendiary—and *antagonistic*—brief op-ed pieces into reckless, wrong-headed books. Nevertheless, though neither reckless nor wrong-headed, Taylor's book is a paralogical provocation that probably raises more questions than provides definitive answers. Still, discussion of this form is more productive than efforts like Nelson's and Schrecker's that encourage us to go "back to the future" in spite of the noticeable faculty and disciplinary fragmentation of the university.

University dialogue is often its richest when motivated by negative commentary. Perhaps provoking some of the hallmarks of academic progress like tenure and traditional disciplinary structures might be "taboo" and annoying to some; but it is also one of the most effective ways of generating academic dialogue in a time of crisis.[69] Not only do such comments draw more public attention to the problems facing higher education, but they also are instrumental in sparking spirited dialogue among students, faculty, and administrators. To be sure, more attention is usually given to negative dialogue than positive dialogue. Consequently, one of our aims at this time should be to strive for an expanded role for negative dialogue in the academy—and perhaps paralogical public intellectuals like Taylor should be championed, rather than chastised. Public intellectuals like Taylor are the antithesis of the modern academic—and perhaps our best hope for the fall of the neoliberal university and the rise of its postmodern counterpart.

4

APOCALYPTIC FEAR

Your courses are expendable; your scholarship inessential; and your discipline is not worth saving. You are micromanaged and maximally measured. Assessment is your culture and audit is your worry. Research must raise revenue and ranking is the prime directive. Professional performance only involves that which is quantifiable—and that which is not quantifiable, such as your feelings and emotional state, do not really matter. The continuous surveillance and obsessive managerialism wears you down, but you dare not speak out against it because you are afraid of retaliation. You are a docile subject. This is life in the neoliberal university—a life where fear is the dominant emotion.

The university in the age of neoliberalism is emotionally stressful not only because of the unreasonable expectation that its participants be able to do anything at any point, but also because at any moment they can be rendered obsolete and expelled from the system. How do you function in an academic environment where you are continually subject to unreasonable expectations? How do you think it feels to be continuously threatened with elimination at any moment? Or to believe that negative dialogue is unwelcome? Or to know that economic imperatives always already override faculty imperatives—and that your academic freedom and shared governance are severely constrained?

It is within these conditions, namely, the rise of the neoliberal university—and the fall of modern university culture as we have known it—that I would like to briefly consider the politics of emotion in academe. Though a relatively neglected area of metaprofessional and educational inquiry, the emotional world created within higher education is an important aspect of academic life.[1] Students pursuing their studies with a preponderance of joy and a feeling of optimism are preferable to those pursuing them with fear and a feeling of nervousness.[2] But how can one expect joy and optimism from today's student population when we know, for example, that many of these students are accumulating massive levels of debt—and we know as well that some of them will even take this debt to their graves?[3]

A similar situation holds for the faculty that teach the students of "generation debt" and the administrators who facilitate relations among students and faculty. Faculty conducting teaching, scholarship, and service with joy and feelings of pride and optimism are becoming more difficult to find; and administrators relaying fearful messages and projecting nervousness and apprehension about academe's future are in no short supply. The neoliberal university most definitely does not bring forth feelings of pride and optimism from its participants—rather it elicits feelings of shame, pessimism, and fear.[4]

The emotional condition of higher education in America has taken a turn for the worse in the new millennium, particularly after the attacks of September 11, 2001—and this is having a debilitating effect on efforts to confront the consequences of the corporate university and educational neoliberalism. Whereas even just a few years ago it may have been appropriate for us to meditate more generally on the role of emotions in academe, today this does not seem as urgent given the dominant and powerful role played by one particular emotion, namely, fear.

In this chapter, I'd like to propose that it is no accident that fear has become the dominant emotion in academe. Rather, the rise of fear in academe can be linked to the rise of neoliberalism in higher education. To be sure, the primary emotional effect of neoliberalism in education is *fear*. Moreover, it can be further established that the promotion of neoliberal academic policies shares a specific and unpleasant characteristic with the attacks of September 11, 2001, namely, both involve acts of *terrorism*. More specifically, where the September 11, 2001, attacks might be termed *political* terrorism,[5] the promotion of neoliberal academic policies might be termed *academic* terrorism. While the latter appellation may seem inappropriate and extreme—as you shall see—it is not only necessary, but also fully warranted.

We need to focus our attention on articulating solutions to the problems facing higher education, rather than avoiding them or merely repeating shopworn assessments of those problems—assessments that more often than not do not get us any closer to getting out of the current abysmal academic condition. Furthermore, we can use the unpleasant intensification of fear and terror in higher education brought about by neoliberal responses to the attacks of September 11, 2001, as an opportunity to bring about the twilight of the corporate university—and dawn of the postmodern university. Studies of the university that offer no speculative position out of the neoliberal abyss are not necessary and only serve to promote academic fear and terror—which is itself the primary fuel for educational neoliberalism.

Power and Emotion

The primary emotional effect of neoliberalism in education is *fear*—if not *extreme* fear, that is, *terror*. Why? Because neoliberalism takes much academic decision making out of the hands of academics, and places it into the invisible hands of the market—and this terrifies academics.

Absolute academic values such as shared governance and academic freedom are rendered contingent under neoliberalism, which is to say, if faculty-driven decisions do not serve the requirements of the market, then they are rendered disposable, or if the fruits of scholarly deliberation are in conflict with the free-flow of the market, then they too are rejected. Moreover, the conjunction of neoliberal educational policy with the demands of a militarized state only exacerbates the fear in academe.

Lyotard's comment from chapter 3 about terror being "the efficiency gained by eliminating, or threatening to eliminate, a player from the language game one shares with him"[6] is apropos here. Neoliberal managerialism is nothing if not efficient. Hence the terror of working under conditions where at any moment one's agency can be, so to speak, "eliminated from the academic game," is emotionally debilitating. This emotional affect manifests itself most obviously in the docility and consent characteristic of the neoliberal academic. "He is silenced or consents," again writes Lyotard, "not because he has been refuted, but because his ability to participate has been threatened (there are many ways to prevent someone from playing)."[7] Even if one takes umbrage with the comparison of academic life to a language game, the terrifying fact remains that academic agency is terminable at any moment in the neoliberal academy—and this is an important part of its modus operandi.

A neoliberal educational system gains much of its power through its control of academic emotions. It projects the state of mind in academe that at any moment one's academic way of life can be interrupted—or, if you will, terminated. "Terror is an emotion, a state of mind,"[8] writes George Lakoff. But, he adds, it is a state of mind that can be extended indefinitely. "Because extreme fear can be provoked at any time," comments Lakoff, "terror cannot be ended."[9] This means that neoliberal terror in academe gains its power by continuously projecting *possible* academic ways of life or worlds much worse than the ones we currently inhabit. If these apocalyptic academic ways of life or worlds were ever to become real, then neoliberalism in education would lose much of its emotional impact on academics. Aristotle seems to confirm this later point in his description of how the emotion of terror works.

In his *Rhetoric*, Aristotle uses the term *phobos* for "a sort of pain or agitation derived from imagination of a future destructive or painful evil."[10] For him, the evil is always near at hand, and not far off, and the persons threatened are ourselves. Often translated as "terror," Aristotle's *phobos* captures well the emotion felt by many academics today faced with the increasing neoliberalization of higher education. Few things in academic life are more painful than *imagining* academe without academic freedom or shared governance. And many of us know firsthand the feeling of being a liberal arts scholar whose courses—if not department—does not *appear* to have a future in the neoliberal universe. This feeling is quite the opposite of the feeling of the scholar whose academic agency is not continuously haunted by the specter of course or program elimination—a feeling among humanities scholars that is becoming increasingly more difficult to find.

But again, note the emphasis on *imagination* in Aristotle's notion of *phobos*. Extreme fear for him involves thinking about a situation that is near at hand, but not *in hand*. The fall of the liberal arts *is about to occur*; the end of the university as we know it *is near at hand*. Arguably, apocalyptic narratives that support these positions are key aspects of neoliberal educational power. The more academics believe that the end of academic ways of life that they love and enjoy are just around the corner, the stronger the ability of neoliberalism to promote a controlling fear. It is a controlling fear that encourages compliance and compromise with neoliberal educational practices—compliance and compromise that can be as simple as "corporatizing" literature courses or as complicated as changing scholarly focus to meet the demands of the education market.

What is interesting is the way in which, on this notion of "terror," allegedly "progressive" narratives about the university become agents of neoliberal terror in the academy. Without widely read narratives like Frank Donoghue's, which project academic events such as the end of the professoriate and offer no hope for a way out, it would be much more difficult for neoliberalism in education to manufacture fear. The imagination, however, uses narratives like Donoghue's to motivate belief in a "future destructive or painful evil" regarding academic life—a belief that conveniently fuels the fear and terror that is arguably the warp and woof of neoliberal educational practice.

The educational nightmare of neoliberalism is made even more intense when coupled with accounts by leading educational commentators like Louis Menand who assert—as he does in the epigraph to this book—that change and reform in higher education is or should be slow. Unlike Donoghue, who is simply content to rehearse the reasons why academia as we know it is about to end, Menand goes one step further in his study when he argues why it is next to impossible to reform the aspects of higher education that are not working well.

Menand revealed his position on changing the current educational system in America early in his book when he said that he was "in favor of reform when it shakes the system and not when it breaks the system."[11] However, he immediately follows this conservative statement with a progressive one: "I do think that intellectual life should involve taking chances."[12] While I fully agree with the latter statement, I could not disagree more with the former statement.

The juxtaposition of these two statements is problematic. One of the wonderful things about intellectual life *is* that it allows us to take chances: to exercise our academic freedom in collaboration with our colleagues; and to exert our academic agency for the betterment of our students and university. Why then should we not aim, for example, to "break" the neoliberal educational system—and to move beyond it? It seems to me to be a chance worth taking. The alternative, that is, working in a neoliberal educational system that is widely despised is not tenable. Therefore, seeking a new system is a risk worth taking.

It is interesting that Menand gives very little attention to elaborating exactly what the "system" is. While one would hope that it is more than Columbia, Harvard, and Yale Universities—the most frequently mentioned institutions of higher education in the book—given the paltry range of schools discussed or mentioned (which are primarily Ivy League schools), there is little evidence that the system amounts to more than these and similar universities. Again, unfortunately, hard questions about the university system in America such as its elitism and its flawed logic of prestige and affiliation are not discussed.[13] Nor are there many thoughts about reforming the American university system based on the educational needs and financial constraints of students—let alone the current negative emotional condition of academics.

It is in the context of fear-invoking accounts of no way out of the neoliberal educational nightmare and accounts maintaining that even if there is a way out, it will take such a long time to come to fruition that effectively it is out of the question, that optimism and hope is found in an account like Mark Taylor's—an account that at least implores us to seek new models for higher education and encourages paralogical inquiry. Taylor's full-embrace of bold educational reform is the polar opposite of Menand's approach—and it is quite empowering, particularly for neoliberal academe's docile subject. But, it still should be noted that Taylor's way is not all sweetness and light for academic emotions.

Recalibrating academe in the wake of its destruction by neoliberalism and the promotion of the postmodern university where paralogy is the preferred mode of dialogue can also invoke fear among academics—fear of change. And while changing neoliberal university culture is the order of the day, some may still be concerned about the type of university culture that will emerge out of the ashes of the neoliberal university. We should look to this emergent culture with a sense of optimism and joy, particularly if we approach it with a sense of justice tempered by intellectual creativity. Engaging in the creation of a new vision for the university is an opportunity to open up new vistas for academic freedom. If it is approached with a sense of opportunity to move beyond the neoliberal academy, then fear of the unknown might be assuaged—and the joys of creation embraced.

Accounts like Menand's that argue that reform in academe is—and should be—slow have the unintended effect of providing the conditions for the continuous suspension of academic terror. If prominent educational commentators and public intellectuals like Menand are suggesting that we should not make a radical break with the widely despised (but apparently long-standing) corporate university system, then the ability to promote fear and terror within academe gets a longer lease on life.

Accounts of the emotional lives of academics are important windows to what works and does not work in academe. If collectively the main emotion that emerges from these accounts is extreme fear about their academic way of life, then every effort should be made to eliminate the conditions that bring about that emotion. Narratives of the imminent demise of the university and the alleged inability for academics to do anything about it only play into neoliberalism's repressive structures—and make academic life more fearful than it needs to be. What is needed in hard educational times such as these are narratives that imagine academe beyond its despised and repressive structures—not additional accounts of future destructive or painful academic evils.

Coercive Acts

Terrorism is usually regarded as a form—and perhaps the most extreme form—of political violence. It is violence that is generally regarded as "unofficial" or "unauthorized" though always said to be in pursuit of some political end or ends. In many ways, it is commonly regarded as the paradigmatic form of political violence in a group of violent acts that include demonstrations, revolutions, and civil war. As such, for an event to count as terrorism, it needs to be not only a violent or intimidating action, but, more importantly, an unofficial or unauthorized operation. An authorized or official action using violence and intimidation in the pursuit of political aims is not terrorism but war. As an act of war, such an official action can count on indignation and an attempt at retaliation. The official warrant of an act of violence provides it with a comprehension of moral clarity that is denied the act of terrorism, or that terrorism, it might be more accurate to say, denies its target.

Regarded as such, the concept of terrorism seems remote to the everyday life of the academy. While the shooting of students at Virginia Tech, for example, may fit the received concept of terrorism, the emotional terror wrought upon academics by neoliberalism does not. Why? Because even though the emotional terror experienced by academics is intimidating to them, there is no physical violence associated with it. Nonetheless, there is something wrong with a concept that does not allow for the type of terror perpetrated by the presence of neoliberalism in academia to be considered terrorism. Perhaps at another time in history, it would be reasonable to allow the noninclusive concept of terrorism to stand. However, these are not "normal" times, particularly given their proximity to an historical event that has changed our understanding of "terror" and "terrorism," if not also many of the other terms through which we view the world.

Prior to September 11, 2001, "terror" was simply a state of mind, that is, an emotional state describable as being greatly frightened or being in a state of intense fear. However, after the attacks, terror became more than simply a mental state that most seek to avoid—or to experience through artworks such as horror movies or tragic plays in an act of catharsis. Rather, it was *hypostatized* into something that exists—or persists—in the world. It became something with which we are at "war."

To notice this transformation is to notice the way in which historical events can redefine and become disassociable with particular terms and concepts. For example, after the French Revolution, "liberty" became disassociable with this historical event in the same way that "holocaust" became indistinguishable from the genocidal events that occurred during World War II. Moreover, these major—or better yet "extreme"—historical events tend to reify terms and concepts. "Liberty," for example, became reified by the French Revolution in the same way "terror" has come to be reified as a consequence of the events of September 11, 2001. However, just because terms and concepts become reified or hypostatized by events does not mean that they provide any more insight on the event. In fact, as we know in the case of "holocaust," sometimes not even decades of reflection and response can solve the enigmas signified by the term. Nonetheless, reification is a sign of a basic change in the being of the term, or what the medieval philosopher Duns Scotus called its *haecceitas*.

In the weeks after the September 11, 2001, attacks, French philosopher Jacques Derrida commented that received concepts such as "war," "terror," and "terrorism" do not adequately account for what happened. In a way, the changes in their *haecceitas*—their *hereness* and *nowness*—facilitated by the events of September 11, 2001, call for a reconsideration of them. Writes Derrida,

> Such an "event" surely calls for a philosophical response. Better, a response that calls into question, at their most fundamental level, the most deep-seated conceptual presuppositions in philosophical discourse. The concepts with which this "event" has most often been described, named, categorized, are the products of a "dogmatic slumber" from which only a new philosophical reflection can awaken us, a reflection *on* philosophy, most notably on political philosophy and its heritage. The prevailing discourse, that of the media and of the official rhetoric, relies too readily on received concepts like "war" or "terrorism" (national or international).[14]

It is from within this space of "new philosophical reflection" awakened or brought about by the events of September 11, 2001, that the reconceptualization of terrorism is warranted.

Not only did the events of September 11, 2001, reawaken "reflection *on* philosophy" in America, they also called into question the very nature of the key concepts associated with these events. In the case of "terror," the events of September 11, 2001, reclaimed this emotion from the realm of the aesthetic (viz., catharsis and the sublime), and pulled it back into the social and political realm. After 9/11, to speak of infliction of the emotion of "terror" is to call upon social and political thinking—if not also neoliberal thinking—rather than aesthetic feeling. As such, given the dominance of the emotion of "terror" within the academy, and a window in philosophical history open to rethinking the concept of terrorism, it seems appropriate to take the opportunity to imagine a concept of terrorism that accommodates both violent and (merely) intimidating acts of terror.[15]

One place to begin to motivate such a concept of terrorism is an article published over 30 years ago by the philosopher Carl Wellman. In "On Terrorism Itself," [16] Wellman avoids "violence" as a necessary condition of terrorism. Rather, he defines terrorism as "the use or attempted use of terror as a means of coercion."[17] In providing this definition, Wellman was well aware that it is much broader (and idiosyncratic) than most. However, Wellman believed that it "is illuminating just because it points to certain morally significant features that paradigm cases of terrorism share with other similar acts that fall outside the usual sphere of attention."[18] The academic terrorism promoted by neoliberalism would most definitely be one of the cases that falls outside the usual sphere of attention.

Though Wellman concedes that "[o]ne of the most effective ways of creating terror is by violent actions, both because such actions characteristically inflict great harm and because they inflict it in a striking manner,"[19] he is not willing to entertain violence as a necessary condition of terrorism. "When the terrorist engages in violence, this feature of his act becomes an important factor in our moral assessment of it," writes Wellman. "But the ethics of terrorism is not a mere footnote to the ethics of violence," continues Wellman, "because violence is not essential to terrorism and, in fact, most acts of terrorism are nonviolent."[20] An example he uses to motivate this atypical claim regarding the link between terrorism and violence is that of a "judge sentencing a condemned criminal to death."[21] This action on the part of the judge is considered by Wellman to be a type of terrorism "if he is deterring or attempting to deter potential criminals by using the terror of death innate in human nature."[22]

While Wellman's example of the use of deterrence in capital punishment cases as a form of (nonviolent) terrorism may seem far from the type of terror instilled by the practice of neoliberal educational policy (as there is no threat of death), his example of the classroom practice of threatening to flunk students is not. "I must confess," says Wellman, "that I often engage in nonviolent terrorism myself, for I often threaten to flunk any student who hands in his paper after the due date."[23] "Anyone who doubts that my acts are genuine instances of the coercive use of terror," continues Wellman, "is invited to observe the unwillingness of my students to hand in assigned papers on time in the absence of any such threat and the panic in my classroom when I issue my ultimatum."[24]

Wellman's example of "classroom terrorism" is not much different than the neoliberal administrator who threatens to cut faculty, courses, programs, and salaries, *if* neoliberal educational policies and values are not adhered to. It makes no difference to the neoliberal administrator that philosophy has been part of the academy since the days of Plato and Aristotle.[25] All that matters is that *if* students pursuing vocational majors are not interested in it, the program is expendable. On Wellman's view of terrorism, the threat of course and program elimination is clearly a form of terrorism—albeit a nonviolent form.

Efforts to "corporatize" liberal arts courses (such as described earlier in the case of literature courses) or programs (such as turning a master's program in English into a "writing" or "publishing" program, viz., one that is vocationally aimed at training students to work in the publishing industry rather than disciplinarily based)[26] should be viewed as responses to academic terrorism: professors threatened with course and program elimination who "corporatize" them do so to protect themselves and their curricular areas from imminent destruction by neoliberal administrators. Corporatized liberal arts curriculum, though the product of neoliberal coercion, still keep the hope alive that they will inspire new generations of students to pursue the liberal arts—even if the task becomes more difficult when the liberal arts are introduced with a neoliberal haze.

It is the use of *coercion*—not violence—that drives Wellman's notion of terrorism. "Coercion," says Wellman, "actual or attempted, is the essence of terrorism."[27] For him, terrorism requires three elements: (1) some terrifying or potentially terrifying action; (2) some future harm or evil ("though not the harm or evil of the past action that created the terror"[28]); and (3) the threat a harm will occur if the coercion is resisted. Academic terrorism in the context of neoliberalism fits squarely into Wellman's three elements model: (1) the introduction of neoliberal educational policies into academe has been a terrifying action; (2) future harm to courses, programs, and faculty freedoms; and (3) termination of courses, programs, and faculty who resist *embracing* neoliberal changes. Under neoliberalism, academic tradition is no longer king; rather, whatever the market can validate takes academic precedence. In the case of the liberal arts, the coercion to vocationalize—or eliminate—them is a major political end of contemporary academic terrorism.

Wellman's concept of terrorism gives but one possible way to express the type of terrorism occurring in the academy. It is by no means the only way, nor is it not without its own difficulties. The point though of bringing it to our attention is to show one possible way to conceptualize how the kind of neoliberal terrorism now found in academe may be squared with the kind of terrorism where buildings are blown up and lives are lost. Both types of terrorism share the use of intimidation through terror though one does this through violence and the other does not. While this may be uncomfortable to some political philosophers who require violence with their terrorism, it should come as comfort to those in academe who every day feel the coercion but have not been able to put a term to it. They can now call it what it is: academic terrorism.[29]

Conclusion

The politics of academic emotions can reveal disturbing features of academe. The reality that most academics today work in fear of loss of academic freedom and shared governance reveals fundamental problems with higher education today. The practice of altering courses and programs to avoid cancellation has become more common as an academic survival response to neoliberal educational practices. State and federal economic pressures and legislative mandates have only intensified the level of coercion in academe. The pursuit of knowledge should be a joyful event where one does not have to continuously look over one's shoulder in fear of saying or doing the wrong thing. To see terror as an emotion that pervades academe today is to recognize the degree to which higher education is in need of fundamental reform. To deny the possibility of reform is to extend indefinitely the current reign of terror in academe; to continue to present narratives (or "studies") of the academy that offer no exit to its neoliberal conditions is to subject it to a form of academic terrorism.

There has been and continues to be a blindness to the emotional lives of academics. The recognition that the emotional condition of many in higher education is best described as "terror" and that a notion of "academic terrorism" not only makes sense, but is probably more active in academe than many realize is very troubling. The events of September 11, 2001, have brought about an intense investigation as to the contemporary meaning of concepts like "terror" and "terrorism." "Fear makes people inclined to deliberation," said Aristotle.[30] Academe must use this tragic historical window as an opportunity for revaluation and resistance to the destructive forces of neoliberal educational policies—and bring an end to the current emotional condition of the academy.

5

CRITICAL AFFILIATIONS

Academic culture in the age of neoliberalism favors students and faculty that are passive, docile and compliant. Critical resistance is not welcome in an educational environment that avoids reform and prefers conformity. The neoliberal university views the freedom to critically inquire and to explore subjects wherever they may lead as an intellectual ideal that does not square well with a teaching-to-the-test approach to higher education. The practical ends of the university in the age of neoliberalism are more closely associated with vocational training than preparation for critical citizenship and intellectual exchange.

In this context, it should be apparent that the effects of this emaciation of academic freedom will be devastating. Martha Nussbaum and others are rightly concerned that the "technically trained docility"[1] that results from much of our current higher education works to "threaten the very life of democracy itself" and to "impede the creation of a decent world culture."[2] Nussbaum warns—as you will recall—that if we continue to "ask our schools to turn out useful profit-makers rather than thoughtful citizens,"[3] our world will become one comprised of "technically trained people who do not know how to criticize authority, useful profit-makers with obtuse imaginations,"[4] that is, "people who do not recognize the individual, who speak group-speak, who behave, and see the world, like docile bureaucrats."[5] The critical implications of neoliberalism in education are clear. The question remains though as to how to avoid them.

Active and engaged academic subjects are not only necessary for progressive education to occur, but are also important to the creation of a world inhabited by thoughtful citizens. If the academy is not committed to the latter—and we know that values determined by pursuit of the extreme free market are not geared toward the production of thoughtful citizens—then we must take very seriously the emaciating effects of neoliberalism on critical exchange. Much hangs on the type of critical exchange with which we choose to affiliate: whereas the docile subjectivity of neoliberal academic culture would seem to favor a type of uncritical exchange, the active subjectivity of the postmodern academic culture described earlier would seem to favor a more robust form of critical exchange.

It also may be the case that the only way out of the neoliberal educational abyss is by way of subjects who reject docile academic subjectivities—and who take on more combative or agonistic ones. Again, think of Lyotard's notion of paralogism where "to speak is to fight"—and where what is being fought against is neoliberalism and its contemporary variations, rather than "the massive and repressive Order of Aristotle and his successors" noted earlier. It must also be pointed out that with agonism comes freedom and power. "At the very heart of the power relationship, and constantly provoking it," writes French philosopher Michel Foucault, "are the recalcitrance of the will and the intransigence of freedom." "Rather than speaking of an essential freedom," continues Foucault, "it would be better to speak of an 'agonism'—of a relationship which is at the same time reciprocal incitation and struggle; less of a face-to-face confrontation which paralyzes both sides than a permanent provocation."[6]

The words and thoughts of Lyotard and Foucault are important to recall as they suggest to us that docile dialogue has much less chance prevailing in a power struggle against neoliberalism than its paralogical counterpart. This chapter will outline these two different types of critical exchange, and examine how they function and what kind of response they can expect to receive within academe. It will be proposed that academic culture in the age of neoliberalism may require a reevaluation of our largely negative perception of tough criticism and paralogical inquiry—a proposal that may not be popular, but may also be necessary.

CRITICAL SPECTACLES

Professor Jones is well known for his generosity in his critical exchanges with his colleagues. He encourages nonconfrontational public exchanges of ideas and is always supportive of his colleagues in his assessments of them. He is also extremely patient with his graduate students, and encourages them to be the same way with each other. For example, if a graduate student makes a comment in class that is weak or off base, unlike some other faculty in his department, he will not make a big fuss about it in class. Rather, when the appropriate opportunity presents itself, he will try to work with the student outside of class to improve his or her line of thinking. Same goes for his colleagues. In print and at presentations, he is known for being upbeat and positive regarding the work of his colleagues—even if he disagrees with their line of thought. His assessments of his colleagues always accentuate the positive aspects of their work, and downplay or dismiss the negative aspects. His critical credo is "If you don't have something positive to say about a student or a colleague, then it is best not to say anything at all—at least not in public." His colleague, Professor Smith, however, thinks quite differently about critical exchange.

Smith has made a career out of telling people that they are wrong, in particular, everyone that does not believe the same thing that he believes. For him, critical exchange is about trying to get the other person to see the world his way, and if they don't, then he will do everything he can to prove to them—and anyone else who will listen—that they are wrong. Critical exchange for him is a struggle among competing ideas. It is a nasty business where it is acceptable to be a brute. In his opinion, strong ideas survive and weak ones perish. The same goes for graduate students and faculty.[7] The academy for him has no room for what he perceives are "wishy-washy" opinions and people. His assessments of his students and colleagues tend to be harsh, but are always well argued and persuasive. Tell things the way they are, and let the chips fall where they may. For him, it is just as acceptable to publicly praise one's colleagues as it is to publicly berate them—students included.[8]

Both of these professors are well known for their affiliation with a specific type of critical exchange, or what might be called in short their "critical affiliation." Their highly different styles of critical exchange with their students and colleagues confer a particular value and identity on them both among their students and colleagues as well as within their discipline and institutions. Or, alternately put, their respective affiliations with highly different styles of critical exchange confer upon them distinctive academic identities and reveal differing professional values.

Most of us probably know someone like Jones. Others have probably either heard of someone like Smith—or might have even been on the receiving end of the behavior of someone like him. While both Jones and Smith deeply value critical exchange, each goes about it very differently. Jones aims for what might be described as a "compassionate, caring" type of critical exchange, which tends to favor "exchange" over "critique." Smith strives for what might be called a more "combative, confrontational" style of critical exchange, which tends to favor "critique" over "exchange." In many ways, each represents a different pole of the critical exchange spectrum. Both have a lot of graduate students and colleagues that affiliate with them, even if those who affiliate with Smith tend to either share his general style of critical exchange or agree more with his opinions than those who affiliate with Jones tend to agree with his opinions.

If asked, one would wager that most scholars and critics in the humanities, especially literary studies, would say that they would like to see more academics like Jones in our profession than academics like Smith—more compassion, less confrontation. Major critics like Americanist and former Duke University English professor Jane Tompkins have recently bemoaned scholarly attacks as evidence of a "decline of civility" in literary studies, and Herbert S. Lindenberger, a professor emeritus of Humanities at Stanford University, has lamented the "warlike atmosphere" of English studies. Comments such as these are indicative of a general dissatisfaction with harsh public criticism in literary studies—criticism that is frowned upon both because of its potential for emotional disruption and for its alleged divisiveness. Critics like Jones believe that solidarity is not possible in a critical climate where ideas are publicly dismantling or where scholars feel a sense of shame for argumentative infelicities. Therefore, in order to avoid any emotional disturbance or division among colleagues, those like Jones who "care" for the welfare of their peers call for the adoption of a more "civil" form of criticism.

I also think that most scholars today in the humanities would say that our profession would be a *better* one if the type of critical exchange practiced by Jones became more commonplace than that of Smith. Why? Because few people in our profession—or most, for that matter—want to be wrong or negatively assessed. Fewer still like to *be told* that they are wrong. And just about no one wants their positions publicly dismantled in a combative, confrontational manner. Most academics in our profession seem to value public critical exchange to the point at which it reveals their own shortcomings, at which point they want it to stop before they are called out or become part of a professional spectacle. The same misgivings also hold for telling others that they are wrong or publicly taking apart the positions of their peers. There are, however, a few like the critic Stanley Fish, who seem to thrive on these professional spectacles, but they are the exception, not the norm.[9]

Is affiliating with a compassionate, caring form of critical exchange more desirable for the future of the humanities, particularly situated as it is in the age of neoliberalism, than affiliating with a combative, confrontational style? Is a compassionate, caring form of critical exchange more collegial than a combative, confrontational style? Does a compassionate, caring form of critical exchange provide the conditions for a stronger or better profession? Answering these and related questions takes one into the formation of normative behavior in the scholarly community—something that is only recently beginning to be understood more completely. It is an area of metaprofessional investigation that takes us into both the ethics of critical exchange and the politics of affiliation.

I would like to maintain that if a compassionate, caring form of critical exchange entails removing the "critical" from "critical exchange," then I would rather see our profession move toward a more combative, confrontational style of critical exchange even if it means rumpling a few feathers. This is particularly important in the face of the challenges to our profession from the neoliberal university. Corporate humanities is already a compromised version of the humanities—one that implies that within the parameters of the neoliberal university, the humanities is required to function differently than it did in the modern university. If one of the consequences of the neoliberal university is the gradual erasure of critical inquiry, then part of the role of corporate humanities needs to be to preserve—if not intensify—the task of critical education in the humanities.

Though the suggestion of moving toward a more combative, confrontational style of critical exchange may not sit well in literary studies, it is not an uncommon style of critical exchange in other disciplines in the humanities. Philosophy, for example, is notorious for its combative, confrontational style of critical exchange. This is so much the case that in philosophy, the mere presence of certain professors in a room can make a speaker quake in their shoes in anticipation of an expected confrontational exchange—and an audience await in high suspense for the eventual critical spectacle. As such, in philosophy, the move toward a more combative, confrontational style of critical exchange would be no big thing—in fact, it probably would not even be worth much discussion. Socrates, the father of Western philosophy, after all, prided himself on a highly confrontational style of critical exchange—and many contemporary philosophers are more than ready to carry on the tradition. In literary studies, however, the suggestion that we adopt a more combative, confrontational style of critical exchange will probably be a much more controversial and unwelcome one.[10]

Normative Behavior

The scholarly community is a closed and tight-knit community both in terms of ideas and values—a situation that is more than likely not to change in the near future. Some go so far as to maintain that professors are of a like mind. Louis Menand, as you will recall, argued for this position, writing "Professors tend to think alike because the profession is increasingly self-selected."[11] He even takes the next step and suggests that the similarities might even go beyond more than just "thinking." Adds Menand, "The university may not explicitly require conformity on more than scholarly matters, but the existing system implicitly demands and constructs it."[12] Menand's point leads one to see the scholarly community as one wherein the rules of normative behavior, while not explicitly stated, are tacitly understood. In other words, behavioral norms are constructed and enforced by the academy—albeit very quietly.

Young professionals are introduced to them in graduate school, master them as (successful) junior faculty, and become protectors and advocates of them as senior faculty. One's success in academe is in large part based on ones' ability to comprehend and observe entrenched protocols—from how one responds to colleagues and approaches scholarly matters, to how one fosters professional relationships and develops disciplinary affiliations; the mastering of professional protocols is a key to scholarly success.

Some of the rules of membership in the scholarly community are fairly straightforward and noncontroversial. For example, we are never prohibited from using the ideas of another scholar in our community just so long as we acknowledge their use. Elaborate mechanisms for citation such as the *MLA Handbook* and *Chicago Manual of Style* map out the citation protocols. Every so many years these protocols are updated or changed to account for things like new sources or forms of information. Membership in the scholarly community requires not only that we acknowledge using the ideas of others but also that we do it in the proper manner.

Nonetheless, while failure to properly utilize the *MLA Handbook* in citing use of another's ideas is generally not grounds for expulsion from the community, failure to even attempt to acknowledge use of another's ideas is.[13] Moreover, few scholars advance in the scholarly community without using the ideas of others. One could not, for example, write an article or book about say Virginia Woolf without at least acknowledging the relationship of one's own ideas about Woolf to those of others. While one does not have to cite everything that has ever been published by Woolf scholars, one has to at least be cognizant of the critical trends in Woolf scholarship.

In fact, one could argue that the more one is able to situate successfully one's own work within the complete body of Woolf scholarship, *ceteris paribus*, the more favorably one's own work will be viewed by the scholarly community. Complete acknowledgment and awareness of the work in one's field in many cases trumps innovative and heterodox thinking and writing. Nonetheless, in spite of the privileged position of orthodox thinking and scholarship, one could not imagine, for example, the formally innovative novels and criticism of Raymond Federman, or the heterodox thinking of Gilles Deleuze, coming from scholars who were expected to make sure that every last article on Spinoza or Beckett were acknowledged before offering their own critical contributions and opinions on these writers. Innovative and heterodox contemporary thinkers like Federman and Deleuze who close out the tail end of the last century, or even Ferdinand de Saussure and Charles Peirce, who closed out (or opened up) the previous one, often have little time or interest in keeping up with the scholarship—and as such create work that has a problematic relationship to more orthodox lines of scholarship.[14]

We are all familiar with the types of works that situate themselves outside of the scholarly community or disciplinary "box." As editor of the *American Book Review*, a publication that is dedicated to publishing reviews of small press books,[15] and editor of *symplokē*, a journal that publishes interdisciplinary work, I probably see much more of this type of work than most. Many of the books of this type come from non-scholarly sources, and are either self-published or come from vanity presses. Many of the manuscripts of this type come from either pre-formative or non-formative sources, namely, from either graduate students whose identity is still to be formed, or from those who make their living outside of academia and have little use for or sense of professional scholarly identity. Few pieces of this sort come from people with fully established academic identities. Or if they do, they tend to be academics very late in their careers.

If one agrees that utilizing the work of others in the scholarly community is a tacit rule of membership in a scholarly community, then so too is acknowledging it in the proper way. But scholarly acknowledgment is not as straightforward as it might seem. In print, it is far easier to acknowledge the positive influence of one's scholarly peers than the negative influence. For example, thanking people for contributing ideas that helped to establish one's point is fraught with fewer potential difficulties than noting the ideas of people that one seeks to set straight or correct. In fact, arguably, critical philosophy was born out of such an acknowledgment when Immanuel Kant thanked David Hume for "awakening him from his dogmatic slumbers."[16] By the same token, how many acknowledgments actually *thank* the folks that are corrected by the work? Still, the latter items are in many regards the modus operandi of critical scholarship: find a published, if not respected position, and set one's own position up *against* it. If everyone thinks that Professor Jackson's reading of *Hamlet* is brilliant, then one can enter the scholarly fray by opposing or rejecting it. But criticism of this type is much more complicated than one would assume on first blush, particularly when the politics of affiliation intersects with the ethics of criticism.

The ethics of criticism, at least in a critically robust scholarly community, will advocate the position that if one finds fault in a line of thinking, then one has a moral obligation to call it out, if not correct it. This, however, presents a problem for those who affiliate with what has been termed the "compassionate, caring" critical affiliation—that is, critics who are often loathe to point out frailties in their colleagues' work. Such critics would rather not say anything about it than make a "negative" comment about it. Here's an actual example (though using a different name) from my work as editor of *American Book Review*.

Professor Jones reads a review of one of his colleagues' works, and is appalled by the "negative" and "dismissive" tone of the review. Feeling a sense of filial obligation (which we did not know at the time of review assignment), Jones offers to review the book for us. However, after assigning the review to Jones, we receive a letter from Jones asking to be relieved from the duty of reviewing the book because after reading it Jones *concurs* with the "negative" review. Says Jones, "I just can't say anything negative about my colleague's book." Remember, Jones's critical credo is "don't say anything if you can't say something positive." Well, he couldn't find anything positive to say about his colleague's book, so decided to beg off reviewing it. This didn't—and still doesn't—seem right to me.

This example illustrates both the consequences of someone like Jones exerting his "critical affiliations," as well as an example of how "affiliation" in itself can present a double-normative-bind for the compassionate, caring critic. Not only is this type of critic normatively predisposed to *not* be publicly critical, he is also bound by his "filial" commitment to his colleagues. In this example, critical affiliation not only short-circuited the critical process, but also contributed to the construction of conformity (and paternalism) in the academy.

Critical affiliation in a robust scholarly community requires not only that we be true to our critical commitments, but also that we use them to advance our scholarly and creative activity. The weakness in Jones's critical affiliations is not the fact that he strives to be compassionate or caring in his dealings with his colleagues (only a cad would maintain that these are not admirable values). The weakness, rather, is that he believes that giving anything but praise to them in print is a violation or betrayal of filiality—or even collegiality.

Anonymous Care

The scenario that was set up involving a book review is not an uncommon one, particularly when the identity of the reviewer is going to be known to the reviewed. Many compassionate, caring critical affiliators would rather not review a book than say something critical about it in public, especially when it is the work of someone with whom they feel a strong sense of affiliation. Short of not saying anything at all about the book or refusing to review it, some prefer instead to give it "faint praise" in this situation. This is one of the ways in which the compassionate, caring critic can get around violating the critical credo "If you don't have something positive to say about a student or colleague, then it is best not to say anything at all—at least not in public."

Faint praise involves criticizing someone indirectly by not directly praising them enthusiastically. It allows the compassionate, caring critic to say something about the work without revealing the true nature of their critical feelings. It is, by many indications, a dangerous but common practice. In her book *Faint Praise: The Plight of Book Reviewing in America* (2007), Gail Pool notes that "praise rather than nastiness has generally been the central problem in American reviewing," and advises editors "to look for writers who are above all critics."[17] Her study draws attention to the ways in which American reviewers have gravitated away from harsh criticism because they are "[w]ary of being viewed as jealous" or of "being considered enviously unfair."[18] By "bending over backwards to praise books more than they deserve," Pool is describing critical behavior that not even Jones would condone: namely, praising something that is actually believed to be unpraiseworthy.[19] Pool seems to believe—and I definitely believe this—that what readers really want in book reviews are honest and direct opinions about books.

However, the problem of faint praise (as well as overpraise) extends deeper into literary studies than just the level of the book review.

From letters of recommendation, to peer reviews of performances and manuscripts, faint praise runs rampant. Instead of saying what one really thinks about a person's scholarly work, faint praise allows people to comment on the matter at hand without saying what they really think.

Scholars like Jones prefer faint praise because it allows them to engage fully in critical exchanges—albeit a rather watered-down version of them—without coming across as overly or hypercritical. However, in my estimation, giving "faint praise" is far worse than just saying nothing at all. Why? Because when we say nothing, we have not rendered a verbal critical judgment (even though we are misleading our audience into believing that we *might* think favorably of someone or something). When we offer faint praise—instead of honest and direct criticism—we are merely offering empty criticism—and the last thing the humanities in the age of neoliberalism needs is a growth in empty criticism. Words chosen so as not to render any critical commentary are tantamount to the emptiest and most banal form of criticism imaginable—and only serve to make the contested space of the humanities today even more vulnerable to neoliberal assault.

Another way that compassionate, caring critical affiliators get around the critical credo "If you don't have something positive to say about a student or colleague, then it is best not to say anything at all—at least not in public" is to shroud negative commentary in anonymity. While it is, for example, difficult today to publish a book review anonymously in print (whereas in the nineteenth century, for example, it was commonplace), it is possible to offer commentary on students' and colleagues' work without revealing one's identity. The question is would Jones have offered negative commentary on his colleague's book if his identity were concealed through anonymity?

What is interesting about this proposition is that if Jones *did* choose to use anonymity to conceal his identity when offering comments that were negative, then he would in effect be revealing himself to be false to his ostensive critical affiliations. Remember, Jones is identified with a compassionate, caring approach in his public critical exchanges. Thus, to conceal his "name" in the case of offering negative assessment of a student or colleague might serve to protect the integrity of his professional identity and affiliations, but it would at the same time reveal hypocrisy at the core of his critical affiliation. Namely, when offering positive assessment, he affiliates himself with the assessment; when offering negative assessment, he disaffiliates himself from the assessment.

One would hope that Jones would choose not to use anonymity to protect the integrity of his critical affiliation, however, it seems more than likely that he would in cases where his assessment threatens to undermine his identity as a compassionate, caring academic, and where it also threatens to undermine his affiliations with his colleagues.[20] If it is then the case that Jones offers negative critical assessments anonymously—and positive ones non-anonymously—then it seems wrongheaded to hold him in higher esteem than his colleague Smith who doles out praise and censure with equal zeal and transparency. Whereas Smith does not shy away from negatively assessing his colleagues, at least he lets his colleagues know that *he* is offering this critical assessment (and not some unidentified source).

Like faint praise, anonymous criticism is also empty criticism. Consider an example from *The Chronicle Review*. Carlin Romano's article "Heil Heidegger!" (2009) was savaged in numerous anonymous letters to the editor. "Romano writes like an undergrad convinced by the argument of the last book he has read," wrote one anonymous critic. S/he continues, "And, yes, he is a professor of philosophy, and yes, he was a Pulitzer Prize finalist, but his understanding of philosophy is so paltry that it beggars belief."[21] To this and other similar comments, Romano responds: "Those who savage me and my article from behind anonymous [I]nternet tags emulate the cowardice, dishonesty, and taste for mobbing of the Nazi thinker they revere. It has often been that way with dupes who defend Heidegger—an abysmal thinker and writer, an immoral monster, and a disgrace to the historic enterprise of philosophy."[22]

Whether or not one agrees with Romano's views on Heidegger, his take on anonymous commentary is worth thinking about. Anonymity does indeed have more in common with cowardice than courage—particularly when it comes to offering our views on the work of others—and is antithetical to critical dialogue. The common rationale for academic anonymity, however, is quite clear: if one were required to accompany one's assessment with one's true identity, one would not always speak the truth. If this is the case, then the problem is not with the critical judgment, but rather with the critical affiliation. Offering critical judgment anonymously, or, in Foucault's words from "The Discourse on Language" (1972), as "a nameless voice,"[23] allows one to stand outside of the order of discourse, dialogue, and language. "I don't want to have to enter this risky world of discourse; I want nothing to do with it insofar as it is decisive and final; I would like to feel it all around me, calm and transparent, profound, infinitely open, with others responding to my expectations, and truth emerging, one by one," writes Foucault.[24] "All I want is to allow myself to be borne along, within it, and by it, a happy wreck," he continues.[25] In other words, it might be said that in the critical arena, anonymity is more calming and less risky—or even more cowardly—than "named" discourse. Moreover, Romano might also be right that it has more in common with dishonesty than honesty. At least in the case of Jones cloaking his negative assessments in anonymity it does.

Conclusion

If one truly cares about their students and colleagues—if not the humanities and their profession—they will offer cogent and respectful critical assessments of them when they are appropriate, and will never resort to faint praise. "Like faculty, students also merit personal respect, but that does not protect their ideas from severe critique," comments Cary Nelson.[26] "Not all ideas merit respect."[27] Moreover, they will never cloak their criticism in anonymity—if they at the same time choose to affiliate praise with their name. Anonymity deflates critical exchange for it does not allow the recipient of anonymous comments to respond to their true source. Robust critical exchange requires a level of honesty and transparency that anonymity simply does not allow.

The future of critical exchange stands at a crossroads where the increased use of faint praise in print and critical anonymity through the Internet threatens to enervate the paralogical imperatives of the academy. While critical affiliation akin to Smith's is not warm and snuggly, it at least furthers the ends of honest critical exchange and robust knowledge production. When critics such as Pool are noting the overuse of "praise" and "faint praise," and critics such as Menand believe that the professor's tend to think alike and that the future of the academy only holds more of the same, then perhaps it is time for us to call into question some of our critical affiliations, particularly those that provide the normative conditions for this type of academic behavior. Perhaps we need to call into question normative behavior in the academy that encourages conformity rather than nonconformity, faint praise over criticism, anonymity over transparency. Perhaps encouraging academics to say "You're wrong" shows more critical compassion than avoiding negative commentary or hiding it behind the cloak of anonymity. Perhaps it is more collegial to share with our colleagues and students what we really think about their work than rather trying to hide it from them or to give it faint praise.

Compassionate criticism is not the critical care that the humanities needs. Rather, we need to grow thicker critical skin. Backslapping and false praise only encourage conformity, mediocrity, and dishonesty. Why? Because encouraging critical behavior that always results in a chorus of affirmative responses is nothing more than conformity; allowing views that need to be challenged to persist is nothing less than critical mediocrity; and failure to tell our colleagues what we truly think about their work is simply dishonest. While it is true that hearing what others really think of our work may be emotionally unsettling, there is no shame in this unless we as a profession regard it as shameful. It is the duty of those like us whose lives are tempered by thinking, reading, and writing to utilize or exercise our critical acumen—and to come to expect that we will not always be right.

If academics are already generally regarded as being too critical of received opinion as compared to those in the public sphere, then a criticism tempered by transparency, motivated by increased scholarly dialogue, and reenergized by the force of intellectual curiosity runs the risk of widening the gap between the academy and the public sphere. But this is a risk worth bearing if the alternative is a generally flaccid, apathetic, and anti-dialogical profession. In my opinion, reassessing our critical affiliations is as good a place as any to start fashioning a more robust, honest, and progressive academy. Moreover, it is going to take all the power of our critical capacities to prevail in our struggle against neoliberalism, so why not put them in the foreground now when they are most needed, rather than hide them? Docile subjectivities cannot lead us out of the neoliberal abyss—and may even in fact prolong it. Academic culture in the age of neoliberalism calls for sustained paralogical inquiry and tough criticism as they give us our best chance for university reform.

6

Wrangling with Rank

American higher education under the spell of neoliberalism is obsessed with ranks and brands. Data collected on student and faculty performance informs internal and external rankings that are then used to position and determine the value of nearly all aspects of academic culture. To be highly ranked is one of the greatest forms of visibility, prestige, and value in neoliberal academic culture; to be lowly ranked—or worse yet, unranked—is a sign of nonperformance, if not also nonexistence. Ranking is both a tangible fruit of neoliberalism's obsession with measurement and performance display, and a somewhat self-fulfilling affirmation of the importance of assessment—as assessment is used to validate rank, but so too is rank used to validate assessment.

It is not uncommon today to find university administrations creating strategic plans specifically aimed at increasing their overall and program rankings, and hiring marketing consultants to improve their branding. One reason for this is that rank and brand are used to lure students (as well as faculty and donors) to universities. College-bound high school students probably know more about university ranks and brands than things they should know, such as the names of all the US presidents or state capitals. College students themselves are most likely better at reciting the top ten football programs in America than the ten poorest countries. And graduate students aim to study at top-ranked schools, while faculty compete for positions at the top-ranked research universities. In the neoliberal day and age, high-ranking and iconic branding are seen as irrefutable signs of excellence and the warp and woof of success.[1]

While most aspects of the American university have been hard hit by neoliberalism's rank and brand "fever," a few have not yet been affected by it. In this chapter, focus will be placed on one of them, and an argument will be made as to why it is hoped that it never catches the fever. The area under consideration will be scholarly journals in the humanities. As an editor of two scholarly journals in the humanities—the *American Book Review* and *symplokē*—perhaps I have more at stake than most when it comes to journal ranking than others. High rankings of journals have the potential to increase the quality of the contributions to these journals as well as increase their readership and sales; low rankings have the potential of driving potential contributors away from these journals to more highly ranked journals as well as decreasing their readership and sales—and few things are as sad as a journal that is seldom read and lowly regarded.

Nevertheless, the argument that will be advanced in this chapter will be one against ranking humanities journals—an argument grounded less on the success of individual or particular journals, and more on the ultimate value of journal rankings. It will be shown that even though journal ranking may be of value in some of the other disciplines, the stated reasons for ranking journals do not hold in the humanities. Journal rankings are neither a reliable sign of scholarly excellence in the humanities, nor do they have very much value in disciplines such as philosophy or literary studies.[2] However, assuming their continued and growing presence (as rank and brand fever shows no signs of breaking), journal rankings may play a useful role in transforming cultural attitudes toward the changing material conditions of humanities scholarship, and help usher in a new era of environmentally responsible scholarly journal publishing.

Deflating Rank

The practice of ranking scholarly journals is fairly widespread in the United States for just about every discipline *except* the humanities. It is one sign of the nonconformity or noncompliance of the humanities with neoliberal culture that they *have not* caught rank and brand fever like many of the other disciplines in the American academy. Whereas one can readily find, for example, rankings of science or business journals, there is a roaring silence when it comes to rankings of humanities journals.[3] Why? While I would like to say that it is because of the ideological opposition of the humanities to all neoliberal practices, I cannot. So, again, why?

For one thing, unlike in business and the sciences, where accreditation and funding are directly linked to publication in more highly ranked journals, in the humanities there is little accreditation and even less funding. If a business professor in an Association to Advance Collegiate Schools of Business (AACSB) accredited program does not publish in highly ranked business journals, then she puts her program at risk of losing its accreditation. However, if a comparative literature professor publishes their work in a little-known journal, they are neither putting their program's accreditation at risk (even though some believe that they are putting their program's *reputation* at risk) nor jeopardizing its funding (state and federal grants in support of comparative literature are about as common as snow in south Florida). The only real danger of the comparative literature professor publishing their scholarship in a little-known journal as opposed to a well-known journal is that it has a lower chance of being read (assuming of course that well-known journals are more widely read than little-known journals—an assumption that some may want to challenge). Compared to other disciplines, where funding and accreditation are linked to journal rank, publishing one's work in the journal *Comparative Literature* (one of the better-known journals in the field) as opposed to say the *South Texas Journal of Comparative Literature* (an imaginary little-known journal) is more a matter of preference in the humanities than of professional necessity.[4]

Another reason for the roaring silence regarding the ranking of humanities journals regards the high level of subdisciplinary specialization.[5] In philosophy, for example, there are journals devoted to general areas of philosophy (e.g., logic, metaphysics, ethics, aesthetics, etc.), to subareas of general areas of philosophy (e.g., medical ethics, business ethics, bioethics, criminal justice ethics, metaethics, environmental ethics, Buddhist ethics, etc.), to the work of individual philosophers (e.g., Thomas Hobbes, David Hume, Bertrand Russell, Charles Peirce, Martin Heidegger, Gilles Deleuze, etc.), to the work of historical periods (e.g., ancient, medieval, modern, etc.), to various philosophical approaches (e.g., phenomenological, analytic, pragmatic, Marxist, historicist, continental, etc.), and so on. Given the heterogeneity of types of philosophy journals, while there is a high chance of at least some agreement on the top ten journals in each of the areas or subdisciplines, there will be very little chance of much agreement beyond this. Why?

A scholar of the nineteenth-century American pragmatist philosopher Charles Peirce, such as me, must list the *Transactions of the Charles S. Peirce Society* as one of the top journals in the discipline. However, this will probably only be the case for someone who works on Peirce in particular, or American philosophy in general. A scholar of the contemporary French continental philosopher Gilles Deleuze will have little use for or interest in the *Transactions of the Charles S. Peirce Society*, and would probably not even consider ranking it as one of the top journals in his discipline. There are plenty of very good French and continental philosophy journals that would quickly take up any ranking slots possibly left over for the *Transactions*. The majority of the philosophy journals in print speak more strongly to subgroups of philosophers than to all professional philosophers. The scholarly narrowness or philosophical focus of these journals is necessary to advance scholarship in their subfield or subdiscipline—which, in turn, advances scholarship in the discipline of philosophy at large. However, this situation makes it very difficult (if not impossible) to provide a general ranking of philosophy journals that has any real merit or validity for *all* professional philosophers. As such, journal ranking within philosophy is of little value if it cannot account in any robust way for philosophical specialization.[6]

Moreover, this situation is not even solved by simply ranking philosophy journals by specialization because rankings of philosophy journals in this way only leads to more splintering into sub-groups and subspecializations: even within Peirce studies, there are logicians, ethicists, phenomenologists, mathematicians, historians, metaphysicians, and epistemologists. All will have their own highly idiosyncratic list of journals based on their particular philosophical interest in Peirce. Consequently, journal ranking is not very useful in academic philosophy—or for that matter, in the humanities in general.

In the humanities, whereas one's views on say Friedrich Nietzsche may find a larger immediate audience in one journal over another, if they are worthwhile ideas, it really makes little real difference if they are publishing in journal A as opposed to journal B—assuming, of course, that the quality of the scholarship is sound and the journal is well edited. With no accreditation or funding implications hanging in the balance, one humanities journal is arguably just as good a home as the other for a paper on Nietzsche.

There is, however, a high level of *prestige* associated with publishing in some journals in the humanities rather than others. For example, all things being equal, publication in the *Journal of Philosophy*, which has been around for over a century, is much more prestigious than publication in *Auslegung: A Journal of Philosophy*, which is "primarily interested in publishing the work of new Ph.D.'s and advanced students pursuing a Ph.D. degree in Philosophy."[7] Nevertheless, I am fairly confident that *Auslegung* would not reject an article accepted by the *Journal of Philosophy*.[8]

What this means is that even though publication of the same article in the *Journal of Philosophy* would be more prestigious than its publication in *Auslegung*, the content of the article would be the same. Therefore, determinations of quality based only on the rank, brand, or prestige of the journal would in instances like this be empty or inaccurate. Just as one cannot necessarily determine the quality of a faculty member based on the rank, brand, and prestige of the university where they teach, so too can one not determine the quality of a scholarly article merely by the rank, brand, or prestige of the journal in which it is published.[9]

Nevertheless, rank, brand, and prestige have to speak at least to tendencies toward quality lest they lose their meaning and value entirely. If the *Journal of Philosophy* all of a sudden began publishing articles rejected by *Auslegung*, then one would begin to lose faith that an article published in the *Journal of Philosophy* is one that would for all intents and purposes is publishable in just about *any* philosophy journal. The *JP brand* is high-quality philosophy scholarship—and its rank, if such a thing were viable and available, would hopefully reflect this. But even this argument has holes in it.

The *Journal of Philosophy*, for example, regularly publishes high-quality works of *analytic* philosophy (in addition to articles employing other philosophical approaches). However, such articles would probably not even be considered for publication in philosophy journals such as the *Continental Philosophy Review*, the *Journal of French Philosophy*, or *Deleuze Studies*. Now does, for example, the fact that *Deleuze Studies* does not publish high-quality works of analytic philosophy make it a low-quality journal? Of course not—and any ranking that would reveal a bias against "specialty" journals or journals that delimit the range of works published by area or specialization is not very useful or valuable.[10]

Aside from providing a resource for philosophers to determine possible venues for publication, ranked journal lists in philosophy are not very worthwhile endeavors. Consequently, similar arguments and cases can be extended to the other disciplines and sub-disciplines in the humanities as well. Humanities scholars in the United States should be proud that they have, to date, avoided at least one of the consequences of neoliberalism's rank and brand fever, namely, scholarly journal ranking.[11]

INFLATING RANK

Even though the ranking of humanities journals has not yet occurred in the United States, rank and brand fever in the humanities has hit Europe and Australia hard in the past few years. Consequently, because of recent and aggressive ranking initiatives by the European Science Foundation (ESF) and Australian Research Council (ARC), there is some concern today among humanities scholars in the states of a carryover effect.[12]

In 2008, the ESF released a ranked index of humanities journals called the "European Reference Index for the Humanities" (ERIH). The ESF notes that the "ERIH is conceived as a tool to improve access to and assessment of Humanities research in Europe, initially by identifying and categorising good research journals in 15 fields of the Humanities." It further notes that its initial lists will be revised after one year, and "then updated after longer intervals."[13] The aim of the ERIH "initial lists" (which were eventually "first" updated in 2011[14]) is to help "identify excellence in Humanities scholarship." The ESF also says that they "should prove useful for the aggregate benchmarking of national research systems, for example, in determining the international standing of the research activity carried out in a given field in a particular country."[15] In addition, the ESF is careful to point out that

> As they stand, the lists are not a bibliometric tool for the evaluation of individual researchers. The distinction between the categories A, B and C is to be understood as being not primarily qualitative and the categorisation is determined by issues such as scope and audience as explained in the ERIH Guidelines. Thus, such categorisations of journals do not prejudge the scientific quality of individual articles that appear in those journals.
>
> *The ERIH Steering Committee and the Expert Panels advise against using the lists as a basis for assessments of individual candidates, be it for positions, promotions, research grant awards etc.*[16]

These comments by the ESF get to the heart of some of the problems with rankings in general. For one, rankings do not speak to the individual quality of articles in journals: in theory, an ERIH "A" journal is just as capable of publishing an excellent piece of research as an ERIH "C" journal. Furthermore, the ESF clearly (and with emphasis) advises against using these rankings as a substitute for assessment of scholarly publications. If one wants to determine the quality of a scholarly article for the purposes of, for example, promotions or grants, then there is no substitute for reading and individually assessing the article itself. While publication in particular journals may reflect the general scholarly values of the journal's editors, advisory board, and peer reviewers, it does not speak to the specific strengths and weaknesses of individual publications. As such, the mere fact of publication in an ERIH "A" journal (or "C" journal, for that matter) is not—and should never be—a substitute for scholarly publication assessment. Journal article publication is never tantamount to assessment, and scholarly publication assessment should never be simply left to journal rankings—even those done by well-meaning and well-respected organizations such as the ESF.

Assessment of the "initial" or pilot phase of the ERIH was done between November 2008 and January 2011. It revealed two major challenges for the ERIH Lists: first, the "A," "B," and "C" designations were misunderstood by many as "qualitative" designations, rather than designations of "kind." This was corrected by the ERIH by dropping them in favor of three new categories, "which indicate the crucial difference between the NATional journals and the INTernational journals."[17] The renamed and reordered categories based on verbal descriptions are as follows:

> *NATional (NAT):* European publications with a recognised scholarly significance among researchers in the respective research domains in a particular (mostly linguistically circumscribed) readership group in Europe; occasionally cited outside the publishing country, though their main target group is the domestic academic community.
>
> *INTernational (INT):* both European and non-European publications with an internationally recognised scholarly significance among researchers in the respective research domains, and which are regularly cited worldwide.
>
> International journals are themselves classified into two sub-categories based on a combination of two criteria: influence and scope:
>
> *INT1 Sub-Category:* international publications with high visibility and influence among researchers in the various research domains in different countries, regularly cited all over the world.
>
> *INT2 Sub-Category:* international publications with significant visibility and influence in the various research domains in different countries.
>
> *W Category Journals:* journals which published their first issue three years or less before the closing date for feedbacks for a given panel.[18]

A solution to the second challenge though proved more serious, namely, "how to represent expertise in sub-disciplines within panels which cover very large and diverse fields, like History, Literature and Linguistics."[19] And while the ERIH says, "In the future it may be advisable to consider dividing these large disciplines into smaller ones to achieve better expertise coverage,"[20] it will not be as simple as renaming and reordering the designations of kind so as they do not appear to be designations of qualitative hierarchy. Advisable, yes; possible, no—as the process of subdividing large and diverse fields will most certainly prove to be intractable.

With all of these provisos, it is unclear just how the ERIH *improves* "assessment" of scholarly journals, particularly those in the humanities. However, what is interesting about the ERIH index is its potential to *improve*—at least in some way—"access." Lists of journals in the humanities such as those found in the ERIH provide scholars with a potentially sure means of locating relevant scholarship in their discipline. These lists of journals should aim to be as complete as possible, and any shortcoming in completeness should be treated as shortcomings in access.

What then should one make of the fact that both the ERIH "initial list" *and* the revised 2011 list not only omits the major journal for Peirce studies (the *Transactions*), but also does not include *Auslegung*, *Deleuze Studies*, and the *Journal of French Philosophy*? What then should this particular scholar think of the ERIH list(s)? Well, not very much, as it does not provide very much access to (nor assessment of) some of the philosophy journals with which he is familiar. On the basis of my own experience with the list, I'm confident that other scholars in the humanities will find it wanting as well in terms of access.

Much like the ESF, the Australian Research Council also recently released lists ranking journals in the humanities. The ARC reports that "the lists are a result of consultations with the sector and rigorous review by leading researchers and the ARC."[21] Overall, 20,605 peer reviewed journals are included in the Excellence in Research for Australia (ERA) 2010 Journal List that includes the Humanities and Creative Arts (HCA) Journal Lists. Developed in consultation with over 700 expert reviewers, the ERA designates a "quality rating" for each and every journal on their list. Their quality ratings are described as follows:

*A**

Typically an A* journal would be one of the best in its field or subfield in which to publish and would typically cover the entire field/subfield. Virtually all papers they publish will be of a very high quality. These are journals where most of the work is important (it will really shape the field) and where researchers boast about getting accepted. Acceptance rates would typically be low and the editorial board would be dominated by field leaders, including many from top institutions.

A

The majority of papers in a Tier A journal will be of very high quality. Publishing in an A journal would enhance the author's standing, showing they have real engagement with the global research community and that they have something to say about problems of some significance. Typical signs of an A journal are lowish acceptance rates and an editorial board which includes a reasonable fraction of well-known researchers from top institutions.

B

Tier B covers journals with a solid, though not outstanding, reputation. Generally, in a Tier B journal, one would expect only a few papers of very high quality. They are often important outlets for the work of PhD students and early career researchers. Typical examples would be regional journals with high acceptance rates, and editorial boards that have few leading researchers from top international institutions.

C

Tier C includes quality, peer reviewed, journals that do not meet the criteria of the higher tiers.[22]

What is interesting though is the highly deflationary comment that accompanies the ERA's four-tiered ranking system:

> A journal's quality rating represents the *overall quality* of the journal. This is defined in terms of how it compares with other journals and should not be confused with its relevance or importance to a particular discipline.[23]

So, on the one hand, "an A* journal would be one of the best in its field or subfield in which to publish," and on the other, an A* ranking should not be confused with "relevance or importance to a particular discipline." As such, by the ERA's own admission, it is possible to have A* journals that are both *irrelevant* and *unimportant*. Now, that certainly tops the assessment provisos of the ESF.

Nonetheless, the ERA's HCA Journal Lists are quite extensive, and include rankings of 7,219 publications.[24] Curiously (and unexplainably), however, one of the journals that I edit, *American Book Review* (which has been in existence for nearly 40 years) is omitted from the subarea "literary studies," while the other journal that I edit, *symplokē* (which has been around about half as long as the other journal), is included. Of the 772 literary studies journals listed in the HCA, 55 received an "A*," 195 received an "A," 192 received a "B," and 385 received a "C." Roughly speaking, each sublist is ranked in such a way that the A* journals represent the top 5 percent, A represent the next 15 percent, B the next 30 percent, and C the final 50 percent.

Assessment of the pilot phase of the ERA's HCA Journal Lists though came to an even more severe conclusion than the ERIH's assessment. The ERA 2012 Journal List was based on the 2010 Journal list that took two years to develop. From February 14, 2011 to April 4, 2011, the revised ERA 2012 Journal List was opened for "Public Consultation," wherein "members of the public were invited to comment on a journal's eligibility for inclusion in the list; a journal's bibliographic data; a journal's assigned rank; and a journal's Field of Research (FoR) code assignment(s)."[25] Then, on May 30, 2011, the ARC made a stunning announcement: the ERA 2012 Journal List would not rank journals. So, the ARC considered all of the public feedback on the ERA 2012 Journal List except that concerning ranks—because there would be no journal ranking done on the 2012 list.

While I *was* pleased that *symplokē* was placed in the A-tier on the 2010 ERA Journal List (the journal did not even make it into the ERIH list), it still is difficult to determine the value of this ranking *if* it is not attached to accreditation, funding, or evaluation—or even associated with "relevance or importance to a particular discipline." In North America, to be sure, rankings such as the fine one afforded *symplokē* by the ARC do not carry very much weight, for they are attached to nothing more than the list from which they come. However, one can imagine a possible (if not future) world where they *do* carry weight within academe, particularly given neoliberal academic cultures obsession with rank.

In such a world, it might be decreed, for example, that only scholarship in A* or A journals would, say, count as acceptable for merit purposes; or that accredited programs in the humanities are those with professors who publish a particular number of articles in A* or A journals; or that state and federal funding for the humanities is tied to publication in A* or A journals. In such a world, the stakes in the humanities regarding ranking *would* be completely different. Perhaps now that the ERIH lists do not even give the pretense of *qualitative* ranking, and the ARC has done away with ranking entirely, there is no reason to consider further journal rank. Still, it seems worth asking whether there is *any* value to or use for rankings that are not connected in the states to accreditation, funding, or evaluation, and whose validity and usefulness to individual scholars is (as noted above) dubious. I think so—albeit in a tangential and indirect way.

Greening Rank

From 1665, the year in which the first scholarly journal, *Journal des Scavans*, was published, until the 1990s, scholarly journals have *only* appeared in paper and ink format. However, in the mid-1970s, experimentation with "electronic journals" or "e-journals" began, and by the 1990s, the first full-text electronic journal, *Online Journal of Current Clinical Trials*, appeared.[26] Today, not only are e-journals commonplace, they are on pace to send print journals to their extinction. However, in spite of the imminent demise of the print journal, scholars in the humanities still tend to reveal a bias toward print journals—and against digital journals. One possible transformative use for journal rankings—if organizations such as the ESF and ARC continue to insist that we have them, particularly in the humanities—is to use them to leverage a full transition from print to digital journal culture in the academy.

To be sure, nothing has changed the process of editing and publishing more positively than the recent progress in digital technology. For both of the journals that I edit, everything from manuscript submission and copy edit to page proofs and layout are done digitally. Even though both *American Book Review* and *symplokē* continue to enjoy solid print runs and distribution, they are quickly being surpassed by their digital formats. While the "brand" of both of these publications was established through paper and ink formats, the addition of digital platforms has only increased the brand and name recognition of both of these publications.

However, my suspicion is that without the prior existence of branded paper and ink publications—particularly at this moment in material cultural history—we would not have enjoyed our "supplemental" digital success. In many ways, paper-and-ink versions are still the gold standard of publication: they legitimate publication in a way that digital-only formats, particularly those that have never been in print, continue to struggle to achieve. Still, for publications such as *symplokē* and *American Book Review*, which are dominated by a digital editorial process and more widely disseminated in digital form, the question seems to be *when* (not *if*) we should go completely digital. The question becomes even more pronounced when one considers that going completely (or solely) digital would probably not negatively affect the rank or brand of these journals (given that it has already been established)—and might even improve it. What then stops us?

Formerly print-only objects such as books, newspapers, and journals are quickly also becoming available as digital objects. The rise of the digital age and the increased availability of digital objects has presented a strong case that because paper-and-ink objects are more expensive to produce and reproduce than digital objects, are not as easily searched and distributed as their digital-twins, and are more difficult to destroy and recycle than their electronic counterparts,[27] that digital objects should be the dominant means of disseminating verbal information. Given then all the advantages of digital objects over print objects, *why has the transition to digital media been so slow? And why do editors such as me hesitate to make the complete transition, that is, do away with paper-and-ink journal publication?*

There are some who argue that digital objects do not have the same quality or feel as print objects. My favorite quote in this regard comes from the celebrated writer E. Annie Proulx, who won an O. Henry Prize for her short story "Brokeback Mountain" in 1998. A few years earlier, Proulx echoed a feeling held by many at that time that the information superhighway might be good for "bulletin boards on esoteric subjects, reference works, lists and news—timely utilitarian information, efficiently pulled through wires," but "[n]obody is going to sit down and read a novel on a twitchy little screen. Ever."[28] It was May of 1994 when Proulx made these comments in *The New York Times*—comments that echoed the feelings of bibliophiles the world over. She then punctuated them with an even stronger one: "books are forever."

The problem was Proulx's "forever" turned out to be only 14 years. It was by this time that technological reality caught up with reading and research expectations with the release of the first "Kindle Readers" by Amazon. Proulx's prediction that nobody is ever "going to sit down and read a novel on a twitchy little screen" was resoundingly disproved on November 19, 2007, when the first Kindle Readers sold out in four and a half hours—and when nine months later almost a quarter of a million people owned one of the devices. But don't feel too bad for Proulx because at the same time the Kindle was proving her wrong, the film *Brokeback Mountain* was being released to great fanfare all over the world—and eventually the little devices built for book reading allowed for movie viewing as well.

In one sense, though, Proulx got it right. "Books" in the sense of long-form reading material *are* forever. Amazon, the company that first produced the "twitchy little screens," now lists over a quarter million Kindle titles for download including some of my own books—and reports that it sells 114 eBooks for every 100 printed books.[29] In another sense, Proulx like many of us at the time had no idea how appealing the digitized word was to become. Not only are we now seeing companies like Amazon fight for marketshare of digital books,[30] but just recently the first bookless public library in the United States was opened.[31] The marketplace for information has shown that the digitized word is not of intrinsically inferior quality than the printed word—and may in fact be poised to eclipse it.

Other arguments against the digital word may be advanced such as the ease in which it may be used without payment or acknowledgment, but these like the quality arguments against digital media are historical, not natural facts. Stealing and plagiarism are ethical issues, not material ones. If one is comfortable with the notion that words mean the same thing on the page as they do on the screen, then the real difference between the digital word and the printed word is *cultural*. One way to think of this difference is consider it analogous to the cult-like devotion some people place on vinyl recordings of music.

There are many who believe that music sounds better when played on vinyl versus through a digital file. But would anyone go so far as to say that recorded sound or the published word is not the same in different information delivery technologies? Truth be told, just as your favorite song is the same song on vinyl and CD, so too is your favorite book. The same case may be made for a scholarly journal made available digitally versus a scholarly journal made available only in paper and ink. Of course, the packaging is different in a journal delivered online versus a journal found on a bookshelf, but the contents are usually the same.[32] The 100 best first lines from novels that *American Book Review* published a few years ago are still the same lines whether they are online or in print. This leads one to conclude that the source of our digital aversion lies in a cultural attitude, not a material condition.

The bibliophile who has a cult-like devotion to the printed word is not unlike the audiophile who swears that music sounds better on vinyl. The same goes for their assignment of a lower value or rank to digital versions of the same information. From the position of the bibliophile, not only is the digital word worth less than the printed word (compare, for example, the cost of a modern first print edition to a digital edition of the same book), but the printed word has a higher cultural and intellectual value also.

The origin of this cultural attitude toward print may be the fact that some still operate from the belief that the culture of paper and ink is *permanent*—or *natural*—and that digital culture is *impermanent*—or *historical*. This cultural attitude is not an ontological or metaphysical one, that is to say, the belief that journals are permanent or natural is not the belief that they cannot be destroyed. Rather, it is the belief that the attitude with which one approaches a printed object such as a journal is fundamentally different than the attitude in which one approaches a digital object. These attitudes are the products of cultural conditioning and habit, and they have a direct correlation with other culturally influenced phenomena such as "branding" and "ranking."

The scholarly publishing world needs to get a handle on the shift from the book to the byte soon for if we take much longer the digital universe is going to completely parallel the print universe—something that surely is not wanted or needed, if for only ecological reasons. After all, trashing a digital file is much "greener" than trashing a glue-bound scholarly journal—the 1,500 scholarly journal issues that you can now carry around on the "twitchy little screen" of your Kindle will never end up in a landfill and have a decidedly much smaller carbon footprint than their pulp-based print versions.[33] And, the iPad, the next generation of "digital reader," allows us to view *any* scholarly journal available online on a highly portable, large, journal-sized, screen.

Rational or philosophical demonstrations of the indiscernibility of printed semantic units and digital ones is not going to solve the shift from print to digital. In fact, there are always ready arguments that may be made on the *cultural* and *semiotic* differences between print and digital information delivery. Rather, the shift from print to digital is only going to be solved through advances in the semiotics of publishing and reading culture. Until we let go of what might be called "the myth of the book," that is, the notion that printed books or journals are permanent (whereas digital culture is impermanent), we will be caught between our digital destiny and our printed purgatory. The problem is not that *intellectually* we cannot understand the difference between the package that information comes in and the information in itself: most would agree that iconicly indistinguishable electronic and digital words convey the same information. The problem is that we cannot seem to come to grips with the notion that the *image* of "the scholarly journal" as a printed artifact is no more or less "natural" than its "digital" (and nonprinted) counterpart. Oddly enough, it may be environmental concerns that bring about the final push to a digitally dominant publishing culture.

If anyone is in a position to take a leading role in the cultural "naturalization" of digital publication, it is the editors of scholarly publications. Moreover, if the move to primarily digital formats is *led* by established scholarly presses and journals, that is, fully branded and *highly ranked* scholarly journals (e.g., those with a rank of "recognised scholarly significance" on the ERA Journal List), then not only can other publications follow on their coattails, but also the arguments against the legitimacy of online scholarship become more vacuous. If online platforms are now the primary platforms for the highly ranked journals established in the print age of journal publishing, then the academy has little or no grounds to dismiss online journal scholarship as inferior to printed scholarship.

The downside of this move is that it has the potential to jeopardize the rank and brand of one's publication; the upside is that digital publishing is not only greener than print publishing, but it also has the potential to get the products of the scholarly process in the hands of many more people than print-only publication. This increase in public access coupled with the environmental arguments for digital publishing, form the basis of a strong case that all scholarly publication editors not only become "green editors" (which most of us are already by virtue of the amount of digital editorial work we do) but also leaders in what might be called the "green journals movement."

Conclusion

There are a variety of very convincing arguments against the value of humanities journals rankings. Hopefully, universities and colleges in the United States will heed them, and not cave to the increasing pressure from neoliberal academe to rank. Moreover, given that there are clear signs that Europe and Australia are reversing course with ranking journals,[34] universities and colleges in the states have a precedent from abroad to draw upon. For Australia to have prepared rankings in 2012 only to drop them after consideration of public comment on them speaks volumes about the challenges such efforts face.

Europe's removal of "A," "B," and "C" from their rankings and replacement with the virtually meaningless "NAT," "INT," and "W" categories is akin to a smoker switching over to a nicotine patch: just as the patch allows you to enjoy the pleasures of nicotine without experiencing the harmful physical effects of smoking, ranking journals according to visibility, significance, and influence allows the ERIH to maintain the neoliberal emphasis on rank and visibility without the pretense that ranking is associated with considerations of quality and hierarchy. In other words, the ERIH concedes that ranking does not have much value, but rather than eliminating them entirely, provides a more or less empty form of ranking. Still, these ERIH rankings may be useful in demonstrating the legitimacy of online scholarship in the humanities. If a journal of "recognised scholarly significance" (borrowing from the new ERIH language) from the print age converts to a digital-only format, there are few grounds to deny its legitimacy other than cultural bias against digital scholarly platforms.

In the final analysis, the suggestion to utilize journal rankings from abroad to help transform cultural attitudes toward online journals in America is a pragmatic one. These journal rankings are not simply going to entirely disappear overnight just because they rankle the feathers of humanities scholars though as we have seen in the updates to both the European and Australian lists, they do have the potential to fade away. However, until then, there appears to be little harm—and no inconsistency—then in using them to transform cultural attitudes toward online journal publishing, while at the same time rejecting their ultimate legitimacy as reliable indicators of scholarly excellence. But there is one final consideration here—and it is an important one. Does the non-ranking of humanities journals aide the mission of corporate humanities or does it detract from it? Does a "corporate humanities" approach to neoliberal academic culture require the humanities to rank journals? Is the non-ranking of humanities journals a sign of their irrelevance within neoliberal academic culture or of their resistance to it? These are important questions and well worth consideration.

Rank is one of the greatest forms of visibility and sites of validation in neoliberal academe. However, it is also—like the faint praise and anonymous criticism discussed in chapter 5—ultimately empty. Scratch away at it with critique and rank dissolves. Perhaps the non-ranking of humanities journals in the United States is a sign that not all elements of academic culture have been absorbed by neoliberalism, and can be used as a platform from which to mount resistance to the overreliance on ranking by higher education in America. Perhaps it is the role of *Humanities, Inc.* to pragmatically use journal rankings to bring about a transition to a green journals movement, while at the same time use its rejection of humanities ranking as a platform to convince colleagues in other areas of the university such as business and the sciences to reject rank as well. Corporate humanities should not shy from either task as both play an important role in determining the future of the humanities.

7

Authorial Prestige

Prestige and status are instrumental in shaping the American university. Alumni compete for social status on the basis of the prestige of the universities they attended; faculty base their status on the prestige of the university at which they are employed; and administrators often believe that increasing the prestige of their university will necessarily improve its value.

In *The Higher Learning in America* (1918), written nearly a century ago, American economist and sociologist Thorstein Veblen reflected on the uses and abuses of prestige or notoriety by higher education in America. For Veblen, the pursuit of prestige by university administrators aims at "a growth in the material resources and the volume of traffic" of the university, not the growth of knowledge. Veblen thought these aims were not only misguided, but also of questionable success: "So far as the acquired prestige is designed to serve a pecuniary end it can only be useful in the way of impressing donors,—a highly speculative line of enterprise, offering suggestive parallel to the drawing of a lottery." His ultimate conclusion was that "Whatever will not serve the end of prestige has no secure footing" in the American university.[1]

Contemporary neoliberalism, however, has taken the traditional pursuit of prestige by the American university to entirely new heights. Stanford University law professor Deborah Rhode has argued in *In Pursuit of Knowledge: Scholars, Status, and Academic Culture* (2006) that the mission of higher education in America is becoming even more focused on the achievement of status and prestige. For her, this results in an increasing shift from academic-focused missions to prestige-focused missions. One of the results of this shift in university mission is increasing pressure on faculty to produce higher levels of scholarship, particularly at institutions seeking to raise their status. Rhode terms this shift "upward drift."[2]

In the context of this "upward drift," matters such as university and journal rank are extremely important as they serve as "objective" evidence of prestige and status. But there are other ways too that the neoliberal overvaluation of prestige affects the humanities. This chapter examines how the neoliberal value of prestige undermines poststructuralism's "death of the author"—one of greatest achievements of late-twentieth-century aesthetics and critical theory. This is a significant—and somewhat unexpected—consequence of the rise of neoliberalism in the humanities given that it was over 40 years ago that a box carried within it a message concerning the death of the author. It also carried within it other works that demonstrate what art *after* the author looks like. One would have hoped that by this time the death of the author would have become part of the modus operandi of the arts of the present. That does not appear to be the case, however—at least not within the neoliberal arts.

Not only are some critics, like Jane Gallop and Seán Burke, challenging the notion that the author was ever dead—even for those who coined the "familiar" poststructuralist "slogan"[3]—but contemporary critical, textual, and editorial practices also seem more attuned to asserting the aesthetic prestige of dead authors than allowing "texts" or "writing" to speak on their own behalf. For me, critical and editorial acts that allow the "author" to impede the free circulation of texts and determine textual practices bind us to an aesthetic and critical past we allegedly were supposed to have overcome. Editors and critics today need to strive for textual practices that move beyond the reliance on "authors" and "authorship"—and instead learn to revel in the collaborative textual multitude afforded to us by the age of digital multimedia. A resurrection of the author is simply not acceptable— even if the age of high theory that announced the death of the author is also itself dead.[4] Let's take the opportunity now to turn back to the message in the box—and work our way forward from it to the critical and editorial present.

The Aspen Box

The box that delivered the message of the death of the author was the multimedia magazine *Aspen*, founded in the early 1960s by Phyllis Johnson, an editor at magazines such as *Women's Wear Daily* and *Advertising Age*.[5] Described as "the first three-dimensional magazine," "each issue came in a customized box or folder filled with materials in a variety of formats,"[6] including "booklets, posters, postcards, flipbooks, vinyl recordings, and in one issue, a reel containing four Super-8 films."[7] Johnson, who said that "*Aspen* should be a time capsule of a certain period, point of view, or person," and had different designers and editors for each of its ten issues, published the first issue in the winter of 1965—and its last issue in 1971.[8] While the first two issues contained materials related to the ski resort town from which the magazine took its name, the third issue, edited by Andy Warhol and David Dalton, left the town behind and took up pop art instead. Warhol and Dalton's issue included, among other items, a vinyl recording of guitar feedback by John Cale of the Velvet Underground—and excerpts from 14 papers presented at the Berkeley Conference on LSD.[9]

It is within the context of LSD papers and John Cale feedback that this multimedia magazine released in Issue 5/6 a provocation by Roland Barthes titled "The Death of the Author."[10] Though Barthes's article would also appear the following year in French in *Manteia*, a bound magazine also in its fifth issue,[11] it is wonderfully appropriate that a piece that figuratively unbinds the author from the text and criticism would first appear in a literally unbound magazine—one that Johnson "wanted to get away from the bound magazine format, which is really quite restrictive."[12] Edited by Brian O'Doherty, with art direction by David Dalton and Lynn Letterman, *Aspen* 5/6 was published Fall–Winter 1967 by Roaring Fork Press, New York City. In addition to Barthes's "Death of the Author" (translated from French by Richard Howard), two other essays were included in the box (George Kubler's "Style and Representation in Historical Time" and Susan Sontag's "The Aesthetics of Silence"). In addition, among the vinyl recordings found in the box were Samuel Beckett's "Text for Nothing #8" (1958) read by Jack MacGowan; "Excerpts from *Nova Express*" (1964) read by their author, William S. Burroughs; and an excerpt from Alain Robbe-Grillet's *Jealousy*, "Now the shadow of the southwest column...," which is also read by its author—and as well includes an English translation of the excerpt. If that were not enough, the box also contains a recording of John Cage's "Fontana Mix-Feed, Nov. 6, 1967"—along with Cage's score to the piece.[13]

Amidst excerpts from Beckett, Robbe-Grillet, Burroughs, and Cage, Barthes brashly asserts that all writing contains "several indiscernible voices, and that literature is precisely the invention of this voice, to which we cannot assign a specific origin: literature is that neuter, that composite, that oblique into which every subject escapes, the trap where all identity is lost, beginning with the very identity of the body that writes."[14] "Probably," continues Barthes, "this has always been the case: once an action is recounted, for intransitive ends, and no longer in order to act directly upon reality—that is, finally external to any function but the very exercise of the symbol—this disjunction occurs, the voice loses its origin, the author enters his own death, writing begins."[15] For Barthes, the announcement of the death of the author aims to *recall* a time before the invention of the "author," who he says is "a modern figure, produced no doubt by our society insofar as, at the end of the middle ages, with English empiricism, French rationalism and the personal faith of the Reformation, it discovered the *prestige* of the individual, or, to put it more nobly, of the 'human person.'"[16] Barthes also reminds us in his provocation of the connection between the rise of capitalism and the birth of the author. "Hence," writes Barthes, "it is logical that with regard to literature it should be positivism, resume and the result[17] of capitalist ideology, which has accorded the greatest importance to the author's 'person.'"[18]

Looking back on Barthes's essay, what is remarkable is its prescience. On the one hand, it wipes away the significance of the author to writing and criticism—and opens the pathway for structural and poststructuralist critical approaches to the author. On the other hand, it restores the position of the author by saying that it will be very difficult to eliminate the author from criticism:

> The author still rules in manuals of literary history, in biographies of writers, in magazine interviews, and even in the awareness of literary men, anxious to unite, by their private journals, their person and their work; the image of literature to be found in contemporary culture is tyrannically centered on the author, his person, his history, his tastes, his passions; criticism still consists, most of the time, in saying that Baudelaire's work is the failure of the man Baudelaire, Van Gogh's work his madness, Tchaikovsky's his vice.[19]

And, interestingly enough, for Barthes, the prestige of these positivistic links to the author are bolstered by their affiliation with capitalist ideology.[20] While the post-1967 theoretical ethos was to assert the death of the author, time has shown that we have found it very difficult—if not impossible—to live without the author. In hindsight, Barthes seems to be aware of this at the very moment he is burying the author in the *Aspen* box. Nevertheless, it seems important at this point to recall the rich theoretical context that couched Barthes' proclamation.

Texting the Author

The death of the author must be understood in the context of the birth of the text. In some ways, Barthes's provocation was announcing a death that had already occurred over the past quarter century with the advent of the New Criticism—and a birth that was emerging in the contemporary concept of text.[21] During its heyday in the 1930s through 1960s, the New Criticism had a monumental effect on the focus of literary studies.[22] While the members of this movement differ on many of the specifics of criticism, they were united in the view that literature should be treated objectively, and that works of literature are self-contained, autonomous, and exist for their own sake. Extrinsic factors such as authorial intention are not important for a determination of identity and meaning as they serve only to divert the reader from the text. Monroe Beardsley and W. K. Wimsatt dubbed such diversions "the intentional fallacy."[23] Oddly enough, with regard to authorship, there is some similarity of view between the New Critical and the seemingly antithetical poststructuralist position on authorship that was presented by Barthes in "The Death of the Author."

The New Critics sought to replace biographical and philological approaches to literary works with a text-centered approach. In this regard, they stood squarely in opposition to philological views of the text that not only emphasized the material boundaries of the text, but also insisted that understanding texts involved determining the intentions of the writer. The New Critics insisted that emphasis be placed on close reading of the text with an eye toward the complex interrelations of form and content—a distinction that would later be dismantled by the contemporary, semiological concept of text advanced by Barthes and others. By championing the beauty, complexity, and speciality of literary language, the New Criticism foregrounded the text as an object of aesthetic appreciation. Both the aesthetic qualities and the meaning of the literature come from its text and not its author, and form and content are inexorably linked.

One of the major debates in twentieth-century aesthetics, especially in the United States and Britain, has been over the source of the identity of the autonomous, stable, and coherent classical notion of text.[24] For some, from Roman Ingarden in *The Literary Work of Art* (1931) to Wolfgang Iser in *The Implied Reader* (1974), the text is a set of schemata with indeterminacies awaiting our concretization. For Stanley Fish, a reception theorist like Ingarden and Iser, the identity of the artistic text is bestowed upon it by its interpreter, and is not an inherent property of the object. Fish's position that textual identity is a social construction implies, for example, that authorial intention plays little role in the identity of the text. It also implies that different interpretations entail different texts. For Fish, there is no difference between explaining a text and changing it. His view then might be said to conflate questions of interpretation with those of identity.[25]

Other theorists of the classical text associate textual identity with inherent properties of the text. Nelson Goodman, for example, argues that the identity of a text is defined by the identity of its syntax and its language—the former involves all of the characters and marks that constitute the text, and the latter implies that translation, for example, will yield a text with a different identity.[26]

Between the flexibility of Fish's classical concept of text and the rigidity of Goodman's, there have been a number of attempts made in Anglo-American aesthetics to define a text that stands somewhere between these two extremes. However disparate the definitions may seem, at the center remains a text with some type of an essence and identity—a notion of text that we will see is squarely opposed to notions of the text developing on the continent. Some theorists, such as Richard Rorty, have tried to find some type of middle ground for texts between essentialistic Anglo-American positions and antiessentialist, continental views.[27] One particularly rich source in this area is the work on text by Umberto Eco.

A text, for Eco, is a "lazy machinery"[28] that asks someone to do part of its job, and is meant to be an experience of transformation for its reader. Aesthetic or open texts serve as "the structured model for an unstructured process of communicative interplay."[29] Labyrinthine structures can be located at the foundation of every aesthetic text, as well as every sign-function. These maze-like structures of the aesthetic text stimulate reactions, rather than communicate contents. Open texts are organized such that their interpretation by a reader forms a significant part of the compositional and narrative strategy of the author. The completion of the open text is possible only through the participation of the reader, yet even so, the completion of a truly open work is only temporary and provisional. The opposite of the open text—the closed text—elicits almost a predetermined response from its reader. A good example of a closed text would be Ian Fleming's James Bond novels, and an exemplary open text would be James Joyce's *Finnegan's Wake* (1939). Open texts lack the specific, privileged point of view of closed texts from which the message may be interpreted. Nevertheless, for Eco, closed texts, like open texts, are always texts, and, as such, can elicit infinite readings without allowing any possible reading.

Classical conceptions of text, then, are closely associated with criticism's demand for a fixed textual meaning. And, if meaning necessarily involves some degree of identity, then classical notions of text must determine the amount and source of textual identity. While each of the positions defended necessarily involves maintaining some degree of stability and determinate identity between the signifier and the signified, there is no consensus as to the source of that identity. As we have seen, it is located to varying degrees and combinations, in the text, the author, and the critic.

By the 1960s, however, and the time of Barthes's provocation, the domain of text had extended from its traditionally delimited space of written discourse to that of any object whatsoever—written or spoken, aesthetic or otherwise. And, some theorists, including Juri Lotman[30] and Jacques Derrida, went so far as to view the world itself as text. Why did this shift take place? What compelled theorists to broaden the scope of text to such a degree?

The key to understanding this shift is to recognize that it involves nothing less than a rejection of the classical notion of text, and a reconceptionalization of the linguistic and philosophical foundations of language. The contemporary concept of text departs from the classical concept by following through on some of the implications of the structural linguistics of Ferdinand de Saussure. He held that the material and nonmaterial differences among signs determine language, and that language is not representational. The sign system is a convention, and signs have neither an existential nor analogical relation to what is represented. Saussure began nothing less than a revolution in the way in which we view the structure of the elements of language—a revolution that in turn compelled many to explore a new conception of text.[31]

Saussure and the structuralists proposed that it is only through functional structures that we are in any sense aware of reality, and maintained that language including art abstracts utterances or cultural products from their existential and historical context. Language, in effect, imposes form on nature, and makes it manifest as the given of a certain structure. For some structuralists, like Michel Foucault, codes are the sum total of a discourse, while for others, like Barthes, the forms of the already given order themselves into the cultural codes of the language. For Barthes, then, codes are the forms imposed by language on reality that determine our perception of it, and the text of art amounts to nothing more than a set of codes that control its production. All told, then, the structuralist text can be said to be motivated by three elements: (1) the sign; (2) the codes that order the signs into the already said of a culture; and (3) the discourses to which sets of codes belong.

In the twentieth century, it has been the multifarious semiological movements and their successors that have been the major forces shaping the contemporary concept of text. From the philological tradition, the semiologists inherited a reverence for the materiality of the text. However, they also removed it from an idealism that philologists contended stabilized and fixed textual meaning. One of the major figures in the semiological reshaping of our concept of text was Louis Hjelmslev. In the early 1960s, Hjelmslev proposed the innovative view of text as process. By replacing Ferdinand de Saussure's opposition of langue to parole with an opposition of system to process, that is to say, language itself to the text, Hjelmslev was able to argue that language cannot be individuated and defined except by starting from processes. Texts come into existence against the background of systems that govern and determine their development. The tradition established by Hjelmslev regarded texts as related to linguistic systems, but not coextensive with them.[32]

Clearly, though, the most influential group of writers on the contemporary concept of text this century has been the Tel Quel group. Founded in 1960, the avant-garde journal *Tel Quel* included among its associates three seminal theorists of the text: Julia Kristeva, Jacques Derrida—and Barthes. The Tel Quel group's contemporary concept of text as *écriture* displaced the idea that the meaning of a text is singular and upheld the notion that textual meaning is polysemic. Derrida's view of écriture is based on the idea that the meaning of texts is not stable or fixed, but is rather a series of supplements, deferrals, and substitutions. Derrida contests long-standing philosophical tradition when he argues that speech is not to be privileged over writing. For Derrida, speech is always already writing, and both speech and writing lack presence and are indeterminate.[33]

According to Tel Quel member Barthes, texts are structures of language in which authorial intention has no role in the meaning of the text. Meaning not only is produced independently of the author, but also resists closure. The reader interacts with the text to produce meaning that is many times a source of *jouissance*.[34] Barthes makes a sharp distinction between this type of entity, which he calls a text, and something he calls a *work*. The latter is laden with authorial intent, finitely meaningful, and ultimately interpretable. Whereas a text is an unstable entity that is produced by the reader, a work is a stable entity consumed by the reader.[35] The predominant view among Anglo-American aestheticians is that the objects of aesthetic inquiry are works, whereas among continental theorists, the view is quite the opposite: the objects of aesthetics are more like Barthes's texts.

Generally speaking, the differences between works and texts mirror the differences between classical and contemporary concepts of text.

It should be noted that even though Barthes restricts the domain of text to written entities only, and treats spoken entities as the domain of discourse, many of the poststructuralists who succeeded him do not follow this practice. Rather, they use the term text to refer to any entity—written, spoken, or otherwise—that produces meaning through the infinite play of signs. Others, like Emile Benveniste, extend the range of discourse to include both spoken and written entities, thus using text synonymously with discourse.[36]

Julia Kristeva treats the text not as a communicative process of social exchange based on the sender–receiver model of communication, but rather as a generative activity that she calls productivity. As productivity, texts—aesthetic and otherwise—have a redistributive relationship to the language in which they are situated, and because of this are regarded by her as translinguistic entities. For Kristeva, texts are regarded as revolutionary transformations of the language because of the dialectical relationship that she establishes between language and text. Of primary concern is the dynamics of the production of texts, rather than the actual product. One of the factors determining the polyphonous character of texts, intertextuality, is not simply a matter of literary influence. The text is an intersection, absorption, and transformation of other texts and codes, and comprises in some sense the entirety of contemporary and historical language. The analytical process, comprising the phenotext and genotext stages, is one of dissolution that inevitably leads us to the hidden meanings of the text. The phenotext is the textual surface structure that can be described empirically by the methods of structural linguistics. The genotext is the level of textual deep structure wherein the production of signification takes place. Characteristics of the genotext include exteriority to the subject, timelessness, and a lack of structure. Genotext contains the possibilities of all languages and signifying practices as its predisposition before it is masked or censured by the phenotext. Textual analysis, for Kristeva, shows us that whenever a text signifies it participates in the transformation of reality by capturing it at the moment of its non-closure.[37]

Prestige of the Author

If Barthes essay announced the death of the author, then the various notions of text developed over the course of the twentieth century demonstrated it. In fact, given their variety, it might be said that the author died a different death in each variant notion. Together they leave no doubt that twentieth-century theory and aesthetics were well placed to critically proceed without the author—both after *and* before Barthes's death pronouncement. On the one hand, the classical concept of text allows us to conceive of text as an autonomous object capable of being evaluated in terms of its formal unity, and as integrating various historical, literary, and sociological influences and sources into a new unity. On the other hand, the contemporary concept of text pushes us to reveal the codes that integrate the text into a whole of signification, and suggests that we view text as a function of linguistic and ideological discourse. Both directions provide pathways for criticism and aesthetics without what Barthes called the "modern figure" of the "author" produced in the context of the "prestige of the individual." Why then does the author continue to find its way back into our textual and critical work?

In her book, *The Deaths of the Author: Reading and Writing in Time*, Jane Gallop claims that Barthes actually writes about two types of authorial death: the first is "the abstract, polemical death of the slogan" found in his 1967 essay, and the second is "a moving, more bodily death of the mortal author."[38] Gallop shows how just three years after his essay, Barthes "announced the author's return" "in his book *Sade, Fourier, Loyola*."[39] She also cites a passage from Barthes's *The Pleasure of the Text* where he says, "As institution, the author is dead; his person...has disappeared...but in the text, in a certain way, *I desire* the author."[40] Gallop's project is to connect the two deaths (the "abstract" and the bodily) and help explain Barthes's "perverse desire for the author he nonetheless knows to be dead"—a desire she terms "'perverse' to connect it to the celebration of non-normative sexuality that is central to *The Pleasure of the Text*."[41]

Gallop, of course, is right that Barthes waffles on the death of the author—as was Seán Burke 19 years before her in his book *The Death and Return of the Author: Criticism and Subjectivity in Barthes, Foucault and Derrida* (1992).[42] In fact, one sees similar struggles in the work of other theorists between the death of the abstract, postulated author who died in text theory, and the death of actual persons who were writers and friends. Derrida, for example, who famously argued in the 1960s and 1970s that there is nothing outside of the text (*il n'y a pas de hors-texte*)[43] and that aesthetic texts as well as all others are a place of the effaced trace—the play of presence and absence, found himself from the late 1980s onward in books such as *Memoires for Paul de Man* (1986), *Specters of Marx* (1994), *Adieu to Emmanuel Levinas* (1997), and *The Work of Mourning* (2001), very much discussing mortality and the death of persons—if not also authors.

Still, he comments that this was something that he long ago promised himself he would never do. "But what I thought impossible, indecent, and unjustifiable," writes Derrida in "The Deaths of Roland Barthes,"

> what long ago and more or less secretly and resolutely I had promised myself never to do (out of a concern for rigor or fidelity, if you will, and because it is in this case *too* serious), was to write *following the death*, not after, not long after the death *by returning* to it, but just following the death, *upon or on the occasion of the death*, as the commemorative gatherings and tributes, in the writings 'in memory' of those who while living would have been my friends, still present enough to me that some 'declaration,' indeed some analysis or 'study,' would seem at the moment completely unbearable.[44]

But my target in this essay is not to retrace ground traveled by Burke and Gallop—even though their work does constitute a case for the continuing prestige of the author in aesthetics in spite of developments in the concept of text. Rather, what I'd like to offer is a different way of approaching the continuing prestige of the author in aesthetics in spite of her multiple deaths over the course of the twentieth century. The kernel of this way is found in a point that Barthes inadvertently alludes to in his essay when he reminds us of the connection between the birth of the author and the rise of capitalism. I can think of no better place to demonstrate this in the arts of the present than the recent publication of postmodern master David Foster Wallace's final novel.

The Profit of Prestige

On April 15, 2011—"tax day" in the United States—Little Brown published David Foster Wallace's unfinished novel, *The Pale King*. Wallace, who ended his own life in September of 2008, supposedly left 250 pages from the novel in the center of his desk. What was missing were instructions for the executors about what to do with the unfinished manuscript. According to Michael Pietsch, the editor charged with creating a publishable book from piles of manuscript pages and notes, "the fact that he left those pages on his work table is proof he wanted the book published."[45] Your guess though is as good as mine how this is "proof." Proof is a yellow sticky note bearing the lines: "Please publish posthumously—DFW" or a comment to his wife or agent about publication. Positivistic as it may be, anything less is only proof that Hachette Livre UK, the parent company of

Little Brown, the largest trade publisher in the United Kingdom, has found yet another way to cash in on the growing demand for everything Wallace (even Wallace's undergraduate philosophy dissertation on Richard Taylor has found its way into print of late.[46]

Wallace's longtime agent, Bonnie Nadell, also speculated on the author's intentions, saying "If there had been a spotlight on those pages it could not have been more obvious."[47] "I felt in my heart," continued Nadell, "and so did Karen Green, David's widow, that he wanted people to see it, and ultimately the reasons to publish outweighed the reasons not to."[48] But there is a big difference between providing access to the manuscript and the many handwritten journals and notebooks associated with the composition of the novel, and publishing it as a posthumous novel. Funny how authorial prestige conveniently emerges when there is an opportunity for corporate profit. For me, the fate of Wallace's unfinished manuscript is the perfect window to the role of the author in the critical and editorial present.

Posthumous materials such as letters, diaries, drafts, and notebooks are the common—and expected—literary residua of a writer's life tragically interrupted in *media res*. And these moments of authorial incompleteness and fragments of the writerly process reveal a different aspect of the writer than their published works. For writers of Wallace's stature, one expects these items to be catalogued and made publically accessible in a library's or center's archives. There they would be preserved for scholarly pursuits and creative engagements—and perpetual nourishment for the literary—and textual—imagination. Anyone who has spent time in an archive knows the singular joy of discovering new dimensions of writers through unseen and unpublished manuscripts. However, between archival access and publication of unfinished works as finished work, there is a great difference.

My general feeling is that if the author does not read the page proofs, then publishers should not publish the work with the author's name on it—especially if the only proof of authorial desire to publish was leaving an incomplete manuscript on their desk. Or, if the unfinished work is published, it should be as close to a reproduction of the original materials left behind by the author as possible. Though a "scholarly" edition or "facsimile" version is much less polished and duller than a creative projection of the final manuscript such as Pietsch's, it still is a more powerful work. Why?

For one, unless the narrative structure is clear, any effort to establish it is merely speculation. In the case of *The Pale King*, the Little Brown editor really had no idea how to order the manuscript material because the novel has only the palest glimmer of a plot. "Nowhere in all these pages," writes Pietsch in his editor's note to the novel, "was there an outline or other indication of what order David intended for these chapters."[49] However, instead of releasing the material in a more fluid form à la a "shuffle novel" or allowing aleatoric instincts to disorder it, Pietsch used a spreadsheet to establish a chronology of events, which was then used to order the sections. When things did not fit in chronological order, he then followed his instincts. "It was not an easy task," comments Pietsch, "even a chapter that appeared to be the novel's obvious starting point is revealed in a footnote, and even more directly in an earlier version of that chapter, to be intended to arrive well after the novel begins."[50]

Moreover, Pietsch took the liberty of adding 20 percent of the material contained in Little Brown's version of *The Pale King* from material that was not available in typescript. He also edited out Wallace's material that he felt was unnecessarily repetitive or slowed down the novel.[51] While the editor's role in shaping the final volume is always considerable (and in turn raises another level of contention about "authorship"), in this case, the author has no final read through. In theoretical effect, Pietsch aimed to transform a paradigmatic contemporary text into a classical text through the editorial imposition of chronological order, speculation on authorial intent, and other textual liberties.

Like the Nabokov family's decision to publish Vladimir Nabokov's *The Original of Laura* (2009) in spite of the author's directions to destroy any unfinished work upon his death, the publication of Wallace's abandoned manuscript seems like the creation a "literary event" to squeeze a few more bucks out of a popular author's industry. Thus far, it seems thankfully that critics will be kinder to Wallace than they were to Nabokov.[52] However, I think the case of Wallace's novel (and, for that matter, Nabokov's novel as well) goes to the heart of why the author has not yet died in spite of the myriad of challenges to the notion. The issue has less to do with demonstrating their independence from the text than seeing the ways others—in this case, one of the wealthiest publishing corporations in the world—profit from the notion and prestige of authorship.

Perhaps, publishing the 250 pages as found would have been the most theoretically sound step. Better yet, give them to us in facsimile form—perhaps even in a box set akin to those produced by *Aspen* magazine complete with handwritten journals and notebooks associated with the composition. Allow us to see a Wallace novel taking shape, and let the Wallace-heads argue how to fill in the gaps—or in theory-talk, the schemata with indeterminacies awaiting our concretization. Let the plotlessness and disunity engage our textual imaginations, rather than projecting this authorial mirage in the desert of postmodern literary history. I don't doubt that Wallace wanted readers to engage the novel that he was writing and the process he used to build his maximal fictions. But I wonder how a writer who fretted over punctuation would have acquiesced to the Frankenstein released by Little Brown.

If nothing else, the twentieth-century death of the author gives us a clear direction on the fate of unfinished posthumous novels. The question of whether they should be edited and published under the prestige of the author or should they be relegated to library archives for study and commentary never arises. We should use the legacy of writers like Wallace to drive readers back to libraries and archives to see the formative "stuff" of great writers. Let incomplete final efforts such as Wallace's stand as examples of the painstaking process that artistic creation often is. While I have not yet seen the mountain of materials from which Pietsch created *his* Wallace novel, I look forward to the day when I can spend time with them in the University of Texas's Harry Ransom Center. I may not be able to form as complete a structure for the novel as Pietsch did, but I would rather engage it in its disorganized, textual glory.[53]

In this age of new media and shifting intellectual property rights, creative people are struggling to maintain material rights and creative control—and the concept of authorship provides convenient cover for capitalist, or better yet, neoliberal, publishing aspirations. While having more David Foster Wallace on the shelf will be welcomed by many readers, there remains a tinge of exploitation that leaves me with reservations. I understand the executors' dilemma, and the perils of "proof of intent," but I retain strong overriding sympathies for any artist who is unable to reclaim creative rights. Let dead authors live in completeness through their published work—and leave unpublished work in its valuable incompleteness.[54]

Conclusion

After the death of the author and the birth of the text, it is much more difficult to make a compelling case that it is possible to "finish" unfinished novels. For that matter, contemporary notions of text opened up the possibility that texts are never finished—and that authors—alive or dead—bear little significant relation to them. Why then the continuing prestige of the author in aesthetics? While surely an "abstract" case can be made concerning our desire and mourning for dead authors, a stronger economic case can be made for their presence. I think the case of Wallace's *The Pale King* illustrates this. The prestige of the author plays an important role in the current neoliberal capitalist publishing economy. Summoning the specter of Wallace is akin to calculating the profits to be made on a final completed manuscript by him. While publishing his final unorganized manuscript and notebooks in an *Aspen* box might have pleased Barthes, it would have effectively buried its sales. The prestige of the author in aesthetics has less to do with mourning—and more to do with money.

While the rebirth of the author may not be the worst consequence of neoliberalism in academe, it still has the power to reshape the humanities by reversing the critical advances of the twentieth century. The author died scores of different deaths in the previous century—and there is no good reason why we should allow the potential profits from his prestige to awaken him from the dead. The neoliberal publishing industry uses the prestige of the author to sell books,[55] whereas neoliberal academic culture uses the prestige of the university to sell education. Cut from the same neoliberal mold, both—in the words of Veblen—aim at "a growth in the material resources," not the growth of knowledge. The resurgence of authorial prestige ultimately takes the humanities backwards, and is a prime example of how "corporate humanities" significantly differs from its noncorporate alternative. The post-corporate humanities of the postmodern university must honor the death of the author lest it be accused of pandering to, what Barthes called, "the prestige of the individual" and all its attendant affiliation with (late-)capitalist ideology.

8

The Publishing Market

Neoliberalism was a part of publishing culture long before it hit academic culture. Its ascent in the publishing world is one of a gradual intensification of market considerations over aesthetic or scholarly ones—a story that holds to varying degrees both within the corporate publishing industry and now within the university and small press publishing world. However, it is not one that has been widely considered—though it needs to be. The aim of this chapter is to provide a prolegomenon to neoliberalism in publishing and to establish its inroads to and convergences with academic culture.[1]

As with the academic world, the rise of neoliberalism within the publishing world has displaced many of its traditional ways of operating. For example, today most authors do not deal directly with large presses anymore, rather this is left to their agents;[2] market data rather than aesthetics drives most large press decision making; the large presses essentially "own" the major book review outlets; multinational publishing corporations control the distribution of books to the majority of stores; and the advances offered by large presses many times exceed the lifetime income of many authors. These and other factors centered upon increased control of the book market have created a disbalance in the publishing world wherein the big presses keep getting bigger, more powerful, and fewer in number, and the smaller presses either get absorbed by the bigger ones or get smaller and more marginalized.

Moreover, the recent shift from a print to a digital book culture has only intensified the effects of neoliberalism in publishing. Not only are presses—both large *and* small—increasingly refusing to publish books that they fear will lose money or only appeal to a limited share of the market such as one of the scholarly subfields or subdisciplines discussed earlier, but the number of physical venues to purchase these books is decreasing. As it becomes increasingly possible to find and purchase just about any book one is looking for through an online vendor such as Amazon, it becomes increasingly impossible to run a bricks-and-mortar bookstore. Not only are private bookstores gradually disappearing from towns and cities across America, so too are the large chain bookstores that hastened the decline of the private bookstores. Bookstores like public libraries should be treated as public spaces where people can gather and seek out written entertainment, edification, and enlightenment, or, if you will, *infotainment*. They are also often the site of readings, book signings, discussion groups, and other activities grounded in dialogue and critical inquiry—two of the cornerstones of democratic culture. The demise of the bookstore is a major setback for academic and democratic culture, and yet another example of the way in which public spaces are privatized under neoliberalism.

"Neoliberalism," writes Alfredo Saad-Filho and Deborah Johnston, "strattles a wide range of social, political, and economic phenomena at different levels of complexity."[3] Inquiry into the ways in which it strattles the publishing world both inside and outside of academe will reveal some of the ultimate constraints neoliberalism places on the marketplace for ideas. If profit generation and market considerations are the primary drivers of the publishing industry, and the publishing industry controls a major section of information and creative dissemination including major book review outlets and other media, then there is not much hope that heterodox, innovative, and transformative thinking will be supported by it. Furthermore, the monopoly of this industry on knowledge dissemination threatens to render silent major avenues of creative innovation and critical dissent. In a way, small presses today are our best hope for overcoming the neoliberal publishing stranglehold, but they are also the most vulnerable, particularly those affiliated with a higher educational world that supports them less and less. But how did the publishing world get here? What follows are a few snapshots from the story—a story that oddly enough can be said to begin with arguably the greatest—and most innovative—book of the twentieth century: James Joyce's *Ulysses*.

Publishing with One Eye

In 1932, when Random House sought to legally publish *Ulysses* in the United States, it was Bennett Cerf, one of the co-owners of the publishing house that contacted the Irish novelist. After receiving Joyce's consent to publish, Cerf had a copy of the book sent from Paris to New York, and then arranged for customs officials to seize it at the docks so that he could prepare for a court battle over it. Ten minutes after Judge John Woolsey of the New York district court delivered his verdict that the book was not legally obscene, Cerf had the typesetters at Random House working on Joyce's masterpiece.[4]

To many, Cerf, who cofounded Random House in 1925 with Donald Klopfer, and whose press also published Sinclair Lewis, William Faulkner, Gertrude Stein, Truman Capote, and John O'Hara, is one of the heroes of American publishing. Though Joyce's book had been published some ten years earlier by Sylvia Beach's Shakespeare & Co. in Paris, because it was banned in the English-speaking world, Joyce did not profit from it until Cerf stood up for it in court. The legal publication of *Ulysses* by Random House finally allowed Joyce—rather than the *Ulysses* bootleggers—to reap more of the financial rewards of its publication.

In hindsight—and from a less flattering perspective—moves like Cerf's acquisition of *Ulysses* and the building of a top-tier list of authors by his press can be seen as laying the groundwork for the rise of contemporary corporate publishing. That is to say, it foreshadows a publishing world where Simon & Schuster is a subsidiary of CBS, and HarperCollins is owned by News Corporation, the multimedia conglomerate founded by Rupert Murdoch; where 12 publishers out of approximately 85,000 account for almost two-thirds of US trade and mass-market book sales;[5] where 90 percent of active publishers account for less than 10 percent of total book sales;[6] where Random House alone accounts for over 13 percent of all US book sales and has worldwide sales revenues of almost 2.4 *billion* dollars;[7] and where Random House *alone* almost sells more books than 58,795 US trade and mass-market publishers *combined*.[8] How did this happen? How did it come to be that a few publishing corporations now control the majority of book sales in the United States? And what does it mean for the 58,795 "small" presses that reside in the shadows of corporate publishing giants like Random House?

In the case of Random House, by the 1950s, the co-owners began to worry about what would happen to the company if one of them died. Cerf said, "Donald and I knew that the real value of the company had increased each year, but nobody knew by how much."[9] He continued, "If its value was too high, how could the survivor afford to buy the other half, and how could the widow of the one who died raise enough cash to pay the estate tax?"[10] Worries about the future of their company if one of them died led Cerf and Klopfer to sell 30 percent of their stock to the public in 1959. "From then on," writes Cerf, "we were publishing with one eye and watching our stock with the other."[11] "Instead of working for yourself and doing what you damn please, willing to risk a loss on something you want to do, if you're any kind of honest man, you feel a responsibility to your stockholders," wrote Cerf.[12]

Going public opened the door to expanding the business, which it did shortly after going public by acquiring both Knopf[13] and Pantheon.[14] Soon Time-Life took an interest in merging with Random House—a deal that eventually fell through when it became clear that the US Department of Justice would most likely oppose the merger on antitrust grounds.[15] In 1965, however, Random House was sold to RCA for 40 million dollars, at which point Cerf stepped down as president. Cerf said they accepted RCA's offer because "it was one of the great corporations of the country."[16] And who would disagree—the sale even allowed one of RCA's writers, Truman Capote, to become one of its recording artists, releasing an album of readings of scenes from *In Cold Blood* in 1966.

By the time Random House was acquired by RCA, it was a much different publishing house from the one where Cerf wrote to Joyce about publishing *Ulysses*. Further acquisitions and mergers followed including its sale in 1980 from RCA to S. I. Newhouse, a wealthy businessman and owner of a range of television stations, newspapers, and magazines, to its sale again in 1998 to Bertelsmann.[17] Today "Random House" consists of over 60 imprints, divisions, and groups in the United States and United Kingdom alone—with one of the imprints of "Random House" called by the same name.[18]

Random House is a perfect example of the effects of the rise of a ruthless new form of market capitalism that scholars have been warning us about for years. "It reifies and glorifies the reign of what are called the financial markets," comments Pierre Bourdieu, "in other words the return to a kind of radical capitalism, with no other law than that of maximum profit, and unfettered capitalism without any disguise, but rationalized, pushed to the limit of its economic efficacy by the introduction of modern forms of domination, such as 'business administration,' and techniques of manipulation, such as market research and advertising."[19] Moreover, Random House's recent merger with another of the largest publishing houses in the world, Penguin, is only further evidence of the continuing ruthlessness of this new form of market capitalism.[20] The new Penguin Random House will account for about one in four books sold—in the world.[21]

This form of unfettered capitalism, says Bourdieu, "sets up as the norm of all practices, and therefore as ideal rules, the real regularities of the economic world abandoned to its own logic, the so-called laws of the market."[22] While it has its roots in the classical liberal economic theories of Adam Smith and David Ricardo, it is more closely associated with the neoliberalism of Friedrich Hayek and Milton Friedman. As a consequence, it has resulted in among other things, the rise of authoritarianism, the suspension of civil liberties, the privatization of public spaces, the upward distribution of wealth—and in our case, the disfigurement of the book publishing industry. Again, as Henry Giroux succinctly puts it, "neoliberalism is an ideology and politics buoyed by the spirit of a market fundamentalism that subordinates the art of democratic politics to the rapacious laws of a market economy that expands its reach to include all aspects of social life within the dictates and values of market-driven society."[23] The case of publishing is yet another sad chapter in the subordination of social life by neoliberalism—as the books that we read are an integral part of it.

There is no doubt that the publishing industry has been forever changed by the rise of neoliberalism. To be sure, there is no aspect of the publishing world that has not been affected by its economic control and cultural domination of the market. What though does the rise of neoliberalism and corporate publishing mean for the 58,795 "small" presses[24] that reside in the shadows of corporate publishing giants like Random House? Is their position any different than it was before Random House went public and was purchased by RCA? And what is the effect of the rise of neoliberalism in publishing on fiction writing, reading habits, and bookselling? Is writing for Cerf and Klopfer any different than writing for Rupert Murdoch[25] or RCA? These and related questions go straight to the foundation of creative writing culture in America and—as many of these projects fall within the domain of the humanities—to the heart of academic culture as well.

Neoliberal Aesthetics

The rise of neoliberalism has forever changed mainstream fiction writing, reading habits, and bookselling in America. Writing fiction in the age of corporate mega-publishing is now more than ever a business affair, not a creative one. In *Acts of Resistance*, Bourdieu writes "neo-liberal ideologues want us to believe that the economic and social world is structured by equations."[26] In terms of the publishing world, they likewise want us to believe that it too is structured by equations.

Now that reading habit data can be tracked through data mining of e-books, publishers can determine everything from how long it took you to read a page to specifically what you read.[27] What then will stop them from feeding this data back into their publishing equations to determine things like the economically optimal narrative aesthetics? How far are we from aesthetics being more than just *influenced* by market fundamentalism, but rather *determined* by it? After all, this and other data determined the books stocked by the fistful of chains that dominated the national landscape (though, we shall see later where it got them). Using data now to determine the shape of narrative seems like a logical next step.[28]

Nearly three-quarters of active publishers in the United States have annual revenues between zero and $50,000; roughly another 20 percent put their annual revenues between $50,000 and 1 million dollars. In total, these figures represent the annual revenues of almost 60,000—or 95 percent —of US publishers.[29] Considering the large percentage of publishers with annual revenues less than $50,000, it could be argued that small press publishing *populates* the national landscape though corporate publishing *controls* it. How else can you describe the difference between a Penguin Random House that will now produce one in every four new books and a small press like the Fiction Collective Two that only publishes six books per year total?

One might argue that what separates a corporate publisher from a small press publisher is that the former want people to *buy* books, however the latter want people to *read* them—or even *believe* in them. In a way, the American political landscape mirrors the publishing landscape. Namely, a case could be made that political power is concentrated among the wealthiest 5 percent of our nation, while the remaining 95 percent dominate in numbers. Whereas in American politics wealth yields a disproportionate amount of political power; in American publishing, capital yields a disproportionate amount of market control.

The great myth of American publishing is that it is controlled by aesthetic values. This might have been the case years ago when the Random House of Bennett Cerf pushed to publish a novel that opens with the line "Stately, plump Buck Mulligan came from the stairhead, bearing a bowl of lather on which a mirror and a razor lay crossed." It is not the case when its contemporary neoliberal instantiation outbid itself to publish the next novel of the author whose first novel began with the line "At the first gesture of morning, flies began stirring."[30] Yes, outbid *itself.* Which is either like tripping over your own shoelaces—or tripping over the outstretched foot of the editor in the cubicle next to you.

The novel that got Random House tripping over its own feet was a first novel whose hardback sales in the late 1990s had exceeded 1.6 million copies. Such things capture the attention of market-driven corporate publishers—"At first gesture of a market, calculators began stirring." Based on what is said to have been a one-page proposal, one of Random House's 60 imprints, divisions, and groups offered an advance of over 5 million dollars to the author. However, not to be outdone by one of their co-division rivals, another division of Random House offered over *eight* million dollars.[31] The name of the novelist and whether the advance paid off for Random House are irrelevant to the conditions that they exemplify: the effects of neoliberal-based decision making in the publishing world.[32]

A climate of publishing where the advance for a second novel exceeds by eight times the annual publishing revenue of 95 percent of American publishing houses—or roughly 60,000 publishers—presents a sad state for American letters. If Random House was willing to offer the author of this second novel an 8-million-dollar advance, one can only imagine how much they were willing to invest in marketing the book. That is, for example, in purchasing mainstream media interest in this author and their work as "essential summer reading" or buying national distribution support to ensure that "the next great American novel" is available for purchase in your local Walmart or Borders. To say that hearing this book news over and over again in major media outlets, and seeing this book prominently displayed in every big-box bookstore in America does not affect reading habits and impact sales would be naïve. However, to say that it *fashions* reading and buying behavior would be closer to the truth.

American publishing in the age of neoliberalism is controlled by markets, equations, and calculators—not aesthetic value, literary contribution, or scholarly impact. The more that mega-publishers invest in large market fiction and avoid small market fiction, the more that aesthetic innovation and narrative diversity will flourish among small presses. In the neoliberal climate of corporate publishing, it is not surprising to see a rise in small press publishers devoted to diversity and innovation—and a widening of the financial gap between small presses and the corporate giants. Moreover, even among the big house publishers, one is beginning to see more capital distance among them.

Of the 4,000 publishers that have annual sales over 1 million dollars, less than 20 percent have annual sales over 50 million dollars[33]— and only 12 have annual sales over 150 million.[34] And among the Big 12, the twelfth largest has only one-tenth of the sales of the largest. This kind of concentration of publishing capital entails a type of power akin to that held by the Bush and Kennedy families in American politics. Again, that Random House *alone* sells more books than 76,500

US trade and mass-market publishers *combined* is as much a cause for celebration among writers as is the fact that McDonald's serves more hamburgers than any other restaurant in America. So, one might ask, would you like to supersize that novel?[35]

Bookstore Simulacra

One of the more visible signs of neoliberalism in publishing has been the decline of independent booksellers—and the corresponding rise of the book superstore. While corporate publisher mergers, market-based editorial decision making, and multi-million dollar author advances are less visible to the general public, huge book megastores—often near boarded up independent bookstores—are a part of the American landscape. Book superstores are as common now to American strip malls as Walmart and Target, and in some cities are even found among luxury stores such as Louis Vuitton and Tiffany's.

Fifty years ago, three quarters of trade books were purchased at independent bookstores. Thirty years ago, competition from mall bookstores slashed this number in half. The meteoric rise of superstores like Barnes and Noble and Borders cut this number in half again five years ago.[36] What's not to like about cappuccino machines, cozy leather chairs, and a mountain of the Tom Clancy novels? But now it seems even the megastores have overreached their rise.

One half of the contemporary book-superstore dynamic duo recently filed for bankruptcy.[37] It seems that while everyone did enjoy the cappuccino machines, cozy chairs, and free reading materials, this didn't necessarily translate into the actual *sale* of books. And while Borders's recent filing for Chapter 11 might be sweet revenge to those who ran and loved the independents, one should not expect a renaissance of the independent bookstore. Consumers increasingly prefer to shop for books online, where they can find big discounts and take advantage of immediate download.

The demise of Borders only strengthens online bookselling giant Amazon, which was positioned in 2011 to account for 50 percent of US trade sales *in all formats* by 2012.[38] To get a perspective on this number, consider that only five years ago, all of the superstores and chains in the United States combined only accounted for 45 percent of the US book retail market.[39] Soon Amazon *alone* will be responsible for half of all book sales in the United States—with and without cappuccino.

If there is a silver lining to this development, at least Amazon makes available many more small press books than Borders and its corporate companions—and easily fills your order for a title by Raymond Federman or Cris Mazza. Shopping at the chains never did that (I make a habit of looking for my favorite *American Book Review*-reviewed authors in every bookstore I visit). Much like Random House, whose transformation from premier literary publishing house to market fundamentalist megacorporation can be linked to its going public and its corporate takeover by RCA, the metamorphosis of Borders from darling of the independent bookstore world to its pariah can be associated with its purchase by another large corporation—in this case, Kmart.

In 1971, Tom and Louis Borders opened a small bookstore in the college town of Ann Arbor, Michigan. Its success over the years encouraged the owners to open a second store in 1985 in nearby Detroit. When this store did well, they opened others. The stores were known throughout the Midwest and Northeast for their wide selection of new titles, but Borders stores retained their roots as academic booksellers. At any Borders, one could find piles of bestsellers alongside thousands of individual copies of scholarly titles—something unusual at the time for a bookstore chain. Kmart, renowned for its "blue-light specials" on underwear and soap, acquired Borders in 1992, and merged it with Waldenbooks, the mall bookstore staple that it had acquired in 1984. The merger, called Borders Group (though I think "Kbooks" would have been more appropriate), went public in 1995.[40]

While the acquisition of bookstore chains by a department store might sound strange, it seems fitting given that at one point department stores in the United States were among the leading sellers of books. Shortly after they first started selling books in late nineteenth century, department stores likes Macy's of New York became national leaders in book sales. And by the early 1950s, it had been estimated that around 20 to 40 percent of trade books were sold by department stores. These businesses favored books in their inventory because they were believed to raise the class of the store, and appealed to a more cultured—and wealthy—clientele.[41]

One of the consequences of this corporate merger with Kmart was that the Borders Group started closing many of its Waldenbooks, and opening up more Borders superstores. From 1993 to 1994 alone, Borders went from 44 to 85 superstores—whereas Waldenbooks was reduced by nearly 60 stores during the same period.[42] And Borders was not the only bookstore increasing its number of superstores at the time: so too was Barnes and Noble, which had bought the other mall chain bookstore staple, B. Dalton Booksellers, in 1986. By 2006, the number of Borders superstores rose to nearly 500 in the United States alone—often in prime locations such as on Chicago's Magnificent Mile or Market Street in San Francisco. But Borders's fall has turned out to be faster than its rise.[43]

To be sure, Borders Group's failings were not just about books. A poor real estate strategy, overinvestment in music (another anguished industry), and inefficient inventory management contributed to the decline. When the company filed for bankruptcy on February 16, 2011, Borders hadn't been profitable for five years. In 1994, Borders Group operated almost 1,200 bookstores. However, just before filing for bankruptcy, there remained one half that number—with another 30 percent set to close.[44] Fittingly, the vacant shells of these large stores in prominent locations like Michigan Avenue in Chicago are as much a visual reminder to all who pass by them of the shortcomings of market-fundamentalist-based decision making as are the piles of remaindered book-mountain titles. These vacated stores are a highly visible sign of the emptiness of neoliberal practices in publishing.

So what now for the independent booksellers? The difference between the book superstore and an independent bookseller ends with the common trait that they both stock and sell books. Whereas independent bookstores are defined for their eclectic and idiosyncratic inventories, mall bookstores like B. Dalton and Waldenbooks, and superstores like Barnes and Noble and Borders are characterized by the consistency and homogeneity of their inventories. While each independent bookstore makes its own inventory decisions, department stores and corporate chains have a few people making purchasing decisions *for all of their stores.*

The recent rise of chains aimed to *simulate* the appearance of high-end independent bookstores by having rows of beautiful bookcases with ladders alongside plush chairs and gourmet coffee, but in the process destroyed the *aura* of the bookstore. By regulating and standardizing the appearance and stock of the corporate bookstore in the same way that McDonald's regulates and standardizes its appearance and menu, they in effect deconstructed the notion of the bookstore they sought to emulate. Just as independent restaurants don't look alike or have the same menu—let alone food that tastes exactly the same—independent bookstores don't all sell the same books or look alike. That's the beauty of independence.[45]

Browsing an independent bookstore for the first time can be an *unsettling* experience. The unfamiliarity with the layout and organization of titles, and with the stock itself, lends an element of adventure. At their best, independent books are unique assertions of aesthetic tastes. Mass market chain stores, however, sacrificed adventure for familiarity. Their overreliance on bestsellers and reluctance to embrace valuable backlist titles led to a homogenizing of offerings. But now even this strategy is failing.

As the industry undergoes a painful contraction, booksellers and publishers will need to reexamine their relationship in a changing market. It is unfortunate that a number of jobs will be lost, and that there will be fewer places to physically browse for books. But perhaps there is a positive element for small press authors. Perhaps, with the decline of the mass market chains, the lure of "big" books for quick bucks will be somewhat lessened. Perhaps booksellers and publishers will reinvest in a long-standing relationship of developing authors and promoting backlist titles, as they did before mass merchandising changed the process. Well-written manuscripts from lesser-known authors might have more of a voice in an environment less dependent on mounds of bestsellers. And who knows, writers and readers just might benefit from some of the recent failures of corporate publishing.

Fall of University Presses

If the decline and fall of corporate and independent booksellers has been one of the more visible signs of neoliberalism in publishing, then one of the least visible signs is the gradual fall and disappearance of university presses. Of all the consequences of neoliberalism in publishing, this is the most devastating to academic culture. While there are only just over 130 university presses in the United States, these presses are the lifeblood of scholarly publishing.[46] The scourge of neoliberalism in higher education has led to a spate of downsizings and closures. One of the latest university presses to face closure is the publisher of *The Collected Works of Langston Hughes* and *The Complete Sermons of Ralph Waldo Emerson*. Starting July 2012, the University of Missouri Press began to phase out operations.[47] The press, which was founded in 1958 by a University of Missouri English professor, William Peden, has published approximately 2,000 titles over the course of its history.

Eclectic in its reach, the press has an impressive catalogue[48] that includes offerings in women's studies, African American studies, creative nonfiction, journalism, and American, British, and Latin American literary criticism. It serves its region with series such as the Missouri Biography Series and Missouri Heritage Readers Series, and American letters in general with series such as the Mark Twain and

His Circle Series and the Southern Women Series. The press's catalogue is deep and rich, and holds gems for both the serious scholar and general interest reader. In addition to the seminal collections of Emerson and Hughes, my own recent favorites are Gail Pool's *Faint Praise: The Plight of Book Reviewing in America* (2007), which was discussed earlier, and Ned Stuckey-French's *The American Essay in the American Century* (2011).[49]

One of the measures of a great university is the strength of its press. Press strength is determined by its catalogue, and its catalogue by the choices of its editors and the impact of its authors. Still, not every excellence indicator is marked in this direction. For example, the existence of a great university press is neither sufficient nor necessary for membership in the revered Association of American Universities (AAU). Last year, University of Nebraska, which operates one of the leading university presses in the country, was ousted from the AAU; and Georgia Institute of Technology, which does not run a press, was recently admitted. The University of Missouri will neither be ousted nor even punished by the AAU for closing its press. The AAU criteria favor competitive research financing, not competitive catalogues; faculty in the National Academies, not award-winning university press titles.

University presses are nonprofit enterprises. Though these presses may reach a level of financial self-sufficiency in their operation, they are by and large underwritten by their host universities. This is part of the investment of higher education. Most of the monographs produced by scholars have a limited audience — and very few make their publishers any money. However, their publication is still an important aspect of scholarly activity and knowledge dissemination.

The University of Missouri system afforded its press a $400,000 annual subsidy.[50] To gain a perspective on this figure and the value of the press to the university, one only has to consider that the head basketball coach at Mizzou makes $1.35 million per year—and the head football coach makes $2.5 million per year.[51] The interim director of the press makes just under $75,000—less than an assistant baseball coach.[52] The acquisitions editor makes just under $35,000—less than an athletic trainer. Closer to the cost of subsidizing the press are the salaries of the assistant head football coach and the linebacker coach/defensive coordinator, who each make just over $340,000 per year.[53] How does one compare a football season to a publishing season? Is an 8–5 season more valuable than 30 books published?[54] Is running a press worth losing an assistant coach or two?

In total, the University of Missouri employs over 17,500 individuals. Currently, the press employs ten people though in 2009 it was nearly twice that number. The economic crash of 2008 forced many state universities such as the University of Missouri to reassess priorities and scale back.[55] Mizzou made their priorities clear: in 2010, the University of Missouri's head football coach received a $650,000 raise.[56] Louisiana State University, another football powerhouse, slated its university press for closure in 2009. Somehow, this press survived the state budget crisis.[57] However, given that it is nowhere near as popular as their football team, I'm sure that it sleeps with one eye open, waiting for the day that university officials have to decide between a subsidy for the press—and a pay raise for the coach. Other presses were not so lucky. Eastern Washington University, Southern Methodist University,[58] and the University of Scranton[59] all closed their presses. And even the celebrated University of California Press tightened its belt by discontinuing a poetry series.[60]

University of Missouri administrators are said to be "hashing out ways to create a new and sustainable model to operate a university press."[61] They also assure us that "any future press won't look like the current operation."[62] "We believe the publication of scholarly work is important," said the president of University of Missouri. "We're working very diligently on what" the new press "will look like."[63] While there is no indication where the University of Missouri administration will go with this, the options here are limited. The most obvious, however, is to go digital. And here there is some precedent.

Though Rice University closed its traditional press in 1996, it reopened in its wake an all-digital press in 2006. According to a 2010 interview with Eugene Levy, who helped finance the revived press during his term as provost at Rice, the all-digital press was costing Rice $150,000 to $200,000 per year. "This was intended as an experiment," said Levy.[64] Coming from the Andrew Hays Buchanan Professor of Astrophysics at Rice, the word "experiment" gains even more gravitas. Rice hoped to save money by not printing books. Comments Levy, "The hope was that, without the burden of having to maintain a print inventory, the press might sustain itself largely on revenues from print-on demand sales." What the university found out was that there "are base costs that are irreducible"—"and that printing is only one of them."[65] By 2010, it was determined that there would be no way to recover even the minimal cost of operations. Combine this with slow sales and a fiscal crisis—and the result is a failed experiment. Rice shut down its all-digital press in the fall of 2010.[66] However, the decision was not without its detractors.

One of the board members—who wished to remain anonymous—commented that new models of academic publishing are not going to be derived from a sales model: "We're moving to a different era of scholarly communication where it's more accessible to more people, and where we don't have to worry about commercial viability." Humanities publishing is being killed by placing emphasis on commercial viability—"there is no commercial viability," added the board member.[67] No matter what the form and how diligent the work, a university press requires resources. Just as it takes resources to run a successful athletic program, so too does it take an investment to run a university press. And comparatively speaking, the costs are negligible: an editor makes less at Mizzou than an athletic trainer, and even the assistant baseball coaches make more than the press director.

Perhaps the solution is not to compare athletic salaries to press salaries but to treat university presses on the same level as athletic programs. Both are auxiliary operations subsidized by the university, and both play an important role in higher education. Perhaps we need to measure the scholarly impact of the books published by the press in the same way we measure the impact of the gymnastics or baseball team winning a game or their division. Or think of the cultural capital and esteem generated by the press as akin to the bowl victories or NCAA titles. And just as we would not scrap athletics if one of our teams loses games or money, we should not scrap university presses if they fail to generate enough revenue to cover their operation. While it may not be the most popular decision for the University of California Press to take one type of book off their list, if it makes their press more viable in some way, it is akin to downsizing or closing down a sport to make an athletics program stronger. Think of the $200,000 invested by Rice or the $400,000 at Mizzou as the cost of being a strong university—a cost that in the big picture is most likely a fraction of the cost of one athletic coach.

What does it mean when a university press fails? It doesn't mean that its authors are not successful or that its press was not run well. Rather it means that its university has abandoned part of its academic or scholarly mission: namely, supporting the publication of books that are the warp and woof of academic culture.

Conclusion

Corporate humanities is always already in the shadow of corporate publishing. As books are the lifeblood of the humanities—be they classics or contemporary works—the fact that much of the scholarly and creative output in the humanities is controlled by corporate interests does not bode well for them. The vast majority of the projects created by humanities scholars have an audience only a fraction of that which is expected by corporate publishers. However, the missteps and failures of the neoliberal publishing regime are reasons to be hopeful that there will be a backlash to McPublishing. There is also a hopeful coda to the University of Missouri Press saga: public outcry over the announcement of the closing of the press resulted in a stay of execution for that press.[68] So there is hope that thoughtful critical resistance can result in a reversal—or at least a reprieve—in neoliberal decision making in academe.

In the end, it may be the acts of resistance of academics that determine the fate of neoliberal publishing. If academics, for example, refuse to utilize the overly priced textbooks of corporate publishers that are re-released every two years in a new edition, this could help derail a very profitable aspect of the publishing industry; if authors in academe, for example, choose to publish their work with small presses rather than corporate presses, this can help cut off their creative supply chain; if people vociferously refuse to accept the closure of university presses, this can perhaps change the behavior of neoliberal administrators and make them more responsive to the needs of the intellectual communities that they represent; and so on. The story of the growth of neoliberalism in publishing can become one of rise and fall more quickly if and only if we in the academy refuse to regard the fruits of our intellectual labors as corporate commodities. This can be accomplished one teacher and one author at a time through the choices we make relative to the intersection of our academic interests and our publishing needs.

9

THE JUNKYARD OF IDEAS

One of the consequences of neoliberalism in higher education is increasing focus on the achievement of status and prestige. As noted earlier, this has resulted in a shift from academic-focused missions to prestige-focused missions. One of the results of this shift in university mission is increasing pressure on faculty to produce higher levels of scholarship, particularly at institutions seeking to raise their status. Deborah Rhode aptly describes this as "upward drift" and notes that "an increasing number of schools have sought to enhance their reputations by supporting research."[1]

However, according to Rhode, this "upward drift" or "mission creep" is not without its costs. Rhode contends that "institutions lower on the prestige pecking order" tend "to imitate rather than innovate and replicate the priorities of more prestigious universities than to develop distinctive strengths."[2] For her, imitation as opposed to *innovation* as a means of achieving status sets up many members of the profession for failure and frustration. "There are, after all," laments Rhode, "so many ways of falling short."[3]

One form of "upward-drift imitation" that can lead to faculty frustration and failure involves increasing the emphasis on research and scholarship. Rhode is rightly quite cynical of the value in itself of more research and scholarship, noting that "estimates of pointless publications run as high as 90 percent."[4] In addition, she charges that the writing style and the highly specialized topics of much contemporary scholarship contribute to its pointlessness. "Too much academic writing is unnecessarily unintelligible and inconsequential," writes Rhode, "directed at too narrow an audience and too insignificant a set of topics."[5]

Rhode's comments on the style of scholarship appear to be more in line with conservative critics than progressive ones. In fact, she even quotes conservative critic Lynne Cheney who charges that these stylistically difficult publications serve "no purpose beyond expanding the author's c.v.'s."[6] Nevertheless, Rhode aims to distance herself from the conservative charge that highly specialized and stylistically difficult scholarship is in itself without value. Her belief is that "more attention should focus on quality rather than quantity."[7] Moreover, the energy and time utilized to produce specialized academic writing "could be usefully redirected to work that has direct application to societal needs and concerns." [8]

Rhode's comments are interesting because they open up an important set of questions regarding neoliberalism in academe: Does higher education in the age of neoliberalism promote "pointless" publication (Rhode's term) or, more bluntly, "junk" (my term)? Does it encourage professors to publish material that they know will end up in the scrapyard of ideas—sooner rather than later? Does the neoliberal professional mandate of "publish or perish" encourage academics to produce material that under other conditions might not be considered worthy of publication? Are academics invested in a model of higher education that encourages *over*publication? Such questions put those of us engaged in academic publication in a defensive position. But such questions may seem overdue to those who do not participate in this highly divisive aspect of the academy—those who see the central role of the academy to be teaching and service.

The word "junk" will sound harsh and inappropriate to many ears. The suggestion that the fruits of our academic labor be regarded as disposable seems disrespectful. It may even seem dangerous in an era where humanities scholarship is already met with derision from colleagues in other fields. But I don't think it is. Rather, I think that it adequately describes the fate of much of what we publish. Much current scholarship is passed over after publication—or is quickly superseded by a faster and shinier idea. The fate of these works is not the trash heap but rather something more like an automotive junkyard: a place where broken down vehicles are kept so that parts can be pulled off for others to use—and where the ultimate fate of the vehicle is recycling or reuse. There is value to be found in small parts, but it requires a persistence of search.

To associate academic publication with the production of material that quickly breaks down or has a relatively short life raises concerns not only about the general value and quality of scholarly output, but also the motivation with which it is produced. But we must acknowledge that part of academic life is to produce work and move on—leaving it for others to pick out threads of ideas. This is the value of the *community of scholars*, namely to process and assess ideas. We rely on fellow scholars scavenging for source material to respond to and develop our ideas. If Louis Menand is right in saying that "[e]clecticism seems to be the fate of the humanities," then a wide search through diverse sources for salvageable ideas seems part of this eclectic fate.[9]

Though we devote considerable time and expense toward preserving and protecting the material existence of our publications in voluminous climate-controlled libraries, and have made great gains in providing easy access to increasing amounts of our scholarship through digital distribution, it does not conceal the fact that the majority of what fills our academic libraries and data servers is seldom accessed. Or that most of the scholarship that we produce only has a brief shelf life. While this scholarship no doubt adds another chapter to a critical conversation or a nuance to a line of scholarship, who really believes that much of what we are writing today will be useful or relevant to scholars five years from now—let alone 50. Like our automobiles, our scholarship is built for the scrap heap—not the long run.

Contemporary academic practices like pressing tenure-track assistant professors for articles and books solely to meet university tenure and promotion requirements or using publication as a means to achieve merit raises can and does bring out the best in some scholars; but it also results in many publications that serve no other end than the furtherance of an individual career. Is this a sustainable model of academic publishing or a glorified "carrot and stick"? Worse yet, is this model of academic publishing only serving to ensure higher levels of mediocrity and obsolescence in scholarly publication? Has the academic industry become so thoroughly corporate that, like companies that design products for obsolescence to accelerate the purchase cycle, it encourages professors to produce scholarship not with the aim of producing ideas with longevity, but rather with the goal of preserving the demand to produce more ideas?

This is not to say that scholarly publication cannot and does not result in material with long-standing interest to the academic community. But think about the classic publications from decades past; those which still have critical purchase or lasting value; and it seems that by comparison, relatively little of what we produce as current scholarship has the same impact.

One reason for this rarity is the sheer difficulty of producing a classic such as *Being and Time* or *The Madwoman in the Attic*. Another might be increasing specialization and a "fractured market" for academic readership. But still another reason is that a lot of what is published in academia today is only produced to forward its author's career—or university's reputation. It is aimed less at solving or making progress on scholarly issues and more at satisfying the demands of careerism.

To be sure, not all of the "junk" publication produced today is the direct consequence of careerism in academia. Part of academic scholarship includes following lines of inquiry to their culmination, and some ideas will be weaker than others; some investigations will prove less fruitful than others. While one can sympathize with honest efforts to scholarly inquiry that end up in the junkyard, it is more difficult to rest easy about weak work produced out of the pressures of careerism.

If too many academic publications serve no other end than the furtherance of individual careers and have little value to anyone aside from a very small coterie of scholars, are we really building a sustainable model of publishing? Do we want to continue to encourage increasing amounts of publishing activity from faculty who only produce this material because they have to? Do we want to sustain a publishing model that essentially encourages the production of increasing amounts of junk publication?

This is especially troublesome when one considers that at no time in the history of higher education in America have there been *more* faculty employed (and underemployed) than the present. This number, which Cary Nelson recently put at 1.4 million (when one takes into account everyone employed to teach at a college or university[10]), is an incredibly large number of people, if all are expected to produce academic publications *with relevance*. Consider that the American Association of University Presses has only about 125 members and publishes only around 10,000 academic books per year. Not only is this a small percentage of the over 150,000 overall titles produced per year, it rings even smaller when one considers the number of faculty vying to publish with these presses. Even if we limited the scholarly community to one book per academic per *career*, it would take 140 years for each member of the community to have his or her book published from an AAUP affiliated press—and 280 years for each to publish two books. Moreover, lowering that number to one book every 25 years would only allow less than one in five faculty to publish a book.

In sum, much of what is currently published does not have scholarly or critical longevity, which opens up questions of value relative to other academic pursuits such as teaching and service. Simultaneously, our academic press system does not have the capacity to publish all of this scholarship anyway—even if it is good—which in turn opens up challenges to the publish or perish model in a world of increasing faculty numbers. These are indicators of a real breakdown in our model for incorporating publication into contemporary academic life: compulsion to publish can result in junk; and expectation to publish be stymied by insufficient capacity to publish all good scholarship. So, where do we go from here?

On the Very Notion of Publishing

There has been quite a bit of discussion of late about the "crisis" in academic book publishing weighed against the increasing pressures on faculty to publish.[11] We need to move on from rehashing the numbers and bemoaning the increasing pressures on scholars and publishing houses alike and move toward reenvisioning the very notion of *publishing* in academe. The scholarly book and the academic article remain the twin-pillars of academic publishing in an age where the exchange of ideas often occurs with tighter insight and more impact in alternate venues such as blogs, Twitter, chatrooms, and websites. Consider as well documentary video, magazine, and newspaper articles and we can see that there are many more portals today than ever to enter the marketplace for ideas—and to demonstrate and make an impact through our disciplinary knowledge.

Why continue to associate academic publication with a limited number of methods of information distribution when (1) we know that much of what is "published" as books and articles in the academy is no more or less valuable to scholarly discourse than some material "presented" in other areas such as blogs and chatrooms, and (2) when we acknowledge that much of what we consider scholarly publication ends up in the same junkyard of ideas as what is presented in these other media. A sustainable model of publishing in the academy needs to both face up to the ultimate value of what we have traditionally regarded as scholarship (books and articles), have traditionally disregarded as legitimate scholarship (essays and book reviews), and now recognize as an increasingly lively and invigorating form of publishing (digital venues). If one judges scholarship by its *impact*, that is, its ability to influence opinions, change arguments, provide information, reach larger audiences, be read, be accessible, be relevant, and be up to date, then we must acknowledge that much of what we have historically privileged as relevant scholarly publication needs reassessment. This will involve nothing less than a complete reconsideration of what is and should be regarded as an academic "publication"—of what "publication" means in and *for* academia.

This transition will require us not only to dismantle our preconceptions and traditions concerning "scholarship and publication"—a process that has already been started by an MLA committee report[12]—but to face up to the fact that much of what we produce as academics—even under a traditional model of academic publication—is ultimately received by a limited audience. Even well-developed and sound scholarship can be of little value beyond a small circle of scholars. But to these scholars, to this corner of a discipline, the value is real.

However, it does not follow from this that if ideas are *not* published in a scholarly article or monograph or other professionally accepted mode they are necessarily any less worthy of consideration as satisfying the requirements of academic scholarship. This is particularly important in an academy that is coming to realize that public access to academic discussions is increasingly important for its future welfare, and that *where* we publish is sometimes just as important as *what* we publish, particularly if it is a venue highly visible to the public. Most, I think, would agree that an opinion piece published, say, on the front page of *The New York Times* or an article in *Harper's* is worth *at least* as much as a publication on the same subject in a scholarly journal.

A more robust sense of academic publication not only will take the pressure off of traditional academic journals and presses to absorb the output of a growing professoriate, but it will also allow us to recognize intellectual work in all of its contemporary variety. A scholar who keeps a blog or maintains a Twitter feed in their field should be recognized for their contributions to the marketplace of ideas as much as one who publishes in an established mode—and even more so if they are able to pull together a significant following for their work in the new media. To publish is to make public one's work: to discriminate on the basis of mode or media without consideration of impact or quality at a time when scholars are able to reach a much wider audience through new media is unacceptable. Any account of sustainable publishing in academia that does not recognize this is flawed.

USE AND MENTION

Another issue lurks in this notion of publication: that of audience. Publication makes a work *public*. The extent to which scholarly work is publicly received is seen to speak to its quality or impact as an academic publication.

A traditional way to discuss impact is to think in terms of the number of "mentions" an article or book receives. The more "mentions," the more "impact" or "importance" the piece is said to have. There is a well-known story in philosophy of a philosopher who was promoted on the basis of a single article amounting to a few brief pages of scholarship. The article had become the subject of much academic discussion, to the point where legend has it that hand trucks piled with journals and books that mentioned the work were presented before the scholar's promotion and tenure committee. The committee was duly impressed, and the absence of other publications in the philosopher's body of work became irrelevant in light of the bounty of work responding to this single article.[13]

The extension of this type of rationale to publication in general encourages and rewards work that generates discussion and response—and does not treat on an equal basis work that does not generate interest. A blog by a faculty member that engages other scholars and generates discussion is not unlike the case of the philosopher who merited promotion on the basis of one publication. That our work is read and used and discussed is still significant as an academic criterion of publication success or impact. What then is the difference between using number of "hits" as evidence of scholarly impact as opposed to number of "mentions"? Really not a lot.

What we are lacking though is a reliable means to track the usage and impact of new media publication. Nonetheless, some online journals are starting to provide information on their articles' online usage, citations, social bookmarks, blog coverage, comments, and "star" ratings. And there are also projects underway to derive valid metrics to assess scholarly impact based on usage, including computer programs that can create spider maps to show an article's reach.[14] While the metrics of measuring responses to scholarly work may change as we transition to new technologies, I would argue that the academy should *continue* to reward faculty whose ideas are read and discussed by others, no matter what the delivery method of publication.[15]

This notion that publication involves making one's work public needs to be taken seriously, especially when contemporary media gives us the opportunity to reach many more people—academics *and* nonacademics—than ever before with our scholarship. Given a robust sense of publication, we might add a condition: namely, a focus on audience. To me this is a more responsible and sustainable way to approach academic publishing than the catalogue of ships model: simply listing published work in a curriculum vitae line tells little of the impact of ideas. Producing material that goes directly into the publishing junkyard is not the future of publishing—at least not the kind that we want to signify as quality, impactful academic publication.

Sustainable Publishing

In its usage within the paper-and-ink manufacturing element of publishing, "sustainable publishing" refers to the extent to which environmentally responsible practices are utilized at every stage of the publishing process. Sustainable editing involves using little paper in the editing process; sustainable production involves the uses of post-consumer paper and nontoxic ink. It is consoling to know that several members of the AAUP (the one for presses, not professors), including the University of Nebraska Press that I work with to publish the journal *symplokē*, have taken the lead on "researching and practicing environmentally sustainable publishing." Erika Kuebler Rippeteau, Nebraska's grants and development specialist, reports that her press "and other university presses are working to decrease our impact on the environment by changing the way we manufacture, distribute, and market our books and journals."[16]

There is considerable economic, environmental, and material pressure for presses to transition to new publishing technologies. Our practices as scholars affect the practices of the publishing houses and presses that print and distribute our work. It is important for everyone involved in publishing—from scholars to editors to printers to tenure committees—to define the "cost" and "value" of publications in the context of changing markets and technologies. But our goal as scholars should be to pursue *professionally* sustainable publishing practices. This includes not only considering new media as potentially legitimate and valuable sites of academic publishing but also giving serious consideration to opportunities such as open access publishing—one which affords us the opportunity to make the products of traditional scholarly modes (articles and monographs) more widely and immediately accessible.[17]

There is considerable irony built into the academy's disdain for electronic publishing and reluctance to recognize online scholarship, since the World Wide Web was conceived as a vehicle to improve scholarly communication. As Michael Clarke writes in "The Scholarly Kitchen," a blog for the Society of Scholarly Publishing:

> When Tim Berners-Lee created the Web in 1991, it was with the aim of better facilitating scientific communication and the dissemination of scientific research. Put another way, *the Web was designed to disrupt scientific publishing*. It was not designed to disrupt bookstores, telecommunications, matchmaking services, newspapers, pornography, stock trading, music distribution, or a great many other industries.[18]

So why, then, have these industries all embraced the Web for product distribution when academics, the original target users, have not?

There's historical practice. There's the simple fact that academic standards are slow to change. And in the humanities, there's a basic love affair with the book itself. In other disciplines, books and articles are used for the dissemination of research done using lab equipment or field research or other materials. For humanities scholars, books are both the research equipment *and* the dissemination vehicle. They are our raw material and our product. It's difficult to raise the value of other methods of publication without feeling that the value of the book is somehow compromised, thus debasing the value of our object of inquiry.

In the end, increasing the number of products and means of academic publication is not as important to a sustainable model as providing products that garner a response, that have longevity as well as currency, and that feed the production of more quality publications. Whether this involves paying closer attention to "mentions" or "page views" or "blog comments" remains an open question. A professionally sustainable model of academic publishing must encourage the publication of impactful scholarship while discouraging the publication of scholarship for scholarship's sake. So how do we accomplish this?

This can only be accomplished with the support of forward-looking academic administrators, that is to say, administrators willing to look beyond the article and the book for sources of scholarly contribution. If department chairs, college deans, and university provosts are not willing to embrace and support more progressive and impactful visions of scholarship—and choose instead to cling to notions of publication as merely scholarship for scholarship's sake—then faculty too will be slow to adopt them or will even avoid them entirely. And who can blame them when their tenure, promotion, and compensation may hang in the balance. Nevertheless, the road to raising the value of other methods of publication is not just contingent on the actions of administrators: faculty members too have a role.

If faculty members come to believe that scholarship for scholarship's sake has become a burden to the humanities rather than a benefit, they can take an active role in changing academic publishing culture by advocating for the implementation of a more impactful and robust sense of scholarship. Advocacy can begin by encouraging the appointment of administrators and tenure committees that support this progressive vision of scholarship. In practice, this may simply amount to demanding a more robust sense of scholarship as one of the criteria for administrative and tenure committee appointment.

But perhaps the best way to raise the value of other methods of publication is the one that individual faculty members have the most control over, namely, choosing to engage in this type of publication themselves.

Producing impactful scholarship whether it is through traditional venues such as the article and the book or untraditional ones such as the blog and the chatroom may involve for many academics a fundamental change in attitude toward access to their work. Far too many academics appear to feel that scholarship always needs to be constructed like a wall intended to keep others out—and that keeping others out of their conversation is an important quality marker. At times this may be unavoidable due to the specialized nature of particular disciplinary languages and topics, but it need not always be the case. The latter is important to note if impact is to be valued: in short, there can be no impact if there is no audience.

Fortunately, there is enough room in academe to support both scholarship constructed like a wall as well as scholarship fashioned like a window, that is, scholarship that is intended to let others in. This access includes not just persons within the discipline and academe in general, but also persons outside of academe entirely. By allowing others to see into one's scholarship, we are affording this scholarship the potential of having an impact—and of being used by others. Whether you consider this kind of access more like a door or a window is less important than the point that it is not a wall—that is, it does not necessarily present by its form and content a barrier to participation.

Scholarship that affords increasingly wider and wider audiences the opportunity to see and participate in it has the potential to support democratic culture and critical citizenship, particularly humanistic discourse dedicated to urgent topics such as social justice and human rights. Moreover, scholarship that provides those outside of the academy a glimpse of life and knowledge within the academy has the potential to start and encourage wider conversations about significant topics such as the future of the humanities and the devastating effects of neoliberalism on the university. In a way, moving beyond the neoliberal academy is integrally connected to the ways in which we communicate with those outside of the academy in our unacceptable current situation. If our scholarship provides a window for the world to see not only the value of higher education as such, but also the ways in which neoliberalism is devastating it, then there is at least some hope of solidarity with a broader audience in support of our academic struggles.

Scholarship that does not provide a window still has a place in the academy, but not to the exclusion of scholarship that does. There are conversations that take years of education and background in which to participate; but there are also conversations that are not or do not need to be as specialized—and that may be no less important though to a different audience. In short, supporting a more robust and impactful sense of scholarship is not only advantageous to faculty, its loud and far-reaching voice may also have the potential to awaken the university from its neoliberal slumbers.

Conclusion

Academics are currently struggling to develop new standards and methods to incorporate and evaluate nontraditional forms of scholarly publication. New media will take time to prove their legitimacy as valid vehicles for communication among scholars. Our goals and challenges remain: to recognize and reward excellence in scholarship, to establish a system for the review and assessment of scholarly work, and to provide guidelines for young scholars. The opening up of alternative ways to satisfy the scholarship and publication dimensions of academic life—for which more pathways must be provided so that more faculty members can contribute—is one way to avoid the crass careerist cynicism that tempers far too much current academic publication. We should write and make our ideas public because we have something to say and believe that others will find it interesting. To treat publication as merely a means to an end (tenure, promotion, pay raises) deflates its value and makes the academic publishing world look more like a junkyard than a bustling highway of ideas.

Moreover, the implementation of a more robust and impactful vision of academic scholarship has the potential to derail the use of status and prestige associated with publication to further the ends of the neoliberal university. The adoption of alternate modes of publication such as blogs, Twitter, chatrooms, websites, documentary video, and magazine and newspaper articles not only provides academics with more pathways to impactful scholarship, but also provides some additional means to disrupt the progress of neoliberal academe. Aiming our scholarship toward impact and relevance serves both our intellectual aspirations as well as the need to use our knowledge to influence opinions, change arguments, and provide information to those outside of the confines of the academy, particularly regarding the nature and value of the humanities.

Coda

To act as though the humanities today are and only should be about the pursuit of literature, history, and philosophy is to jeopardize seriously their future in the academy. Neoliberalism presents a university climate where it is necessary now to think not only about the content of our courses, but also how they comport with the changing mission of most American universities.

If you are fortunate enough to work for an institution of higher education that sees itself as having an educationally driven mission rather than an economically driven one, then you are at a university that is "out of time." Most US institutions of higher education are operated today by some form of economically driven mission. This mission not only places a high value on status and prestige, but also constructs its subjects to be docile ones. The best way to describe the most extreme versions of this economically driven mission is neoliberalism—a discourse whose proponents want us to believe that the academic world—and the social and economic world—is structured by equations. As Bourdieu has warned, the discourse of neoliberalism is not like most other discourses because like psychiatric discourse it is bolstered by a world of power relations. These power relations direct and dominate economic choices making neoliberalism a "strong discourse," that is, a discourse that is very difficult and hard to fight.[1] Hard to fight, but not impossible to fight. How then?

First, there must be an acknowledgment that academe today resides within a culture of neoliberalism. This means that whether or not one agrees or disagrees with a university mission driven by economic imperatives and market forces, the broader context of higher education in the United States *is* a neoliberal one—and it is a strong and dominant one. Bourdieu likens this broader context to a well-known theological one, the great chain of being:

> One of the strengths of neo-liberal thought is that it presents itself as a kind of 'great chain of Being', as in the old theological metaphor, where at one end there is God and then you work your way down, link

by link, to the lowest forms of life. In the neo-liberal universe, right at the top, in the place of God, is a mathematician, and at the bottom there is an ideologue of *Esprit,* who doesn't know much about economics but wants to give the impression of knowing something, with the aid of a varnish of technical vocabulary. This very powerful chain has an authority effect.[2]

So, in the context of academe, the "authority effect" of neoliberalism is an overwhelming and overbearing one couched in both the metaphysics of mathematical necessity and the technical language of assessment, measurement, ranking, reputation, performance measures, and so on. But, if one confronts the technical language of the neoliberal academic ideologue, in many cases, it breaks down quite quickly. The example of rank discussed earlier is a good one for it shows both the weakness of this as a performance metric as well as the difficulties in institutionalizing it.

Second, there must be acts of resistance to neoliberalism in academe. My suggestions have been to use our capacities for critical dialogue as a force of disruption, resistance, and revival. Instead of docile academic subjectivities, ones that play into neoliberal managerialism, we need to adopt a more paralogical approach to academic dialogue. Namely, to use dialogue as a disruptive force rather than an affirmative one. Critical exchange is at the heart of academic freedom, and academic freedom—the freedom to teach as we choose without interference—is predicated on keeping the "critical" in critical exchange (or inquiry) activated. Neoliberal academic culture strives to stifle critical thought and thinking. We can be a force of resistance to neoliberal academe by awakening and privileging our critical capacities—and tough criticism may be the only way to awaken academe from its neoliberal slumbers. Without a strong auto-critique discourse to counteract the strong discourse of neoliberalism, resistance becomes difficult, if not impossible.

Third, there must be a sense of building toward a future vision of academe. This vision though is not one of going "back to the future," nor is it one of "the end of academe." As we have seen, in many ways the character of the humanities and the structure of the university itself has not changed much. This holds not only over the twentieth century, but also going back even further to the eighteenth century of Kant. Whether it is the way we regard disciplinarity and the division of the faculties or the way we understand scholarly contribution, many of our former ways of fashioning academic life and expectations need to be confronted and recalibrated. University reform may be difficult, but we should not let this difficulty thwart our efforts to bring it about, especially in the face of the options provided to us by neoliberal academe. "But all things excellent are as difficult as they are rare,"[3] said Baruch Spinoza. So it is too with university reform.

The university of the twenty-first century will take place under conditions very much unlike that of past centuries. Classrooms have become virtual; books, digital; and media, social. We are endlessly connected and reconnected to each other in the academy of the twenty-first century. How these and other new and emergent technological phenomena will ultimately change higher education is unknown, but that it will do so is not. Let the fear that may result from all these changes and others dissipate into deliberation about the future of academe—not its end.

Fourth, there should be no shame in pragmatic responses to the difficult situation we are facing. In the case of our humanities courses, for example, it is better for us to think of them as always already "corporate" than to have them be eliminated from the curriculum because of our refusal to adapt them to the neoliberal climate. This is not to say that we should roll over and play dead in the humanities; rather it is to say that we can forward our critical agenda albeit with one eye toward the strong discourse of neoliberalism and its vocational aspirations, and the other toward a critical agenda that has been one of the distinctive and long-standing features of the humanities.

And fifth, and finally, there needs to be continuing discussion and examination of the effects of neoliberalism in and around higher education, particularly those areas that have not yet been magnified by the lens of research on neoliberalism. The situation of the publishing market represents a case with direct consequences to academe, but with little or no work done to map out the role of neoliberalism in publishing. Insight into areas like these or areas where the rise of neoliberalism works to thwart progress in other areas as, for example, in the case of the death of the author in aesthetics and critical theory, opens up a fuller picture of the consequences of neoliberalism in academe. This fuller picture of neoliberal culture is empowering as it provides us with a better view of the enemy.

My aim in sharing my thoughts with others is to generate a sense of hope as well as to provide some strategies to pull ourselves out of the neoliberal abyss. While there is reason to believe that there is no going back to future in higher education, this need not be regarded as the "end" or "fate" of higher education. Rather, it needs to be regarded as an opportunity to forge a new beginning. This is only going to happen though through individual efforts—efforts that I have suggested begin with the way we teach our classes, converse with our colleagues, and present our scholarship to the world. Corporate humanities may sound like an oxymoron, but it is meant to call attention to the tough times in which the humanities currently exist as well as the compromises and choices we face in forging a new future for the humanities—if not academe itself.

In sum, my perspective on neoliberalism in academe is based on the experiences of someone who as a student studied economics, philosophy, and literature; who both started a journal as well as adopted one; who advanced from the position of graduate student and lecturer to full professor and dean during the first decade of this century; and who everyday faces the challenges of academic administration in dark times. These and other characteristics provide a unique angle on the workings of the university and the publishing world. From this angle, there are reasons to be excited about the future of the humanities, and to be hopeful that we can effect change in higher education. Nevertheless, I am well aware of the devastating effects of neoliberalism in education, and the ways in which it has negatively impacted many lives. My aim here was to provide a pathway out of the dark woods of academic neoliberalism—and hope for the return of education-based university missions.

NOTES

INTRODUCTION

1. Joëlle Fanghanel, *Being an Academic* (London and New York: Routledge, 2012), 26. The phrase "docile neoliberal subject" quoted by Fanghanel comes from Bronwyn Davies, Michael Gottsche, and Peter Bansel, "The Rise and Fall of the Neoliberal University," *European Journal of Education* 41.2 (2006): 307.
2. See Maurizio Lazzarato, *The Making of the Indebted Man: An Essay on the Neoliberal Condition* (Los Angeles, CA: Semiotext(e), 2012), 9.
3. Pierre Bourdieu, *Acts of Resistance: Against the New Myths of Our Time* (Cambridge: Polity Press, 1998; reprint, 2000), 95.
4. Though the phrase "indebted person" reflects more directly the fact that both men and women are affected by debt culture, I prefer "indebted man" because of its associations with the phrase "existential man." Debt is the current existential condition of both men and women in the neoliberal academy. Using the phrase "indebted man" helps make a semiotic link to philosophical history's "existential man." A similar rationale goes for using "entrepreneurial man" in the next paragraph.
5. Though I am primarily thinking here of the existentialism of Jean-Paul Sartre, there are, of course, a variety of different philosophical senses of the "existential man"—and others may too be apropos. See Walter Kaufmann's *Existentialism: From Dostoevsky to Sartre* (Cleveland and New York: World Publishing, 1956) for an introduction to them.
6. Lazzarato, *The Making of the Indebted Man*, 19.
7. The phrase "post welfare-state" was introduced by Jeffrey J. Williams in his review essay, "The Post-Welfare State University," *American Literary History* 18.1 (Spring 2006): 190–216.
8. Henry Giroux, *The Terror of Neoliberalism: Authoritarianism and the Eclipse of Democracy* (Boulder and London: Paradigm, 2004), xii.
9. Pierre Bourdieu too speaks of the "scourge" of neoliberalism in *Acts of Resistance*. It is a very effective word to describe its consequences in culture. See his *Acts of Resistance*, vii.
10. One of the most critically engaged scholars on student debt over the past ten years has been Jeffrey J. Williams, who has compared student debt to the "spirit of indentured servitude." See, "Student Debt and the Spirit of Indenture," *Dissent* 55.4 (Fall 2008): 73–78. See also, "Debt Education: Bad for the Young, Bad for America," *Dissent* 53.3 (Summer

2006): 53–59, a piece where he outlines, among other things, a number of lessons taught by debt.
11. G. Ardant, *Histoire financière de l'antiquité à nos jours* (Paris: Gallimard, 1976), 320. Quoted by Maurizio Lazzarato, *The Making of the Indebted Man*, 20–21.
12. Bourdieu, *Acts of Resistance*, 34.
13. Giroux, *The Terror of Neoliberalism*, xxii.
14. Plato describes the death of Socrates as follows: "When the poison reaches the heart, that will be the end. He was beginning to grow cold about the groin, when he uncovered his face, for he had covered himself up, and said (they were his last words)—he said: Crito, I owe a cock to Asclepius; will you remember to pay the debt? The debt shall be paid, said Crito; is there anything else? There was no answer to this question; but in a minute or two a movement was heard, and the attendants uncovered him; his eyes were set, and Crito closed his eyes and mouth" (*Phaedo* 118a; trans. Benjamin Jowett, 499).
15. Many students will in fact die without having paid their student loans. For example, it has recently been reported that the fastest growing sector of the population burdened by student loans are the over-60 crowd, many of whom sought graduate degrees during the recession. Within this group, there are many who "fully expect to die" without having repaid their student debt. However, don't expect any of them to be Socratic about their student debt—and to ask on their deathbed for it to be paid. See Stacey Patton, "I Fully Expect to Die with this Debt," *Chronicle of Higher Education*, April 15, 2013.
16. Henry Rosovsky, *The University: An Owner's Manual* (New York: W. W. Norton, 1990), 179–180.
17. Ibid., xii–xiv.
18. For a further examination of the problems caused by neoliberalism, see Jeffrey R. Di Leo and Uppinder Mehan, eds., *Capital at the Brink: Overcoming the Destructive Legacies of Neoliberalism* (Ann Arbor, MI: Open Humanities Press, 2014).
19. See Jeffrey R. Di Leo, "Public Intellectuals, Inc.," in *Academe Degree Zero: Reconsidering the Politics of Higher Education* (Boulder and London: Paradigm, 2012), 13–24.
20. Fanghanel, *Being an Academic*, 26. See also, note 1.
21. See Paul Du Gay, Stuart Hall, Linda Janes, Hugh MacKay and Keith Negus, *Doing Cultural Studies, The Story of the Sony Walkman* (London: Sage, 1997), 3.

1 CORPORATE LITERATURE

1. Andrew Hacker and Claudia Dreifus, *Higher Education? How Colleges Are Wasting Our Money and Failing Our Kids—And What We Can Do about It* (New York: Times Books/Henry Holt, 2010), 3.

2. The American Association of University Professors (AAUP) is the foremost defender of faculty rights and privileges in America. Nelson, past national president of the AAUP and Jubilee Professor of Liberal Arts and Sciences at the University of Illinois at Urbana-Champaign, recently published *No University is an Island: Saving Academic Freedom* (New York University Press, 2010). In addition, Ellen Schrecker, former editor of the *Academe*, the official magazine of the AAUP, and professor of history at Yeshiva University, recently published *The Lost Soul of Higher Education: Corporatization, the Assault on Academic Freedom, and the End of the American University* (New York and London: The New Press, 2010). Both books are excellent surveys of the assaults on academic freedom, and are discussed in chapter 3, "Paralogical Inquiry."
3. An abbreviated list also includes CUNY sociologist Stanley Aronowitz's *The Knowledge Factory: Dismantling the Corporate University and Creating True Higher Learning* (Boston, MA: Beacon Press, 2001), and freelance journalist and New America Foundation fellow Jennifer Washburn's *University, Inc.: The Corporate Corruption of Higher Education* (New York: Basic Books, 2005).
4. Frank Donoghue. *The Last Professors: The Corporate University and the Fate of the Humanities* (New York: Fordham University Press, 2008), xi.
5. Ibid., xi.
6. Ibid., xv.
7. Ibid., 26.
8. One noteworthy recent exception to this trend is philosopher Mark Taylor's *Crisis on Campus: A Bold Plan for Reforming our Colleges and Universities* (New York: Alfred A. Knopf, 2010), which will be taken up later, in chapter 3.
9. Hacker and Dreifus, *Higher Education?*, 3.
10. Ibid.
11. For an excellent introduction to this topic, see Henry Giroux, "The Post-9/11 Militarization of Higher Education and Neoliberalism's Culture of Depravity: Threats to the Future of American Democracy" in Jeffrey R. Di Leo, Henry Giroux, Sophia McClennen, and Ken Saltman, *Terror, Education, Neoliberalism: Contemporary Dialogues* (Boulder, CO, and London: Paradigm, 2012).
12. A recent study from the Project on Student Debt reports that two-thirds of seniors who graduated in 2011 borrowed money to attend college, and that their average debt at graduation is $26,600. This is a 5 percent increase over the previous year, and marks an ever-increasing debt pattern. However, the report also finds that less than 1 percent of students have a loan debt above $100,000—which to some, comes as a relief. Still, $26,600 is a huge debt hole for graduating students considering that the average starting salary for someone with a bachelor's degree is only $43,521. See, Caitlin Peterkin, "Rise in Student-Loan Debt Spurs

Advocates' Call for Frank Discussion, Not Panic Over Extreme Cases," *Chronicle of Higher Education* (October 26, 2012).
13. Daniel Yankelovich's study is cited in Victor E. Ferrall Jr., *Liberal Arts at the Brink* (Cambridge, MA: Harvard University Press, 2011), 50.
14. Ibid., 50.
15. Ibid., 50.
16. Daniel Born, "What is the Crisis in the Humanities?," *Common Review* (Spring 2010), 5.
17. Ferrall Jr., *Liberal Arts at the Brink*, 55.
18. The introduction of film into the philosophy classroom as a way of motivating philosophical discussion and facilitating philosophical understanding has been one of the greatest recent advances in philosophy pedagogy. In large part, this advance was only possible on a wide scale with the advent of video technology. Prior to VHS tapes, reels and projectors made it much more difficult to access films and to utilize film clips in the classroom, let alone to require students to view films as class assignments. See Jeffrey R. Di Leo, *From Socrates to Cinema: An Introduction to Philosophy* (New York: McGraw Hill, 2007) for a more comprehensive treatment of film as an introduction to philosophy. Also, in addition to *Thelma and Louise* as a gloss on *The Second Sex* (pp. 337–345), there are over 140 different films discussed in *From Socrates to Cinema* as glosses on philosophical topics and texts.

2 Humanities, Inc.

1. The logical extension and intensification of the "corporate" university is the "neoliberal" university, that is, one that makes no pretense toward an educationally driven university mission and wholeheartedly adopts an economically driven one.
2. Martha Nussbaum, *Not for Profit: Why Democracy Needs the Humanities* (Princeton and Oxford: Princeton University Press, 2010), 2.
3. Ibid., 2.
4. Ibid., 7.
5. Ibid., 141–142.
6. Ibid., 142.
7. Nussbaum here lends more support for Thesis Two from the Introduction, namely, the position that the neoliberal subject is a docile one because of its emaciated critical skill set.
8. Martha Nussbaum, *Not for Profit*, 142.
9. Ibid., 7.
10. Ibid., 6.
11. Ibid., 142.
12. Ibid., 17.
13. Ibid., 18.

14. Ibid., 10.
15. Ibid., 23.
16. Ibid., 23.
17. Ibid., 23.
18. Ibid., 25.
19. Ibid., 10.
20. Ibid., 15.
21. Ibid., 14.
22. Ibid., 15.
23. Ibid., 7.
24. Ibid., 7.
25. Ibid., 6.
26. Ibid., 6.
27. Toby Miller, *Blow Up the Humanities* (Philadelphia, PA: Temple University Press, 2012), 1.
28. Ibid., 1–2.
29. Ibid., 64.
30. A "prestige" distinction too would have the added value of drawing the humanities directly into the neoliberal debate as it is one of the key factors in neoliberal academic teleology. Chapter 6, "Wrangling with Rank," and chapter 7, "Authorial Prestige," deal more with the role of prestige in neoliberalism.
31. Miller, *Blow Up the Humanities*, 2.
32. An "everyday" state school at least in comparison to the University of Chicago.
33. Miller, *Blow Up the Humanities*, 2.
34. Ibid., 8.
35. Ibid., 6.
36. Ibid., 6.
37. This of course complements the point made in chapter 1 about the use of film and television in the philosophy and literature classrooms. In a way, then, Miller's Humanities Two is connected with what was described as "corporate literature" in chapter 1.
38. Miller, *Blow Up the Humanities*, 77.
39. Ibid., 64.
40. Ibid., 64.
41. Ibid., 67. Miller borrows the phrase "Humanities 2.0" from Cathy N. Davidson's "Humanities 2.0: Promise, Perils, Predictions" (*PMLA* 123.3 [2008]). The rest of the quote is his gloss on Friedrich Kittler's "Universities: Wet, Hard, Soft, and Harder" (*Critical Inquiry* 31.2 [2004]). One of the noteworthy aspects of Miller's book is the sheer number of glosses, quotes, and citations. Miller even cites personal correspondence. The bibliography for 123 pages of narrative is 30 pages long. This means that there is approximately one page of bibliography for every four pages of narrative—something that is perhaps explained through

the following comment by Miller: "My notion of the two humanities comes from elsewhere, like everything I write" (p. 64).
42. Miller, *Blow Up the Humanities*, 79.
43. Ibid., 79.
44. Ibid., 82–88. These are all also connected to the rise of neoliberalism. See, for example, Henry Giroux's *The Terror of Neoliberalism: Authoritarianism and the Eclipse of Democracy* (Boulder, CO, and London: Paradigm, 2004), *The University in Chains: Confronting the Military-Industrial–Academic Complex* (Boulder, CO, and London: Paradigm, 2007), *Hearts of Darkness: Torturing Children in the War on Terror* (Boulder, CO, and London: Paradigm, 2010), as well as other recent work by him.
45. Miller, *Blow Up the Humanities*, 105.
46. Ibid., 95.
47. Ibid., 105.
48. Ibid., 108.
49. Ibid., 107.
50. Ibid., 107.
51. Ibid., 108.
52. Ibid., 108. A few years back, the question was raised as to whether semiotics was trying to gain a second wind by trying to "repackage" itself as cultural studies. Miller's suggestions raise a related question: whether cultural studies is now trying to gain a second wind by trying to "repackage" itself as humanities. See Jeffrey R. Di Leo, "Cultural Studies, Semiotics, and the Politics of Repackaging Theory," in *Academe Degree Zero: Reconsidering the Politics of Higher Education* (Boulder, CO, and London: Paradigm, 2012) for my thoughts on the former question; the latter question is a good one though better left for another occasion.
53. Miller's suggestion that the future of the humanities is held in the hands of cultural studies is somewhat ironic—discussions of the demise of cultural studies have been just as frequent as discussions of the demise of the humanities. As such, whether it is cultural studies that will be reenergizing the humanities *or* the humanities that will be reenergizing cultural studies is still to be determined. In any case, Miller's proposal has the capacity to reenergize both the humanities as well as cultural studies.
54. Miller, *Blow Up the Humanities*, 1.
55. Ibid., 1–2.
56. Louis Menand, *The Marketplace of Ideas: Reform and Resistance in the American University* (New York and London: W. W. Norton, 2010), 17.

3 Paralogical Inquiry

1. Derek Bok, *Universities in the Marketplace: The Commercialization of Higher Education* (Princeton, NJ: Princeton University Press, 2003), x.

2. Frank Donoghue, *The Last Professors: The Corporate University and the Fate of the Humanities* (New York: Fordham University Press, 2008), xi.
3. Ibid., xi.
4. I'd like to thank Danny Postel for introducing me to Ellen Schrecker's, and Andrew Hacker and Claudia Dreifus's work, and for his comments on Mark Taylor's work.
5. Jean-François Lyotard, *The Postmodern Condition: A Report on Knowledge* (Minneapolis: University of Minnesota Press, 1984), 65.
6. Ibid., 65.
7. Ibid., 65.
8. Ibid., 66.
9. Ibid., 63.
10. Ibid., 63–64.
11. Ibid., 64.
12. Ibid., 64.
13. In chapter 4, "Apocalyptic Fear," I expand on the notion of terror within academe. I propose that the primary emotional effect of neoliberalism in education is *fear*, and that the promotion of neoliberal academic policies is itself a type of terrorism, namely, *academic* terrorism.
14. Lyotard, *The Postmodern Condition*, 66.
15. Ibid., 66.
16. Ibid., 65.
17. Ibid., 66.
18. Ibid., 66.
19. Ibid., 66.
20. Ibid., 10.
21. Fredric Jameson, "Foreword" in Jean-François Lyotard, *The Postmodern Condition*, xix.
22. Cary Nelson, *No University Is an Island: Saving Academic Freedom* (New York University Press, 2010), 124.
23. For an extended defense of agonistic critical exchange, see chapter 5, "Critical Affiliations."
24. Nelson, *No University is an Island*, 26.
25. Ibid., 266.
26. Ibid., 266.
27. Ellen Schrecker, *The Lost Soul of Higher Education: Corporatization, the Assault on Academic Freedom, and the End of the American University* (New York and London: New Press, 2010), 5.
28. Ibid., 232.
29. Hacker and Dreifus, *Higher Education? How Colleges Are Wasting Our Money and Failing Our Kids—and What We Can Do about It* (New York: Times Books/Henry Holt, 2010), 168.
30. Ibid., 149.
31. Louis Menand, *The Marketplace for Ideas: Reform and Resistance in the American University* (New York and London: W. W. Norton, 2010), 13.

32. Ibid., 13.
33. Ibid., 17.
34. Ibid., 30n6.
35. Ibid., 20.
36. Ibid., 55.
37. Ibid., 55.
38. Ibid., 56.
39. Ibid., 64.
40. Ibid., 76.
41. Ibid., 81.
42. Ibid., 85.
43. Ibid., 87.
44. Ibid., 87.
45. Ibid., 96–97.
46. Ibid., 119.
47. Ibid., 94.
48. Ibid., 155.
49. Ibid., 152.
50. Ibid., 153.
51. Mark Taylor, *Crisis on Campus: A Bold Plan for Reforming our Colleges and Universities* (New York: Alfred A. Knopf, 2010), 16.
52. Ibid., 17.
53. Ibid., 21.
54. Ibid., 22.
55. Ibid., 45.
56. Ibid., 52. The quote from Immanuel Kant's *The Conflict of the Faculties* is cited on pages 51–52 of Taylor's *Crisis on Campus*.
57. Ibid., 63.
58. Ibid., 63.
59. Ibid., 115.
60. Ibid., 104.
61. Ibid., 204.
62. Ibid., 205.
63. Ibid., 206.
64. Ibid., 213.
65. Ibid., 190.
66. Ibid., 145.
67. Ibid., 43.
68. Mary Pilon, "What's a Degree Really Worth," *Wall Street Journal* (February 2, 2010).
69. To be clear, I am in no way advocating the abolishment of tenure. Rather, what I am advocating is that critical discussion of all aspects of the academy should be embraced—even those aspects like tenure that are highly valued by academics. Critical self-reflection is the heart and soul of all healthy institutions—and academe should be no exception.

4 APOCALYPTIC FEAR

1. For an introduction to this topic, see my "Shame in Academe: On the Politics of Emotion in Academic Culture" in *Academe Degree Zero: Reconsidering the Politics of Higher Education* (Boulder, CO: Paradigm, 2012), 33–42.
2. This is not to say that other emotions such as sadness, anger, and surprise are not a part of academic life. Rather, it is to say that a preponderance of joy rather than fear is preferable. If this is not the case, then the emotional condition of the academy is in very good shape—as fear is the dominant academic emotion today.
3. See, for example, Stacey Patton, "I Fully Expect to Die with this Debt," *Chronicle of Higher Education* (April 15, 2013), http://chronicle.com/article/I-Fully-Expect-to-Die-With/138507/.
4. Shame and shaming are key aspects of academic culture that have been connected to power. For example, shame theorist Gershen Kaufman writes, "There is an inverse relation between shame and power: to the degree that one is powerless in any work environment, one is most vulnerable to shame." However, fear is at least as controlling and powerful an emotion as shame, particularly in the academic workplace. Just replace "shame" with "fear" in the Kaufman quote to get a sense of this. In fact, I would argue that it is an even more powerful emotion: we often blush when we are shamed, whereas we often run when we are fearful. Hence, the discussion of emotion in academe in this chapter focuses more on fear rather than shame. For my thoughts on academic shame, see "Shame in Academe." Kaufman is quoted on page 40 of this article.
5. Or, alternately, albeit more controversially, *religious* terrorism.
6. Jean-François Lyotard, *The Postmodern Condition: A Report on Knowledge*, trans. Geoff Bennington and Brian Massumi (Minneapolis: University of Minnesota Press, 1984), 63.
7. Ibid., 63–64.
8. George Lakoff, "Beyond the *War on Terror*: Understanding Reflexive Thought" in *Transforming Terror: Remembering the Soul of the World*, ed. Karin Lofthus Carrington and Susan Griffin (Berkeley: University of California Press, 2011), 43.
9. Ibid., 43.
10. Aristotle, *On Rhetoric*, trans. George A. Kennedy (New York: Oxford University Press, 1991), 1382a1.
11. Ibid., 20.
12. Ibid., 20.
13. The best account of the flawed logic of prestige is still Thorstein Veblen's *The Higher Learning in America* (New York: B. W. Huebsch, 1918), written nearly a century ago, where he reflected on the uses and abuses of prestige by higher education in America. For Veblen, the pursuit of prestige by university administrators aims at "a growth in the material

resources and the volume of traffic" (228) of the university, not the growth of knowledge. Veblen thought these aims were not only misguided, but also of questionable success: "So far as the acquired prestige is designed to serve a pecuniary end it can only be useful in the way of impressing donors—a highly speculative line of enterprise, offering suggestive parallel to the drawing of a lottery" (139). His ultimate conclusion was that "Whatever will not serve the end of prestige has no secure footing" in the American university (228). In addition, Deborah L. Rhode's *In Pursuit of Knowledge: Scholars, Status, and Academic Culture* (Stanford, CA: Stanford University Press, 2006) is an excellent updating of Veblen's arguments. For an account of the limits and logic of affiliation, see my *Affiliations: Identity in Academic Culture* (Lincoln and London: University of Nebraska Press, 2003).

14. Giovanna Borradori, *Philosophy in a Time of Terror: Dialogues with Jürgen Habermas and Jacques Derrida* (Chicago and London: University of Chicago Press, 2003), 100.
15. The foregoing thoughts on terrorism, 9/11, and conceptual change draw from Jeffrey R. Di Leo and Uppinder Mehan, "Theory Ground Zero: Terror, Theory, and the Humanities after 9/11" in *Terror, Theory, and the Humanities*, ed. Jeffrey R. Di Leo and Uppinder Mehan (Ann Arbor, MI: Open Humanities Press, 2011).
16. Carl Wellman, "On Terrorism Itself," *The Journal of Value Inquiry* 13 (1979): 250–258.
17. Ibid., 250.
18. Ibid., 251.
19. Ibid., 251.
20. Ibid., 251.
21. Ibid., 251.
22. Ibid., 251–252.
23. Ibid., 252.
24. Ibid., 252.
25. Proposed philosophy program eliminations at the University of Nevada, Las Vegas and Middlesex University (UK) are evidence of this. Both proposals for program elimination have drawn international responses against them.
26. Menand extends this comment though uses "non-liberal" rather than "neoliberal": "Almost any liberal arts field can be made non-liberal by turning it in the direction of some practical skill with which it is already associated. English departments can become writing programs, even publishing programs; pure mathematics can become applied mathematics, even engineering; sociology shades into social work; biology shades into medicine; political science and social theory lead to law and political administration; and so on. But conversely, and more importantly, any practical field can be made liberal simply by teaching it historically or theoretically." See Louis Menand, *The Marketplace of Ideas: Reform and*

Resistance in the American University (New York and London: W. W. Norton, 2010), 55.
27. Wellman, "On Terrorism Itself," 252.
28. Ibid., 253.
29. With a more robust notion of violence, it may be possible to establish a form of academic terrorism that involves violence. For example, consider the violence that is unseen and unheard that happens on a temporal scale that is beyond the capacities of our senses. Rob Nixon terms this "slow violence," and describes it as "a violence that occurs gradually and out of sight, a violence of delayed destruction that is dispersed across time and space, an attritional violence that is typically not viewed as violence at all" (2). While Nixon associates this violence with "climate change, the thawing cryosphere, toxic drift, biomagnifications, deforestation, the radioactive aftermath of war, acidifying oceans, and a host of other slowly unfolding environmental catastrophes" (2), it may also be possible to think of violence in the academy in a similar way. See Rob Nixon, *Slow Violence and the Environmentalism of the Poor* (Cambridge, MA: Harvard University Press, 2011). For a more robust sense of the violence attributable to neoliberalism, see Jeffrey R. Di Leo and Sophia McClennen, "Postscript on Violence," *symplokē* 20.1/2 (2012).
30. Aristotle, *Rhetoric*, 1383a14.

5 CRITICAL AFFILIATIONS

1. Nussbaum here lends more support for Thesis Two from the Introduction, namely, the position that the neoliberal subject is a docile one because of its emaciated critical skill set.
2. Martha Nussbaum, *Not for Profit: Why Democracy Needs the Humanities* (Princeton and Oxford: Princeton University Press, 2010), 142.
3. Ibid., 141–142.
4. Ibid., 142.
5. Ibid., 23.
6. Michel Foucault, "The Subject and Power," in *Michel Foucault: Beyond Structuralism and Hermeneutics*, ed. Hubert L. Dreyfus and Paul Rabinow (Chicago: University of Chicago Press, 1983), 221–222.
7. An argument could be made here that praising weak graduate students may be comforting to the students, but it is not in their long-term best interest. Students who believe that their scholarly abilities are stronger create a false sense of their future in the academy. One could argue that it is the task of faculty to be as transparent as possible with their graduate students about their scholarly abilities, particularly students who repeatedly show a lack of promise in graduate school. This argument, however, would seem to go against the grain of critical attitudes of faculty toward their graduate students, especially in the profession of literary studies.

8. It is interesting to imagine Jones and Smith alternately from the point of view of race, class, gender, sexuality, and even academic rank. For example, imagine Jones as a white, male, assistant professor, whereas Smith is an Hispanic, female, full professor. The combinations here are many—and can lead to interesting glosses as to how race, class, gender, sexuality, and rank contribute to their critical affiliation. Under such considerations, many other factors start to come into play regarding their critical approaches—so many in fact that they distract from the basic point about critical affiliation, namely, that one can be more or less extreme in their criticism of others and that this has some important general implications within academic culture. For the sake of what I seek to establish in this chapter, I am going to bracket considerations of the race, class, gender, sexuality, and rank of Jones and Smith, though I do acknowledge that they add an increased and important level of complexity.
9. This is, of course, should not be news to anyone who knows Fish's work. "Stanley Fish is an equal opportunity antagonist," say the promotional materials for his book *The Trouble with Principle* (2001). "A theorist who has taken on theorists, an academician who has riled the academy, a legal scholar and political pundit who has ruffled feathers left and right." http://www.hup.harvard.edu/catalog.php?isbn=9780674005341.
10. I only feel comfortable generalizing about critical attitudes in literature and philosophy, areas that I have studied as a graduate student and now work as a professor. I will leave it to others to fill in as to where on the critical spectrum other areas of the humanities such as history, communication, and media fall, which presumably is somewhere between the extremes of literary studies and philosophy. Also, if one regards Humanities One à la Miller as literature, history, and philosophy, and Humanities Two as communication and media studies, then one may be tempted to make a "house-divided" argument about critical exchange in Humanities One. However, this though is probably better left for another occasion.
11. Louis Menand, *The Marketplace for Ideas: Reform and Resistance in the American University* (New York and London: W. W. Norton, 2010), 155.
12. Ibid., 155.
13. Reflecting on the relationship of the *MLA Handbook* to the MLA itself in terms of its role in the regulation of normative behavior within the MLA would be an interesting project. It often goes unnoticed that the *MLA Handbook* both is and is not the handbook of the profession. In his President's Column for the Winter 2012 MLA Newsletter, Michael Bérubé comments that a young man reacted to his introducing himself as the president of the association with, "You mean the Modern Language Association that does the *Handbook* for research papers?" Bérubé responded, somewhat stunned, "I do...but I have to admit I don't have any jurisdiction over the *Handbook*" (2).

14. See Jeffrey R. Di Leo, *Federman's Fictions: Innovation, Theory, and the Holocaust* (Albany: State University of New York Press, 2011) for an overview of the problematic relationship of his work to more orthodox lines of scholarship.
15. The number of small presses is by no means a small number: it can be estimated to be around 50,000, which is approximately the number of active publishers which received around $50,000 or less in annual revenues. This number is in stark contrast to the number of publishers with over $50,000,000 in annual revenue, which are about 500. There are an estimated 62,815 publishers with at least some reported annual revenues and 85,000 total publishers in the Bowker database. See, *Under the Radar* (Book Industry Study Group, 2005).
16. In the *Prolegomena* of 1783, Immanuel Kant writes, "I freely admit the remembrance of *David Hume* was the very thing that many years ago first interrupted my dogmatic slumber and gave a completely different direction to my researches in the field of speculative philosophy" (*Prolegomena to Any Future Metaphysics*, rev. ed., ed. and trans. Gary Hatfield [Cambridge: Cambridge University Press, 2004], 10). Elsewhere, however, Kant gave another source entire credit for his arousal: "The antinomy of pure reason—'The world has a beginning; it has no beginning, and so on,' right up to the fourth [sic]: 'There is freedom in man, versus there is no freedom, only the necessity of nature'—that is what first aroused me from my dogmatic slumber and drove me to the critique of reason itself, in order to resolve the scandal of ostensible contradiction of reason with itself" (*Emmanuel Kant: Philosophical Correspondence 1759–99*, trans. A. Zweig [Chicago: University of Chicago Press, 1986], 252).
17. Gail Pool, *Faint Praise: The Plight of Book Reviewing in America* (Columbia and London: University of Missouri Press, 2007), 47 and 135.
18. Ibid., 47.
19. Ibid., 47.
20. I've seen this behavior many times with peer-reviewers who ask that their name not be revealed when their comments are negative, but feel differently when their comments are positive.
21. Anonymous letter to the editor in *The Chronicle Review* (November 27, 2009), B18.
22. Carlin Romano's response to the responses to his piece on Heidegger appeared in the *Chronicle Review* (November 27, 2009), B19.
23. Michel Foucault, *The Archeology of Knowledge and the Discourse on Language* (New York: Pantheon Books, 1972), 215.
24. Ibid., 215–216.
25. Ibid., 216.
26. Cary Nelson, *No University is an Island: Saving Academic Freedom* (New York University Press, 2010), 10.
27. Ibid., 10.

6 Wrangling with Rank

1. There has however been a backlash against the obsession with ranks and brands by colleges and universities. Lloyd Thacker's *College Unranked: Ending the College Admissions Frenzy* (Cambridge, MA: Harvard University Press, 2005), for example, convincingly demonstrates many of the dangers of the college ranking system. There is also a growing level of discontent with *US News and World Report's* annual college rankings issue including efforts to boycott it, spearheaded by Thacker's foundation, the Education Conservancy.
2. If they did, then the professional organizations associated with these areas (the American Philosophical Association and the Modern Language Association) would need to produce these rankings. But the fact that they do not says a lot about their general value to the profession.
3. I'm not counting here "informal" surveys such as the Leiter Reports (noted below in note 6) that are more akin to academic fun—than studies that are used by administrators to determine the actual value of the publication based on journal rank.
4. In the 20 years that I have edited *symplokē*, I have only come across one instance of a scholar who refused to publish in the journal because they viewed it as not befitting their "stature." In fact, going back to the earliest numbers of *symplokē*, one finds articles published by some of the most well-known and established scholars in the field: Matei Calinescu (vol. 1.1), David Palumbo-Liu (vol. 1.2), James Guetti (vol. 2.1), Christian Moraru (vol. 2.2), Jeffrey Williams (vol. 3.1), Ewa Ziarek (vol. 3.2), and so on. Throughout its history, *symplokē* has consistently published work from leading scholars in the humanities—a point that lends support to the claim that journal publication in the humanities is more a matter of preference than professional necessity.
5. It must be noted though this is not unique to the humanities: there is also a high level of sub-disciplinary specialization in business and the sciences. However, because there are fewer funding and accreditation links to humanities journals as compared to business and science journals, there is much less motivation for the humanities to deal with the complexities of ranking brought about by sub-disciplinary specialization.
6. A good example of this is the Leiter Reports's "Philosophy Blog," which has posted a poll of the "highest quality 'general' philosophy journals in English." While aimed at helping "graduate students and younger philosophers trying to figure out where to publish," the list of 29 journals based on 400 votes is far too general to be of much use for younger philosophers trying to place their specialized manuscripts. The Leiter Reports rankings make for interesting blog fodder, but nothing more. See http://leiterreports.typepad.com/blog/2009/03/which-are-the-highest-quality-general-philosophy-journals-in-english.html.
7. http://www.philosophy.ku.edu/Auslegung/General.html.

8. The reverse of this though is not true: that is to say, I am fairly confident that the *Journal of Philosophy* would probably reject most of the articles that are usually published in *Auslegung*.
9. Nonetheless, Dan Subotnik and Glen Lazar have shown in "Affiliating the Rejection Letter" in *Affiliations: Identity in Academic Culture*, ed. Jeffrey R. Di Leo (Lincoln and London: University of Nebraska Press, 2003) that the top law journals reveal a bias toward publishing articles on the basis of extraneous factors such as the rank of the author's school. I have long suspected that if the acceptance criteria of the premier humanities journals were studied, a similar situation would hold, namely, weaker articles by authors affiliated with premier research institutions and/or whose names are well known are generally preferred to stronger articles by authors affiliated with less prestigious institutions or whose names are not readily recognizable by the journal's readership. In fact, Stanley Fish has infamously argued his opposition to the blind submission policies often incorporated by journals to avoid the kind of situations studied by Subotnik and Lazar in "No Bias, No Merit: The Case against Blind Submission" in *The Stanley Fish Reader*, ed. H. Aram Veeser (Malden, MA: Blackwell, 1999). Fish not only acknowledges that the chances of his pieces being accepted are greatly increased if he submits it with his name on it but also does not see anything wrong with this form of affiliational bias. "I have paid my dues and earned the benefit of the doubt I now enjoy," says Fish, "and don't see why others shouldn't labor in the vineyards as I did" (p. 253). Rank, brand, and prestige are powerful and persistent forces that often find ways to leak back into journal article publication.
10. Assuming, of course, that bias is something that one aims to avoid in journal article publication—a direction opposite the one established by Fish in "No Bias, No Merit: The Case against Blind Submission."
11. Other aspects such as graduate program ranking have not been avoided and have been commonplace for decades. Sources here include annual rankings by *US News and World Report* and the United States National Research Council, which issues a ranking about every ten years.
12. See, for example, Jennifer Howard, "New Ratings of Humanities Journals Do More than Rank—They Rankle," *Chronicle of Higher Education* (October 10, 2008).
13. European Science Foundation, "ERIH Timeline," http://www.esf.org/research-areas/humanities/erih-european-reference-index-for-the-humanities/erih-timeline.html.
14. European Science Foundation, "ERIH Foreword," http://www.esf.org/research-areas/humanities/erih-european-reference-index-for-the-humanities/erih-foreword.html.
15. Ibid.
16. Bold in original. European Science Foundation, "ERIH 'Initial' Lists," http://www.esf.org/research-areas/humanities/erih-european-reference-index-for-the-humanities/erih-initial-lists.html.

17. http://www.esf.org/research-areas/humanities/erih-european-reference-index-for-the-humanities/erih-foreword.html.
18. Ibid.
19. Ibid.
20. Ibid.
21. Australian Research Council, "ERA PCE and HCA Journal Lists," http://www.arc.gov.au/era/journal_list.htm.
22. Australian Research Council, "Tiers for the Australian Ranking of Journals," http://www.arc.gov.au/era/tiers_ranking.htm.
23. Australian Research Council, "Ranked Journal List Development," http://www.arc.gov.au/era/journal_list_dev.htm.
24. Australian Research Council, "ERA PCE and HCA Journal Lists." http://www.arc.gov.au/era/journal_list.htm.
25. Development of the ERA 2012 Journal List, http://www.arc.gov.au/era/era_2012/journal_list_dev.htm.
26. Stephen P. Harter and Hak Joon Kim, "Electronic Journals and Scholarly Communication: A Citation and Reference Study," *Information Research* 2.1 (1996).
27. The notion that digital objects are more easily recycled and destroyed than print objects is the most debated item from this list of the advantages of print objects to digital objects. There are a variety of studies though few firm conclusions. See, for example, Don Carli's "Is Digital Media Worse for the Environment Than Print?" *Mediashift* (March 31, 2010) and "Print vs. Digital Media: False Dilemmas and Forced Choices," *Institute for Sustainable Communication* [Whitepaper, n.d.], two fine introductions to the issue.
28. E. Annie Proulx, "Books on Top," *New York Times* (May 26, 1994): A13.
29. Mark Sweney, "Penguin and Random House Merger to Create Biggest Book Publisher Ever Seen," *Guardian* (October 29, 2012).
30. The US Department of Justice has accused Apple of leading a conspiracy to fix e-book prices. The coconspirators—Hachette, HarperCollins, Macmillan, Penguin, and Simon & Schuster—have already settled but Apple is still in the crosshairs of the government, which claims that it was the leader of this group of six. According to the Department of Justice, this group of publishing companies were worried that Amazon's $9.99 Kindle e-book prices were too lean for their diet. So, allegedly, Steve Jobs of Apple took the lead in trying to create with them "a real mainstream e-books market at $12.99 and $14.99." The publishers, however, have shot back that they are not the monopolists, rather it is Amazon. See Andrew Albanese, "Penguin and Macmillan Reject Price Fixing Charges," *Publishers Weekly*, May 31, 2012, and Nate Raymond, "Judge says leaning toward U.S. in Apple e-books case," *Reuters*, May 23, 2013.
31. The first fully digital public library opened in San Antonio, Texas, in 2013. With 150 e-readers, 25 laptops, 25 tablets, but no books, San Antonio

now has bragging rights to having launched the first bookless library system in America. The local judge who launched the library got the idea for it after reading a biography of Steve Jobs, founder of Apple. "If you want to get an idea what it looks like, go into an Apple store," said Bexar County Judge Nelson Wolff. See "America's First Bookless Library to Open in Texas," *De Zeen* (January 21, 2013).
32. The major difference that can be found between the digital versions of *symplokē* and *American Book Review* and the print versions of these same journals is that the digital versions do not contain the advertisements for books and journals that are found in the print versions. I assume that this is the case for all of the many journals that utilize Johns Hopkins University Press's Project MUSE for publication and distribution of their journals online, but have not confirmed it.
33. This is not an uncontroversial claim. For example, *The New York Times* has cited a report that "e-readers could have a major impact on improving the sustainability and environmental impact on the publishing industry, one of the world's most polluting sectors." "In 2008," says the *Times* article, "the U.S. book and newspaper industries combined resulted in the harvesting of 125 million trees, not to mention wastewater that was produced or its massive carbon footprint." It also claims "on average, the carbon emitted over the life of" an Amazon Kindle "is offset after the first year of use." However, the article also mentions "none of this means that e-readers are without environmental impact." Part of the problem is identifying what, if any, toxic materials are used in their circuitry as electronic devices like the Kindle "are notorious for containing a variety of toxic materials among their circuitry." See, Joe Hutsko, "Are E-Readers Greener than Books?," *New York Times* (August 31, 2009).
34. It remains to be seen though if the European rankings will entirely disappear. A recent communication from a European scholar who published an article in *symplokē* confirms this and speaks to the pressures put on scholars to publish in ranked journals: "I'm writing to you because, as I'm preparing my annual report of research and publications, I discovered that *symplokē* is not listed on the European Science Foundation Reference Index for the Humanities…As researchers in Europe (as in the United States) are increasingly put under pressure to publish only in officially recognized peer reviewed high impact journals, it might be of strategic interest to you to get *symplokē* on these European lists!"

7 Authorial Prestige

1. Thorstein Veblen, *The Higher Learning in America* (New York: B. W. Huebsch, 1918), 228.
2. Deborah L. Rhode, *In Pursuit of Knowledge: Scholars, Status, and Academic Culture* (Stanford, CA: Stanford University Press, 2006), 32.

3. Jane Gallop, *The Deaths of the Author: Reading and Writing in Time* (Durham and London: Duke University Press, 2011), 1. Gallop uses the terms "familiar" and "slogan" numerous times in this book to describe the phrase "death of the author."
4. Over the past ten years, there has been much discussion on the death of theory. See, for example, Terry Eagleton, *After Theory* (London: Penguin, 2003); Bruno Latour, "Why Has Critique Run out of Steam? From Matters of Fact to Matters of Concern," *Critical Inquiry* 30.2 (2004): 225–248; Daphne Patai and Will H. Corral (eds), *Theory's Empire: An Anthology of Dissent* (New York: Columbia University Press, 2005); and, most recently, Jane Elliott and Derek Attridge (eds), *Theory After "Theory"* (London and New York: Routledge, 2011).
5. *Aspen*, http://www.hofstra.edu/PDF/lib_sc_weingrow_usrp_gann.pdf.
6. http://en.wikipedia.org/wiki/Aspen_(magazine).
7. *Aspen*, http://www.hofstra.edu/PDF/lib_sc_weingrow_usrp_gann.pdf.
8. Ibid.
9. http://www.ubu.com/aspen/aspen3/index.html.
10. Roland Barthes, "The Death of the Author," trans. Richard Howard, *Aspen* 5/6, item 3 (fall/winter 1967), n.p. The original French version of the essay, "La mort de l'auteur" was published the following year in *Manteia* 5 (1968).
11. Barthes, "La mort de l'auteur."
12. *Aspen*, http://www.hofstra.edu/PDF/lib_sc_weingrow_usrp_gann.pdf.
13. The contents of issues 5/6 of *Aspen* may be viewed at http://www.ubu.com/aspen/aspen5and6/index.html. All ten issues are available from the ubu.com/aspen website.
14. Barthes, "The Death of the Author."
15. Ibid.
16. Ibid., my emphasis.
17. Elsewhere Howard translates "resume and conclusion of capitalist ideology" as "crown and conclusion of capitalist ideology." See, Roland Barthes, "The Death of the Author," in *The Rustle of Language*, trans. Richard Howard (New York: Hill and Wang, 1986), 50. In general, the later Howard translation is preferable, however, because the earlier one appeared in *Aspen*, I am quoting from it.
18. Barthes, "The Death of the Author," (1967).
19. Ibid.
20. While it would take this chapter well beyond its scope, it would be interesting to examine the role of post-1967 literary history manuals, writer biographies, writer interviews, etc. in preserving the prestige of the author amidst its theoretical defacement by theory in the late twentieth century.
21. This section draws from my article on "Text" for the *Oxford Encyclopedia of Aesthetics*, vol. 4, ed. Michael Kelly (New York: Oxford University Press, 1998), 370–375.

22. See Vincent Leitch, "The 'New Criticism'" in *American Literary Criticism Since the 1930s*, 2nd ed. (New York: Routledge, 2009).
23. See, W. K. Wimsatt, Jr., and Monroe Beardsley, "The Intentional Fallacy [1946]" in *The Verbal Icon: Studies in the Meaning of Poetry*, ed. W. K. Wimsatt (Lexington: University of Kentucky Press, 1954), 3–18.
24. A fuller statement on the differences between the classical and contemporary notions of text can be found in my article on "Text."
25. See Stanley Fish, *Is There a Text in This Class? The Authority of Interpretive Communities* (Cambridge, MA: Harvard University Press, 1980).
26. See Nelson Goodman, *Languages of Art*, 2nd ed (Indianapolis, IN: Hackett, 1976).
27. See Richard Rorty, "Texts and Lumps" in *Objectivity, Relativism and Truth, Philosophical Papers*, vol. 1 (Cambridge: Cambridge University Press, 1991), 78–92.
28. Umberto Eco, *Six Walks in the Fictional Woods* (Cambridge, MA: Harvard University Press, 1994), 3.
29. Umberto Eco, *A Theory of Semiotics* (Bloomington: Indiana University Press, 1976), 275.
30. See Juri Lotman, *The Structure of the Artistic Text* (Ann Arbor: University of Michigan Press, 1977).
31. See Ferdinand de Saussure, *Course in General Linguistics* (Peru, IL: Open Court, 1986).
32. See Louis Hjelmslev, *Prolegomena to a Theory of Language* (Madison: University of Wisconsin Press, 1962).
33. See Jacques Derrida, *Of Grammatology* (Baltimore, MD: Johns Hopkins University Press, 1974).
34. See Roland Barthes, *The Pleasure of the Text* (New York, NY: Hill and Wang, 1975).
35. See Roland Barthes, "From Work to Text" in *The Rustle of Language* (New York, NY: Hill and Wang, 1986).
36. See Emile Benveniste, "The Semiology of Language" in *Semiotics*, ed. Robert Innis (Bloomington: Indiana University Press, 1985).
37. See Julia Kristeva, *Semeiotike: Recherches pour une sémanalyse* (Paris: Seuil, 1969) and *The Kristeva Reader*, ed. Toril Moi (New York: Columbia University Press, 1986).
38. Gallop, *The Deaths of the Author*, 4–5.
39. Ibid., 5. Gallop dates the return from the 1968 French publication of Barthes's essay, whereas if you date it from the *Aspen* version the return comes four, not three, years later.
40. Gallop, *The Deaths of the Author*, 31, Barthes's emphasis. From Barthes, *The Pleasure of the Text*, 27.
41. Gallop, *The Deaths of the Author*, 5.
42. Burke has subsequently revised his 1992 study two times. A second edition was published in 1998 and a third edition in 2010.
43. See Derrida, *Of Grammatology*, 158–59.

44. Jacques Derrida, "The Deaths of Roland Barthes," *The Work of Mourning*, ed. Pascale-Anne Brault and Michael Nass (Chicago and London: University of Chicago Press, 2001), 50.
45. Charles McGrath, "Piecing Together Wallace's Posthumous Novel," *New York Times*, April 8, 2011.
46. David Foster Wallace, *Fate, Time, and Language: An Essay on Free Will*, ed. Steve M. Cahn and Maureen Eckert (New York: Columbia University Press, 2010).
47. McGrath, "Piecing Together."
48. Ibid.
49. Michael Pietsch, "Editor's Note" in *The Pale King: An Unfinished Novel*, ed. David Foster Wallace (New York: Little, Brown, 2011), viii.
50. Ibid., ix.
51. McGrath, "Piecing Together."
52. According to Dmitri Nabokov, Vladimir's son, his father left unfinished upon his death in 1977 a manuscript consisting of 138 index cards (which amount to about 30 pages of manuscript). See, "Interview with Dmitri Nabokov" on National Public Radio on April 30, 2008. http://www.npr.org/templates/story/story.php?storyId=90073521.
53. Like David Foster Wallace, Ralph Ellison also left behind an unfinished novel. However, while Wallace only left 250 pages upon his death, Ellison left several thousand pages and had spent nearly four decades working on this, his second novel. From the 27 boxes of files related to the novel held in the Library of Congress, two volumes have been published: *Juneteenth* in 1999, five years after his death, and *Three Days Before the Shooting...*, in 2010. *Juneteenth* is noted by its editor to be "the most ambitious and latest, freestanding, compelling, extended fiction in the saga," whereas *Three Days Before the Shooting...* is an 1,100-page edition that "enable[s] scholars and readers alike to follow Ellison's some forty years of work on his novel-in-progress" (xxviii). "For those willing to confront the challenges of the work's fragmentary form," write editors John F. Callahan and Adam Bradley in their "General Introduction to *Three Days Before the Shooting...*, "for those capable of simultaneously grasping multiple versions of the same scene, *Three Days Before the Shooting...* offers unparalleled access to the craft of Ellison's fiction and an unprecedented glimpse into the writer's mind" (xxix). Compared to the edition of Wallace's unfinished novel, *Three Days Before the Shooting...* is much closer to how an unfinished novel might be published. Nonetheless, the fact that *Juneteenth* was published prior to *Three Days Before the Shooting...* might be explained by noting that the publisher of both editions of Ellison's unfinished second novel is the Random House Publishing Group, a division of Random House, Inc.
54. In *Literature as Conduct: Speech Acts in Henry James* (New York: Fordham University Press, 2005), J. Hillis Miller similarly grapples with the issue of unfinished texts and dead authors, specifically, Henry James's unfinished novel, *The Sense of the Past*. Though James died

before he was able to finish *The Sense of the Past*, he left extensive notes regarding it speaking as though he could "see" (324) the finished novel. Says Hillis Miller, James "speaks as if that action has somewhere an ideal existence and his problem is to get access to the already-existing story, so he can write it down correctly, thereby transmitting it to his readers" (323). Hillis Miller compares this "ideal existence" to the ideal object in Edmund Husserl. "A triangle is for Husserl an ideal mathematical object," says Hillis Miller. "It exists independently of its actualization in any triangles in the material world" (324). "In a similar way," continues Hillis Miller, "any work of literature, according to Derrida, would exist somewhere, in a perpetual present, even if it were never to get written down, or even if it has been written down but all copies of it have been destroyed" (324). Hillis Miller's thinking then with regard to James's unfinished manuscript is that it exists finished in a transcendental Husserlian sense, and that the various notes James leaves with regard to it help us to better see it. However, in spite of his comments regarding ideal literary objects, Hillis Miller seems to confer with my own recommendation that we should leave unpublished (and unfinished) work in its valuable incompleteness:

> The thing itself, the unwritten part of *The Sense of the Past*, is lost forever. It still exists somewhere as the possibility of the words James did not write. Only James, however, had direct access to that possibility, that virtual reality, that "ideality." With his death, he took his clear vision of *The Sense of the Past* with him to his grave. There it remains encrypted in unrecoverable secrecy, except for the uncanny access without access to it given us by the "Notes." (324)

If one insists on the notion that there are ideal literary objects, then a similar situation may be said to hold for Wallace's *The Pale King*.

55. Another dimension here of how the neoliberal publishing industry uses prestige to sell books is the rise of prizes in literature and the arts over the past 100 years. James F. English has done a wonderful job of tracking the development of this aspect of cultural history in *The Economy of Prestige: Prizes, Awards, and the Circulation of Cultural Value* (Cambridge, MA: Harvard University Press, 2005).

8 The Publishing Market

1. The two best sources on the role of the market in publishing are John B. Thompson's *Books in the Digital Age: The Transformation of Academic and Higher Education Publishing in Britain and the United States* (Cambridge: Polity Press, 2005) and his *Merchants of Culture: The Publishing Business in the Twenty-First Century*, 2nd ed. (New York: Plume, 2012). However, the association of neoliberalism with publishing has not to date been developed.

2. See Thompson, "The Rise of Literary Agents," *Merchants of Culture*, 59–100. See also, James Hepburn, *The Author's Empty Purse and the Rise of the Literary Agent* (London: Oxford University Press, 1968) for a longer range survey of literary agents.
3. Alfredo Saad-Filho and Deborah Johnston, "Introduction," *Neoliberalism: A Critical Reader*, ed. Alfredo Saad-Filho and Deborah Johnston (London: Pluto Press, 2005), 1.
4. For Cerf's account of the acquisition of *Ulysses*, see Bennett Cerf, *At Random: The Reminiscences of Bennett Cerf* (New York: Random House, 2002), 90–98. Cerf's reminiscences were first published in 1977.
5. Number of publishers in the Bowker database with active ISBNs. Thompson, *Merchants of Culture*, 153.
6. Thompson, *Merchants of Culture*, 153.
7. Thompson, "Table 6—The 12 Largest Trade Publishers in the US, 2007–2008," *Merchants of Culture*, 117.
8. Random House trade and mass market revenues for 2007 were almost 2.4 billion dollars; the combined revenues of the 58,732 "small" presses, that is, presses under 1 million dollars annual sales, was around 2.7 billion dollars. See Thompson, *Merchants of Culture*, 117, 153.
9. Cerf, *At Random*, 276.
10. Ibid., 276.
11. Ibid., 278.
12. Ibid., 278.
13. Ibid., 279.
14. Ibid., 282.
15. Ibid., 285.
16. Ibid., 285.
17. Thompson, *Merchants of Culture*, 113.
18. Thompson, "Appendix 1—Selected Imprints of the Main Publishing Corporations," in *Merchants of Culture*, 410–411.
19. Pierre Bourdieu, *Acts of Resistance: Against the New Myths of Our Time*, trans. Richard Nice (Cambridge: Polity Press, 1998), 35.
20. "Random House" and "Penguin" together will consist of over 100 imprints, divisions, and groups in the United States and United Kingdom alone. See Thompson, "Appendix 1," *Merchants of Culture*, 410–411, for a listing of them.
21. Mark Sweney, "Penguin and Random House Merger to Create Biggest Book Publisher Ever Seen," *Guardian* (October 29, 2012), http://www.guardian.co.uk/books/2012/oct/29/penguin-random-house-book-publisher.
22. Ibid.
23. Henry Giroux, *The Terror of Neoliberalism: Authoritarianism and the Eclipse of Democracy* (Boulder, CO, and London: Paradigm, 2004), xxii.
24. There are 58,795 active publishers in the United States with annual sales revenue of less than 1 million dollars. Thompson, "Table 8—Estimated

Number of Active Publishers in the U.S. by size, 2004," *Merchants of Culture*, 153.
25. Or, more accurately, James Murdoch, the son of Rupert and the former executive vice-president of News Corporation, who is at the center of the conspiracy to fix e-book prices noted earlier. "Throw in with Apple," wrote Steve Jobs to James Murdoch, "and see if we can all make a go of this to create a real mainstream e-books market at $12.99 and $14.99" (Jenny Hendrix and Carolyn Kellogg, "All Eyes on Apple as E-book Price-fixing Trial Begins," *Los Angeles Times* [June 3, 2013]). This is the same Murdoch who was recently at the center of a phone-hacking scandal involving *News of the World* and News International—a scandal where some 90 people have been arrested and 16 charged with crimes. A report from British Parliament rebuked Murdoch, asserting that he "showed willful ignorance of the extent of the phone-hacking" and was "guilty of an astonishing lack of curiosity" regarding the situation (Jason Deans and John Plunkett, "Phone Hacking: Select Committee Report Unveiled" *The Guardian* [May 1, 2012]).
26. Bourdieu, *Acts of Resistance*, 35.
27. See Alexandra Alter, "Your E-Book Is Reading You," *Wall Street Journal* (June 29, 2012).
28. The use of data to determine aesthetics has already begun. A good recent example is the development of miniseries by Netflix. "We know what people watch on Netflix and we're able with a high degree of confidence to understand how big a likely audience is for a given show based on people's viewing habits," said Jonathan Friedland, director of Communications at Netflix (Roberto Baldwin, "Netflix Gambles on Big Data to Become the HBO of Streaming," *Wired* [November 29, 2012]). Every time you "hit the pause button" while viewing something on Netflix, it is a "discrete action that could be logged, recorded and analyzed," writes Andrew Leonard in *Salon* ("How Netflix is turning viewers into puppets" [February 1, 2013]). Continues Leonard:

As a consequence, the company knows more about our viewing habits than many of us realize. Netflix doesn't know merely what we're watching, but when, where and with what kind of device we're watching. It keeps a record of every time we pause the action—or rewind, or fast-forward—and how many of us abandon a show entirely after watching for a few minutes.

Netflix has used this "Big Data" to cast and develop both the *House of Cards* miniseries and the *Arrested Development* miniseries. While the use of Big Data does not guarantee that these shows will be a hit, Netflix "believes it can save big on marketing costs," comments Leonard, because their "recommendation engine will do all the heavy lifting."
29. Thompson, "Table 8," *Merchants of Culture*, 153.
30. Charles Frazier, *Cold Mountain* (New York: Atlantic Monthly Press, 1997), 1.

31. Thompson, *Merchants of Culture*, 178.
32. The first novel was Charles Frazier's *Cold Mountain*. His follow-up novel, *Thirteen Moons*, did not even cover the initial advance, let alone the actual $8.25 million dollar advance. See Thompson, *Merchants of Culture*, 178.
33. Thompson, "Table 8," *Merchants of Culture*, 153.
34. Thompson, "Table 6," *Merchants of Culture*, 117.
35. The recent merger of Random House and Penguin puts even a greater distance between the top of the Big 12, which is now Penguin Random House, and the rest of the group.
36. That is, in 2006. Thompson, *Merchants of Culture*, 31–32.
37. February 16, 2011.
38. Stephen Windwalker, "Amazon Positioned for 50% Overall Market Share by End of 2012," *Seeking Alpha* (February 3, 2011).
39. Thompson, "Table 3—Estimated Shares of U.S. Book Retail Market, 2006," *Merchants of Culture*, 50.
40. Thompson, *Merchants of Culture*, 28.
41. Ibid., 26.
42. Thompson, "Table 1—The Expansion of Borders and Barnes & Noble, 193–1994," *Merchants of Culture*, 30.
43. Thompson, *Merchants of Culture*, 29–30.
44. Julie Bosman and Michael J. De La Merced, "Borders Files for Bankruptcy," *New York Times* (February 16, 2011).
45. The simulated, homogenous bookstore experience has also hit many college and university bookstores. Barnes and Noble College, for example, operates nearly 700 college and university bookstores. Their website notes that they serve 4.5 million students and over 250,000 faculty members. See http://www.bncollege.com/college-partners/.
46. The American Association of University Presses reports just over 130 members. http://www.aaupnet.org/#.
47. Ben Palosaari, "University of Missouri Press Will Close," *The Pitch News* (May 24, 2012), http://www.pitch.com/plog/archives/2012/05/24/university-of-missouri-press-will-close.
48. http://press.umsystem.edu/%28S%28wm1t4d55lz2yogenbmptcjfi%29%29/catalog/CategoryInfo.aspx?cid=152&AspxAutoDetectCookieSupport=1.
49. Stuckey is leading a charge to save the press. Claire Kirch, "Outrage Grows to University of Missouri Shutting Down Press," *Publishers Weekly* (May 28, 2012).
50. Janese Silvey, "Wolf explains UM Press decision, says model sought," *Columbia Daily Tribune* (June 1, 2012).
51. "University of Missouri Coaches, Employee Pay." http://www.stltoday.com/news/local/education/university-of-missouri-coaches-employee-pay/html_c0f4c842-6760-11df-979e-0017a4a78c22.html.

52. MU Salary Database 2011. https://www.google.com/fusiontables/DataSource?snapid=S456793mZOi.
53. Ibid.
54. Palosaari, "University of Missouri Press will close."
55. Carolyn Kellogg, "University of Missouri Press to Close After 54 Years," *Los Angeles Times* (May 24, 2012).
56. "University of Missouri Coaches, Employee Pay."
57. Kellogg, "University of Missouri Press to close, after 54 years."
58. Scott Jaschik, "SMU Suspends Its University Press," *Inside Higher Ed* (May 7, 2010).
59. "University of Scranton Press is Closing," *Inside Higher Ed* (August 16, 2010).
60. Carolyn Kellogg, "Facing Cutbacks, UC Press will Suspend Poetry Series," *Los Angeles Times* (July 19, 2011).
61. Silvey, "Wolf explains."
62. Ibid.
63. Ibid.
64. Scott Jaschik, "Abandoning an Experiment," *Inside Higher Ed* (August 20, 2010).
65. Ibid.
66. Ibid.
67. Ibid.
68. Jennifer Howard, "After Outcry over Closure, U. of Missouri Press is Back to Printing Books," *Chronicle of Higher Education* (August 28, 2012).

9 THE JUNKYARD OF IDEAS

1. Deborah Rhode, *In Pursuit of Knowledge: Scholars, Status, and Academic Culture* (Stanford, CA: Stanford University Press, 2006), 32.
2. Ibid., 10
3. Ibid., 12.
4. Ibid., 30.
5. Ibid., 31.
6. Ibid., 39.
7. Ibid., 46.
8. Ibid., 46.
9. Louis Menand, *The Marketplace for Ideas: Reform and Resistance in the American University* (New York and London: W. W. Norton, 2010), 94.
10. Cary Nelson, *No University Is an Island: Saving Academic Freedom* (New York University Press, 2010), 81.
11. One of the major issues is how to balance the rising cost of producing and publishing books with shrinking university press and library

budgets. The best and most comprehensive survey of this topic is John B. Thompson's *Books in the Digital Age Books in the Digital Age: The Transformation of Academic and Higher Education Publishing in Britain and the United States* (Cambridge: Polity Press, 2005), Parts II and III, 81–308. Another major issue is whether the book should remain the "gold standard for tenure," or, as Lindsay Waters, executive editor for humanities at Harvard University Press has asked, whether the scholarly world should once again make the essay the standard of achievement. See, Lindsay Waters, "Slow Writing; or, Getting Off the Book Standard: What Can Journal Editors Do?" *Journal of Scholarly Publishing* 40.2 (January 2009). See also, Lindsay Waters, *Enemies of Promise: Publishing, Perishing, and the Eclipse of Scholarship* (Chicago: Prickly Paradigm Press, 2004).

12. "MLA Task Force on Evaluating Scholarship for Tenure and Promotion," *Profession 2007* (New York: MLA, 2007).

13. The story gets even stranger as it is rumored that the philosopher was just encouraged by his colleagues to write up any ideas he had to satisfy the administration. Originally written in English, the philosopher had someone translate the paper into Spanish, and it was then published in a South American journal—and only later was published in the United States. The philosopher is Edmund L. Gettier III and his famous three-page paper is "Is Justified True Belief Knowledge?" *Analysis* 23 (1963), 121–123. I was told this story by one of my philosophy professors at Indiana University, Hector-Neri Castañeda, who was a colleague of Gettier at Wayne State University at the time of the incident. As of 2013, the *Philosopher's Index* still only lists one publication by Gettier: "Is Justified True Belief Knowledge?" He is now professor emeritus at the University of Massachusetts, Amherst.

14. For example, a $349,000 grant from the Andrew W. Mellon Foundation to Indiana University Bloomington, in 2010, is funding research to develop a sustainable initiative to create metrics for assessing scholarly impact from large-scale usage data. http://newsinfo.iu.edu/news/page/normal/15040.html.

15. In chapter 8, concern was shown for using data to determine the shape of narrative and the example of Netflix using viewer data to develop miniseries programming was cited. Should we then be concerned with academics using data to determine the shape of academic writing? I don't think so as there is not much to be economically gained by a professor creating well-trafficked writing as opposed to a company like Netflix using it to develop shows like *House of Cards*. Nevertheless, the parallels and opportunities are still there.

16. *University of Nebraska Press Newsletter*, vol. 5. 2, Fall 2008.

17. A good and successful example of an open access scholarly publishing initiative is Open Humanities Press. Run by some of the most respected critical theorists in the world, OHP publishes new scholarly titles and

makes them available to the public at no cost. Open access initiatives like OHP have the potential to reconfigure scholarly publishing. Titles like my own *Terror, Theory, and the Humanities* (coedited with Uppinder Mehan, 2012) are available online from OHP at no cost to digital readers (even though print copies are still made available for purchase).
18. Michael Clarke, "Why Hasn't Scientific Publishing Been Disrupted Already?" *The Scholarly Kitchen* (January 4, 2010).

CODA

1. Pierre Bourdieu, *Acts of Resistance: Against the New Myths of Our Time*, trans. Richard Nice (Cambridge: Polity Press, 1998; reprint, 2000), 95
2. Ibid., 54–55.
3. Baruch Spinoza, "Part V, Proposition 42, Scholium," in *The Ethics and Selected Letters*, ed. Seymour Feldman, trans. Samuel Shirley (Indianapolis and Cambridge: Hackett, 1982), 225.

Bibliography

Albanese, Andrew. "Penguin and Macmillan Reject Price Fixing Charges." *Publishers Weekly* (May 31, 2012). http://www.publishersweekly.com/pw/by-topic/digital/retailing/article/52168-penguin-and-macmillan-reject-price-fixing-charges.html.

Alter, Alexandra. "Your E-Book Is Reading You." *Wall Street Journal* (June 29, 2012).

"America's First Bookless Library to Open in Texas." *De Zeen* (January 21, 2013). http://www.dezeen.com/2013/01/21/bookless-library-based-on-apple-store-planned-in-texas/.

Aronowitz, Stanley. *The Knowledge Factory: Dismantling the Corporate University and Creating True Higher Learning.* Boston, MA: Beacon Press, 2001.

Aspen Magazine. http://www.hofstra.edu/PDF/lib_sc_weingrow_usrp_gann.pdf.

Baldwin, Roberto. "Netflix Gambles on Big Data to Become the HBO of Streaming." *Wired* 29 (November 2012). http://www.wired.com/gadgetlab/2012/11/netflix-data-gamble/.

Barthes, Roland. "From Work to Text." In *The Rustle of Language*. Translated by Richard Howard. New York: Hill and Wang, 1986. 56–64.

———. "The Death of the Author." In *The Rustle of Language*. Translated by Richard Howard. New York: Hill and Wang, 1986.

———. "The Death of the Author." Translated by Richard Howard. *Aspen* 5/6, item 3 (Fall/Winter 1967): n.p. http://www.ubu.com/aspen/aspen5and6/threeEssays.html#barthes.

———. *The Pleasure of the Text.* Translated by Richard Miller. New York: Hill and Wang, 1975.

Bell, David. "Does This Man Deserve Tenure?" *New Republic* (September 6, 2010). http://www.tnr.com/book/review/mark-taylor-crisis-campus-colleges-universities.

Benveniste, Emile. "The Semiology of Language." In *Semiotics*, edited by Robert Innis. Bloomington: Indiana University Press, 1985. 226–246.

Bérubé, Michael. "What Is the MLA, and Where Does it Live?" *MLA Newsletter* 44.4 (Winter 2012): 2–3.

Bok, Derek. *Universities in the Marketplace: The Commercialization of Higher Education.* Princeton, NJ: Princeton University Press, 2003.

Born, Daniel. "What is the Crisis in the Humanities?" *Common Review* (Spring 2010). http://www.thecommonreview.org/article/archive/2010/08/article/what-is-the-crisis-in-the-humanities.html.

Borradori, Giovanna. *Philosophy in a Time of Terror: Dialogues with Jürgen Habermas and Jacques Derrida*. Chicago and London: University of Chicago Press, 2003.

Bosman, Julie, and Michael J. De La Merced. "Borders Files for Bankruptcy." *New York Times* (February 16, 2011). http://dealbook.nytimes.com/2011/02/16/borders-files-for-bankruptcy/.

Bourdieu, Pierre. *Acts of Resistance: Against the New Myths of Our Time*. Translated by Richard Nice. Cambridge: Polity Press, 1998; reprint, 2000.

Burke, Seán. *The Death and Return of the Author: Criticism and Subjectivity in Barthes, Foucault and Derrida*. Edinburgh: Edinburgh University Press, 1992. 2nd ed., 1998. 3rd ed., 2010.

Callahan, John F., and Adam Bradley. "General Introduction to *Three Days Before the Shooting…*" Ralph Ellison, *Three Days Before the Shooting*.…Edited by John F. Callahan and Adam Bradley. New York: The Modern Library, 2011. xv–xxix.

Carli, Don. "Is Digital Media Worse for the Environment than Print?" *Mediashift* (March 31, 2010). http://www.pbs.org/mediashift/2010/03/is-digital-media-worse-for-the-environment-than-print090.html.

———. "Print vs. Digital Media: False Dilemmas and Forced Choices." *Institute for Sustainable Communication* [Whitepaper] (n.d.): 1–10. www.sustainablecommunication.org.

Carman, Taylor. "Do Our Universities Need a Makeover?" *New York Times* (May 2, 2009). http://www.nytimes.com/2009/05/03/opinion/103university.html.

Cerf, Bennett. *At Random: The Reminiscences of Bennett Cerf*. New York: Random House, 2002.

Clarke, Michael. "Why Hasn't Scientific Publishing Been Disrupted Already?" In *The Scholarly Kitchen* (January 4, 2010). http://scholarlykitchen.sspnet.org/2010/01/04/why-hasnt-scientific-publishing-been-disrupted-already/.

Damrosch, David. *We Scholars: Changing the Culture of the University*. Cambridge, MA: Harvard University Press, 1995.

Davidson, Cathy N. "Humanities 2.0: Promise, Perils, Predictions." *PMLA* 123.3 (2008): 707–717.

Davies, Bronwyn, Michael Gottsche, and Peter Bansel. "The Rise and Fall of the Neoliberal University." *European Journal of Education* 41.2 (2006): 305–319.

Deans, Jason, and John Plunkett. "Phone Hacking: Select Committee Report Unveiled." *Guardian* (May 1, 2012). http://www.guardian.co.uk/media/blog/2012/may/01/select-committee-report-james-rupert-murdoch.

Derrida, Jacques. *Adieu to Emmanuel Levinas* [1997]. Translated by Pascale-Anne Brault and Michael Naas. Stanford, CA: Stanford University Press, 1999.

———. *Of Grammatology.* Translated by Gayatri Spivak. Baltimore, MD: The Johns Hopkins University Press, 1974.

———. *Memoires for Paul de Man*, rev. ed. New York: Columbia University Press, 1986.

———. *Spectres of Marx: The State of the Debt, the Work of Mourning, and the New International.* Translated by Peggy Kamuf. New York: Routledge, 1994.

———. "The Deaths of Roland Barthes." In *The Work of Mourning*, edited by. Pascale-Anne Brault and Michael Nass. Chicago and London: University of Chicago Press, 2001.

Di Leo, Jeffrey R. *Academe Degree Zero: Reconsidering the Politics of Higher Education.* Boulder, CO: Paradigm, 2012.

———. *Affiliations: Identity in Academic Culture.* Edited with an introductory essay. Lincoln and London: University of Nebraska Press, 2003.

———. *Federman's Fictions: Innovation, Theory, and the Holocaust.* Edited with an introductory essay. Albany: State University of New York Press, 2011.

———. *From Socrates to Cinema: An Introduction to Philosophy.* New York: McGraw-Hill, 2007.

———. "Text." In *Oxford Encyclopedia of Aesthetics*, edited by Michael Kelly, vol. 4. New York: Oxford University Press, 1998. 370–375.

Di Leo, Jeffrey R., and Sophia McClennen. "Postscript on Violence." *symplokē* 20.1/2 (2012): 182–186.

Di Leo, Jeffrey R., and Uppinder Mehan. "Theory Ground Zero: Terror, Theory, and the Humanities after 9/11." In *Terror, Theory, and the Humanities*, edited by Jeffrey R. Di Leo and Uppinder Mehan. Ann Arbor, MI: Open Humanities Press, 2012.

Di Leo, Jeffrey R., and Uppinder Mehan, eds. *Capital at the Brink: Overcoming the Destructive Legacies of Neoliberalism.* Ann Arbor, MI: Open Humanities Press, 2014.

Donoghue, Frank. *The Last Professors: The Corporate University and the Fate of the Humanities.* New York: Fordham University Press, 2008.

Du Gay, Paul, Stuart Hall, Linda Janes, Hugh MacKay, and Keith Negus. *Doing Cultural Studies: The Story of the Sony Walkman.* London: Sage, 1997.

Eagleton, Terry. *After Theory.* London: Penguin, 2003.

Eco, Umberto. *Six Walks in the Fictional Woods.* Cambridge, MA: Harvard University Press, 1994.

———. *A Theory of Semiotics.* Bloomington: Indiana University Press, 1976.

Elliott, Jane, and Derek Attridge, eds. *Theory After "Theory."* London and New York: Routledge, 2011.

English, James F. *The Economy of Prestige: Prizes, Awards, and the Circulation of Cultural Value*. Cambridge, MA: Harvard University Press, 2005.

Fanghanel, Joëlle. *Being an Academic*. London and New York: Routledge, 2012.

Ferrall, Victor E., Jr. *Liberal Arts at the Brink*. Cambridge, MA: Harvard University Press, 2011.

Fish, Stanley. *Is There a Text in This Class? The Authority of Interpretive Communities*. Cambridge, MA: Harvard University Press, 1980.

———. "No Bias, No Merit: The Case against Blind Submission." In *The Stanley Fish Reader*, edited by H. Aram Veeser. Malden, MA: Blackwell, 1999. 241–258.

———. *The Trouble with Principle*. Cambridge, MA: Harvard University Press, 2001.

———. *Professional Correctness: Literary Studies and Political Change*. Cambridge, MA: Harvard University Press, 1996.

Florida, Richard. *The Rise of the Creative Class: And How It's Transforming Work, Leisure, Community, and Everyday Life*. New York: Basic Books, 2002.

Foucault, Michel. *The Archeology of Knowledge and The Discourse on Language*. Translated by A. M. Sheridan Smith. New York: Pantheon Books, 1972.

———. "The Subject and Power." In *Michel Foucault: Beyond Structuralism and Hermeneutics*, edited by Hubert L. Dreyfus and Paul Rabinow. Chicago: University of Chicago Press, 1983. 208–226.

Frazier, Charles. *Cold Mountain*. New York: Atlantic Monthly Press, 1997.

Gallop, Jane. *The Deaths of the Author: Reading and Writing in Time*. Durham and London: Duke University Press, 2011.

Gettier, Edmund L, III. "Is Justified True Belief Knowledge?" *Analysis* 23 (1963): 121–123.

Giroux, Henry. *Hearts of Darkness: Torturing Children in the War on Terror*. Boulder, CO, and London: Paradigm, 2010.

———. "The Post-9/11 Militarization of Higher Education and Neoliberalism's Culture of Depravity: Threats to the Future of American Democracy." In *Terror, Education, Neoliberalism: Contemporary Dialogues*, edited by Jeffrey R. Di Leo, Henry Giroux, Sophia McClennen, and Ken Saltman. Boulder, CO, and London: Paradigm, 2012. 36–66.

———. *The Terror of Neoliberalism: Authoritarianism and the Eclipse of Democracy*. Boulder, CO, and London: Paradigm, 2004.

———. *The University in Chains: Confronting the Military–Industrial–Academic Complex*. Boulder, CO, and London: Paradigm, 2007.

Goodman, Nelson. *Languages of Art*. 2nd ed. Indianapolis, IN: Hackett, 1976.

Hacker, Andrew, and Claudia Dreifus. *Higher Education? How Colleges Are Wasting Our Money and Failing Our Kids—and What We Can Do about It*. New York: Times Books/Henry Holt, 2010.

Harter, Stephen P., and Hak Joon Kim. "Electronic Journals and Scholarly Communication: A Citation and Reference Study." *Information Research* 2.1 (1996). http://informationr.net/ir/2-1/paper9a.html.

Hendrix, Jenny, and Carolyn Kellogg. "All Eyes on Apple as E-book Price-fixing Trial Begins." *Los Angeles Times* (June 3, 2013). http://www.latimes.com/features/books/jacketcopy/la-et-jc-all-eyes-on-apple-as-ebook-pricefixing-trial-begins-20130603,0,4862944.story.

Hepburn, James. *The Author's Empty Purse and the Rise of the Literary Agent.* London: Oxford University Press, 1968.

Hillis Miller, J. *Literature as Conduct: Speech Acts in Henry James.* New York: Fordham University Press, 2005.

Hitchens, Christopher. "The Minority Report." *Nation* (November 5, 1983).

Hjelmslev, Louis. *Prolegomena to a Theory of Language.* Translated by Francis J. Whitfield. Madison: University of Wisconsin Press, 1962.

Howard, Jennifer. "After Outcry over Closure, U. of Missouri Press is Back to Printing Books." *Chronicle of Higher Education* (August 28, 2012). http://chronicle.com/article/After-Outcry-Over-Closure-U/133988/?cid=at&utm_source=at&utm_medium=en.

———. "New Ratings of Humanities Journals Do More than Rank—They Rankle." *Chronicle of Higher Education* (October 10, 2008). http://chronicle.com/article/New-Ratings-of-Humanities/29072.

http://en.wikipedia.org/wiki/Aspen_(magazine).

http://press.umsystem.edu/%28S%28wm1t4d55lz2yogenbmptcjfi%29%29/catalog/ CategoryInfo.aspx?cid=152&AspxAutoDetectCookieSupport=1.

http://www.aaupnet.org/#.

http://www.bncollege.com/college-partners/.

http://www.ubu.com/aspen/aspen3/index.html.

Hutsko, Joe. "Are E-Readers Greener than Books?" *New York Times* (August 31, 2009). http://green.blogs.nytimes.com/2009/08/31/are-e-readers-greener-than-books/.

Ingarden, Roman. *The Literary Work of Art: An Investigation of the Borderlines of Ontology, Logic, and Theory of Language* [1931]. Translated by Ruth Ann Crowley and Kenneth Olsen. Evanston, IL: Northwestern University Press, 1979.

"Interview with Dmitri Nabokov." National Public Radio, April 30, 2008. http://www.npr.org/templates/story/story.php?storyId=90073521.

Iser, Wolfgang. *The Implied Reader: Patterns of Communication in Prose Fiction from Bunyan to Beckett.* Baltimore, MD: The Johns Hopkins University Press, 1974.

Jameson, Fredric. Foreword by Jean-François Lyotard, vii–xxi. *The Postmodern Condition: A Report on Knowledge.* Translated by Geoff Bennington and Brian Massumi. Minneapolis: University of Minnesota Press, 1984.

Jaschik, Scott. "Abandoning an Experiment." *Inside Higher Ed* (August 20, 2010). http://www.insidehighered.com/news/2010/08/20/rice.

———. "SMU Suspends Its University Press." *Inside Higher Ed* (May 7, 2010). http://www.insidehighered.com/news/2010/05/07/smu.

Joyce, James. *Finnegan's Wake*. London: Faber and Faber, 1939.

Kant, Immanuel. *Emmanuel Kant: Philosophical Correspondence 1759–99*. Translated by A. Zweig. Chicago: University of Chicago Press, 1986.

———. *Prolegomena to Any Future Metaphysics*, rev. ed. Edited and translated by Gary Hatfield. Cambridge: Cambridge University Press, 2004.

———. *The Conflict of the Faculties*. Translated by Mary Gregor. Lincoln: University of Nebraska Press, 1979.

Kaufmann, Walter. *Existentialism: From Dostoevsky to Sartre*. Cleveland and New York: World Publishing, 1956.

Kellogg, Carolyn. "Facing Cutbacks, UC Press will Suspend Poetry Series. *Los Angeles Times* (July 19, 2011). http://latimesblogs.latimes.com/jacketcopy/2011/07/uc-press-poetry-series.html.

———. "University of Missouri Press to Close After 54 Years." *Los Angeles Times* (May 24, 2012). http://latimesblogs.latimes.com/jacketcopy/2012/05/university-of-missouri-press-to-close-after-54-years.html.

Kirch, Claire. "Outrage Grows to University of Missouri Shutting Down Press." *Publishers Weekly* (May 28, 2012). http://www.publishersweekly.com/pw/by-topic/industry-news/publisher-news/article/52140-outrage-grows-to-university-of-missouri-shutting-down-press.html.

Kirp, David L. *Shakespeare, Einstein, and the Bottom Line: The Marketing of Higher Education*. Cambridge, MA: Harvard University Press, 2003.

Kittler, Friedrich. "Universities: Wet, Hard, Soft, and Harder." *Critical Inquiry* 31.2 (2004): 244–255.

Kristeva, Julia. *Semeiotike: Recherches pour une sémanalyse*. Paris: Seuil, 1969.

———. *The Kristeva Reader*. Edited by Toril Moi. New York: Columbia University Press, 1986.

Lakoff, George. "Beyond the War on Terror: Understanding Reflexive Thought." In *Transforming Terror: Remembering the Soul of the World*, edited by Karin Lofthus Carrington and Susan Griffin. Berkeley: University of California Press, 2011. 43–46.

Latour, Bruno. "Why Has Critique Run out of Steam? From Matters of Fact to Matters of Concern." *Critical Inquiry* 30.2 (2004): 225–248.

Lazzarato, Maurizio. *The Making of the Indebted Man: An Essay on the Neoliberal Condition*. Translated by Joshua David Jordan. Los Angeles, CA: Semiotext(e), 2012.

Leitch, Vincent. *American Literary Criticism Since the 1930s*. 2nd ed. New York: Routledge, 2009.

Lemisch, Jesse. "Hacker and Dreifus's Higher Education? A Neocon Screed." *New Politics* (July 27, 2010). http://newpolitics.mayfirst.org/node/358.

Leonard, Andrew. "How Netflix is Turning Viewers into Puppets." *Salon* (February 1, 2013). http://www.salon.com/2013/02/01/how_netflix_is_turning_viewers_into_puppets/.

Lotman, Juri. *The Structure of the Artistic Text*. Translated by Ronald Vroon and Gail Vroon. Ann Arbor: University of Michigan Press, 1977.

Lyotard, Jean-François. *The Postmodern Condition: A Report on Knowledge*. Translated by Geoff Bennington and Brian Massumi. Minneapolis: University of Minnesota Press, 1984.

McGrath, Charles. "Piecing Together Wallace's Posthumous Novel." *New York Times* (April 8, 2011). http://www.nytimes.com/2011/04/09/books/david-foster-wallace-and-the-pale-king.html.

Menand, Louis. *The Marketplace of Ideas: Reform and Resistance in the American University*. New York and London: W. W. Norton, 2010.

Miller, Toby. *Blow Up the Humanities*. Philadelphia, PA: Temple University Press, 2012.

"MLA Task Force on Evaluating Scholarship for Tenure and Promotion." *Profession 2007.* New York: MLA, 2007.

MU Salary Database 2011. https://www.google.com/fusiontables/DataSource?snapid=S456793mZOi.

Nabakov, Vladimir. *The Original of Laura: A Novel in Fragments*. New York: Knopf, 2009.

Nelson, Cary. *No University Is an Island: Saving Academic Freedom*. New York, NY: New York University Press, 2010.

Nixon, Rob. *Slow Violence and the Environmentalism of the Poor*. Cambridge, MA: Harvard University Press, 2011.

Nussbaum, Martha. *Not for Profit: Why Democracy Needs the Humanities*. Princeton and Oxford: Princeton University Press, 2010.

Palosaari, Ben. "University of Missouri Press Will Close." *Pitch News* (May 24, 2012). http://www.pitch.com/plog/archives/2012/05/24/university-of-missouri-press-will-close.

Patai, Daphne, and Will H. Corral, eds. *Theory's Empire: An Anthology of Dissent*. New York: Columbia University Press, 2005.

Patton, Stacey. "I Fully Expect to Die with this Debt." *Chronicle of Higher Education* (April 15, 2013). http://chronicle.com/article/I-Fully-Expect-to-Die-With/138507/.

Peterkin, Caitlin. "Rise in Student-Loan Debt Spurs Advocates' Call for Frank Discussion, Not Panic Over Extreme Cases." *Chronicle of Higher Education* (October 26, 2012), A3.

Pietsch, Michael. Editor's Note by David Foster Wallace. *The Pale King: An Unfinished Novel*. Edited by Michael Pietsch. New York: Little, Brown, 2011. v–xiv.

Pilon, Mary. "What's a Degree Really Worth." *Wall Street Journal* (February 2, 2010). http://online.wsj.com/article/SB10001424052748703822404575019082819966538.html.

Plato, *Phaedo*. *The Dialogues of Plato*. Vol. 1. 2nd ed. Translated by Benjamin Jowett. Oxford: Oxford at the Clarendon Press, 1875.

Pool, Gail. *Faint Praise: The Plight of Book Reviewing in America*. Columbia and London: University of Missouri Press, 2007.

Proulx, E. Annie. "Books on Top." *New York Times* (May 26, 1994), A13.
Raymond, Nate. "Judge says Leaning toward U.S. in Apple E-books Case." *Reuters* (May 23, 2013). http://www.reuters.com/article/2013/05/23/usa-apple-ebooks-idUSL2N0E42FJ20130523.
Readings, Bill. *The University in Ruins*. Cambridge, MA: Harvard University Press, 1996.
Rhode, Deborah L. *In Pursuit of Knowledge: Scholars, Status, and Academic Culture*. Stanford, CA: Stanford University Press, 2006.
Romano, Carlin. "Heil Heidegger!" *Chronicle Review* (October 18, 2009). http://chronicle.com/article/Heil-Heidegger-/48806/.
———. "Response." *Chronicle Review* (November 27, 2009), B19.
Rorty, Richard. "Texts and Lumps." In *Objectivity, Relativism and Truth, Philosophical Papers*, vol. 1. Cambridge: Cambridge University Press, 1991. 78–92.
Saad-Filho, Alfredo, and Deborah Johnston. "Introduction." In *Neoliberalism: A Critical Reader*, edited by Alfredo Saad-Filho and Deborah Johnston. London: Pluto Press, 2005. 1–6.
Saussure, Ferdinand de. *Course in General Linguistics*. Edited by Charles Bally and Albert Sechehaye with the collaboration of Albert Riedlinger. Translated by Roy Harris. Peru, IL: Open Court, 1986.
Schrecker, Ellen. *The Lost Soul of Higher Education: Corporatization, the Assault on Academic Freedom, and the End of the American University*. New York and London: New Press, 2010.
Silvey, Janese. "Wolf explains UM Press Decision, says Model Sought." *Columbia Daily Tribune* (June 1, 2012). http://www.columbiatribune.com/news/education/wolfe-explains-um-press-de-cision-says-better-model-sought/article_79236ece-4ea0-51fb-ae12-f6aa19f813f5.html.
Snow, C. P. *The Two Cultures and the Scientific Revolution*. New York: Cambridge University Press, 1959.
Spinoza, Baruch. *The Ethics and Selected Letters*. Edited and introduced by Seymour Feldman. Translated by Samuel Shirley. Indianapolis and Cambridge: Hackett, 1982.
Stuckey-French, Ned. *The American Essay in the American Century*. Columbia, MO: University of Missouri Press, 2011.
Subotnik, Dan, and Glen Lazar. "Affiliating the Rejection Letter." In *Affiliations: Identity in Academic Culture*, edited by Jeffrey R. Di Leo, 54–72.
Sweney, Mark. "Penguin and Random House Merger to Create Biggest Book Publisher Ever Seen." *Guardian* (October 29, 2012). http://www.guardian.co.uk/books/2012/oct/29/penguin-random-house-book-publisher.
Taylor, Mark. *Crisis on Campus: A Bold Plan for Reforming our Colleges and Universities*. New York: Alfred A. Knopf, 2010.
———. "The End of the University as We Know It." *New York Times* (April 26, 2009). http://www.nytimes.com/2009/04/27/opinion/27taylor.html.
Thacker, Lloyd. *College Unranked: Ending the College Admissions Frenzy*. Cambridge, MA: Harvard University Press, 2005.

Thompson, John B. *Books in the Digital Age: The Transformation of Academic and Higher Education Publishing in Britain and the United States*. Cambridge: Polity Press, 2005.

———. *Merchants of Culture: The Publishing Business in the Twenty-First Century*. 2nd ed. New York: Plume, 2012.

Under the Radar. Book Industry Study Group, 2005.

"University of Missouri Coaches, Employee Pay." http://www.stltoday.com/news/local/education/university-of-missouri-coaches-employee-pay/html_c0f4c842-6760-11df-979e-0017a4a78c22.html.

"University of Scranton Press is Closing." *Inside Higher Ed* (August 16, 2010). http://www.insidehighered.com/quicktakes/2010/08/16/u-scranton-press-closing.

Veblen, Thorstein. *The Higher Learning in America*. New York: B. W. Huebsch, 1918.

Wallace, David Foster. *Fate, Time, and Language: An Essay on Free Will*. Edited by Steve M. Cahn and Maureen Eckert. New York: Columbia University Press, 2010.

———. *The Pale King: An Unfinished Novel*. Large print edition. Edited by Michael Pietsch. New York: Little, Brown, 2011.

Washburn, Jennifer. *University, Inc.: The Corporate Corruption of Higher Education*. New York: Basic Books, 2005.

Waters, Lindsay. *Enemies of Promise: Publishing, Perishing, and the Eclipse of Scholarship*. Chicago: Prickly Paradigm Press, 2004.

———. "Slow Writing; or, Getting Off the Book Standard: What Can Journal Editors Do?" *Journal of Scholarly Publishing* 40.2 (January 2009): 129–143.

Wellman, Carl. "On Terrorism Itself." *Journal of Value Inquiry* 13 (1979): 250–258.

Williams, Jeffrey J. "Debt Education: Bad for the Young, Bad for America." *Dissent* 53.3 (Summer 2006): 53–59.

———. "Student Debt and the Spirit of Indenture." *Dissent* 55.4 (Fall 2008): 73–78.

———. "The Post-Welfare State University." *American Literary History* 18.1 (Spring 2006): 190–216.

Wilshire, Bruce. *The Moral Collapse of the University: Professionalism, Purity, and Alienation*. Albany, NY: State University of New York Press, 1990.

Wimsatt, W. K. *The Verbal Icon: Studies in the Meaning of Poetry*. Lexington: University of Kentucky Press, 1954.

Windwalker, Stephen. "Amazon Positioned for 50% Overall Market Share by End of 2012." *Seeking Alpha* (February 3, 2011). http://seekingalpha.com/article/250507-amazon-positioned-for-50-overall-market-share-by-end-of-2012.

About the Author

Jeffrey R. Di Leo is dean of the School of Arts and Sciences, and professor of English and Philosophy at the University of Houston-Victoria. He is editor and founder of the critical theory journal *symplokē*, editor and publisher of the *American Book Review*, and executive director of the Society for Critical Exchange. His books include *Morality Matters: Race, Class and Gender in Applied Ethics* (2002); *Affiliations: Identity in Academic Culture* (2003); *On Anthologies: Politics and Pedagogy* (2004); *If Classrooms Matter: Progressive Visions of Educational Environments* (2004, with W. Jacobs); *From Socrates to Cinema: An Introduction to Philosophy* (2007); *Fiction's Present: Situating Contemporary Narrative Innovation* (2008, with R. M. Berry); *Federman's Fictions: Innovation, Theory, and the Holocaust* (2010); *Terror, Theory, and the Humanities* (2012, with U. Mehan); *Academe Degree Zero: Reconsidering the Politics of Higher Education* (2012); and *Neoliberalism, Terrorism, Education: Contemporary Dialogues* (2013, with H. Giroux, K. Saltman, and S. McClennen).

Index

Note: Locators followed by 'n' refer to notes.

Academe, 32, 139n. 2
academic culture, ix, xix, 6, 28, 58, 71, 106, 109, 115, 116, 148n. 8
  impact of university presses on, 115
  neoliberal, ix, xvii–xviii, 57–8, 69, 71, 80, 86, 103, 106, 136
academic freedom, ix, xv, xx, 1, 10, 12, 28, 32–4, 45, 47, 48, 49, 50, 55, 57, 134
  assaults on, 32–3, 139n. 2
  future of, 33
academic identity, ix, xi, xv, xvi
  in the neoliberal university, 28
Acts of Resistance (Bourdieu), xv, 109, 137n. 9
Adieu to Emmanuel Levinas (Derrida), 98
Advertising Age, 90
affiliation, 35, 36, 49, 59, 62, 64, 65, 66, 146n. 13
  critical, 57–69, 148n. 8
  politics of, 61, 64
agonism, 41, 58
Amazon, 82–3, 106, 112, 152n. 30, 153n. 33
  see also Kindle
American Association of University Presses (AAUP), 124, 128, 160n. 46
American Association of University Professors (AAUP), 3, 28, 32–3, 41, 139n. 2

American Book Review, 63, 64, 72, 79–80, 81–2, 83, 113, 153n. 32
American Comparative Literature Association (ACLA), 3
American Essay in the American Century, The (Stuckey-French), 116
American Philosophical Association, 150n. 2
Andrew W. Mellon Foundation, 162n. 14
anonymity, 66–8
Aristotle, 48, 54, 56
Arizona State University, 34
Aronowitz, Stanley, 27
Arrested Development (miniseries), 159n. 28
Aspen, 90–1, 92, 101, 103, 154n. 17, 155n. 39
Association of American Universities (AAU), 116
Association to Advance Collegiate Schools of Business (AACSB), 72
Auslegung: A Journal of Philosophy, 74–5, 78, 151n. 8
Australian Research Council (ARC), 76, 78
author, the, 94, 98, 101
  and capitalism, 92, 99, 100, 102, 103
  death of the author, 90–103, 135;
  two types, 98

author, the—*Continued*
  difficulty to eliminate, 92
  intention of, 93, 96, 101, 102
  invention of, 92
  and prestige, 92, 98, 99, 102–3, 154n. 20
  resurrection of, 90, 103
  and text, 92–7

Barnard College, 42
Barnes and Noble, 112, 113, 114
Barnes and Noble College, 160n. 45
Barthes, Roland, 91–3, 95, 96–9, 103
B. Dalton Booksellers, 113, 114
Beach, Sylvia, 107
Beardsley, Monroe, 93
Beauvoir, Simone de, 11
Beckett, Samuel, 63, 91
Being an Academic (Fanghanel), xvii
Being and Time (Heidegger), 123
Benveniste, Emile, 97
Berkeley Conference on LSD, 91
Bertelsmann, 108
Bérubé, Michael, 148n. 13
Birmingham Center for Contemporary Cultural Studies, xix
Blow Up the Humanities (Miller), 18–22, 141n. 41
Bok, Derek, 4, 27, 28
book reviewing, 64–5, 66, 125
  outlets, 105, 106
Books in the Digital Age (Thompson), 157n. 1, 162n. 11
bookstores, 106, 112–15, 160n. 45
  chains, 106, 111, 113–14
  demise of, 106
  independent, 112, 114
  private, 106
  see also individual booksellers
Borders, 111, 112–14
Borders, Louis, 113

Borders, Tom, 113
Bourdieu, Pierre, x, xv, 108, 109, 133–4, 137n. 9
Bowker database, 149n. 15
Bradley, Adam, 156n. 53
branding, 71, 75, 81, 82, 84, 85, 151n. 9
  fever, 71, 72, 75–6, 150n. 1
Brokeback Mountain (film), 82
Burke, Seán, 90, 98, 99, 155n. 41
Burroughs, William S., 91
Bush family, 111
business (discipline), 9, 19, 23, 72, 87, 150n. 5
  journals, 72, 150n. 5

Cage, John, 91
Cal State system, 23
Cale, John, 91
Calinescu, Matei, 150n. 4
Callahan, John F., 156n. 53
capitalism, 39, 108
  and birth of the author, 92, 99
  extreme free market, xvi, xvii
Capote, Truman, 107, 108
careerism, 9, 124
CBS, 107
Cerf, Bennett, 106–8, 109, 110, 158n. 4
Chaucer, Geoffrey, 3
Cheney, Lynne, 121–2
Chicago Manual of Style, 62
Chronicle of Higher Education, 2
Chronicle Review, The, 67
citizenship, ix, 10, 14–15, 16, 17, 20, 57, 130
City University of New York (CUNY), 27, 139n. 3
Clancy, Tom, 112
Clarke, Michael, 128
Cold Mountain (Frazier), 160n. 32
Collected Works of Langston Hughes, The, 115
College Unranked (Thacker), 150n. 1

Columbia University, 38, 49
communication (discipline), 19–20, 21, 22, 148n. 10
see also Humanities Two
Comparative Literature, 73
Complete Sermons of Ralph Waldo Emerson, The, 115
Conflict of the Faculties, The (Kant), 40
Continental Philosophy Review, 75
corporate university, xix, 2, 4, 6, 9–10, 12, 13, 34, 46, 140n. 1
  ascent of, 2
  effect on the humanities, 6
  humanities within, 9–10, 11
  student demand and, 6
  see also neoliberal university
creative class, 20
creative industries, 20–1, 24
Crisis on Campus (Taylor, M.), 38, 139n. 8
critical exchange, 57–61, 66, 68, 134, 143n. 23, 148n. 10
  ethics of, 61
  future of, 68
  in philosophy, 61
  two types of, 58–61, 64, 65, 66
  see also criticism; faint praise
critical inquiry, xiv, xv, xx, xxi, 1, 106
  erasure of, 61
critical thinking, xv, 14, 17
  erosion of, xiv
  importance of, 16
criticism, 60, 64–9, 93, 94, 98, 134, 148n. 8
  anonymous, 67–8, 86
  and author, 91, 92
  civil, 60
  empty, 66, 67
  ethics of, 64
  metaprofessional, 41
  negative perception of, 58, 60
  see also critical exchange; faint praise

cultural studies, 3, 21–2, 38, 142n. 52, 142n. 53
  approach to renewing the humanities, 21–2
  rise of, 3
curriculum, 1, 10, 12, 22, 34, 35–7, 135
  humanities, 2, 12, 15
  liberal arts, 9, 12, 54
  literature, 10
  philosophy, 10, 11
  vocationalism of, 6
  vocationally based, 1, 6, 9

Dalton, David, 91
Damrosch, David, 4
Davidson, Cathy N., 141n. 41
Death and Return of the Author, The (Burke), 98
death of the author, see under author, the
Deaths of the Author, The (Gallop), 98
debt, xiii, xiv, xv
  critical, xv
  student, xi–xii, xiv, xv, 7, 28, 46, 137n. 10, 138n. 15, 139n. 12
  see also debt economy
debt economy, x, xi, xii–xiv
Deleuze, Gilles, 63, 73
Deleuze Studies, 75, 78
Derrida, Jacques, 52, 95, 96, 98–9, 157n. 54
democracy, 14, 16, 17, 20
  importance of humanities to, 14, 15
  see also democratic education; democratic values; citizenship
democratic education, ix, xiv–xv, xviii, xxi, 10, 15, 17
  assaults on, 14
democratic values, 17
  abandonment of, 14, 17
Department of Justice, 108, 152n. 30

Dewey, John, 15
dialogue, 29, 30, 31, 32, 33, 34, 41, 43, 45, 50, 58, 67, 69, 106, 134
  and consensus, 29–30, 33
Donoghue, Frank, xx, 5–7, 27–8, 48–9
Dreifus, Claudia, 2, 6, 7, 29, 34–5, 36, 39, 40, 42
Duke University, 60

Eastern Washington University, 117
Eco, Umberto, 94
economic growth, 14, 15, 16, 17
economy, *see* debt economy; neoliberal economy
Economy of Prestige, The (English), 157n. 55
education (discipline), 23, 24
Education Conservancy, 150n. 1
education games, 30–1
elitism, 36, 49
Ellison, Ralph, 156n. 53
Emerson, Ralph Waldo, 116
English, James F., 157n. 55
entrepreneurial man, x, xi, xiii, xiv, 137n. 4
  see also indebted man
equality, 16, 17
European Reference Index for the Humanities (ERIH), 76–8, 80, 86
  see also European Science Foundation (ESF)
European Science Foundation (ESF), 76–7, 78–9, 81
  see also European Reference Index for the Humanities
Excellence in Research for Australia (ERA) Journal Lists, 78–80, 85
existential man, x–xi, 137n. 4
  see also indebted man
existentialism, 137n. 5

faint praise, 65–6, 67, 68, 86
  see also critical exchange; criticism

Faint Praise (Pool), 65, 116
Fanghanel, Joëlle, xvii
Faulkner, William, 107
fear, 45–7, 48–9, 50, 55
  of change, 50
  see also terror
Federman, Raymond, 63, 113
Fiction Collective Two, 110
Finnegan's Wake (Joyce), 94
Fish, Staley, 4, 60, 93–4, 148n. 9, 151nn. 9, 151n. 10
Fleming, Ian, 94
Florida, Richard, 20
Foucault, Michel, 58, 67–8, 95
funding, 9, 80, 81, 150n. 5, 162n. 14
  for humanities scholarship, 7
  and journal rank, 73, 80–1
  military, 7
  and publishing, 72, 73, 74
  research, 34
Frazier, Charles, 160n. 32
French Revolution, 51–2
Friedland, Jonathan, 159n. 28
Friedman, Milton, 109

Gallop, Jane, 90, 98, 99, 154n. 3, 155n. 39
genotext, 97
Georgia Institute of Technology, 116
Gettier, Edmund L. III, 162n. 13
Giroux, Henry, xii, xv, xvi, 109
Goodman, Nelson, 94
Guetti, James, 150n. 4

Habermas, Jürgen, 29, 30, 31
Hachette, 152n. 30
Hachette Livre UK, 99–100
Hacker, Andrew, 1–2, 6, 7, 29, 34–5, 36, 39, 40, 42
Haecceitas, 52
Hall, Stuart, xix
Hamlet (Shakespeare), 64
HarperCollins, 107, 152n. 30
Harper's, 126
Harry Ransom Center, 102

Index

Harvard Business School, 23
Harvard University, 18, 22, 27, 28, 35, 36, 49
Harvard University Press, 162n. 11
Hayek, Friedrich, 109
Heidegger, Martin, 67, 73
Higher Education? (Hacker & Dreifus), 1–2, 34
Higher Learning in America, The (Veblen), 89, 145n. 13
Hillis Miller, J., 156–7n. 54
history (discipline), 3, 7, 19, 21, 23, 133, 148n. 10
  see also Humanities One
Hjelmslev, Louis, 96
Hobbes, Thomas, 73
House of Cards (miniseries), 159n. 28, 162n. 15
Howard, Richard, 91, 154n. 17
Hughes, Langston, 116
humanism
  American, 6
  liberal, 17, 18
humanities
  comparative global, 15
  condition of, 3
  corporate, 24, 61, 86–7, 103, 118, 136
  crisis in, 11, 12, 17, 22, 24, 35
  critical, 10
  demise of, 6, 142n. 53
  discussion of problems facing, 3
  future of, 87, 142n. 53
  hegemony of, 11
  impact of September 11, 2001, attacks on, 5, 7
  within neoliberal university, 13–14
  value of, 12, 131
  see also Humanities One; Humanities Three; Humanities Two
Humanities and Creative Arts (HCA) Journal Lists, 78, 79–80
Humanities One, 18–19, 20, 21, 22, 23, 148n. 10
  see also Humanities Two; Humanities Three
Humanities Three, 22–3
  see also Humanities One; Humanities Two
Humanities Two, 18–20, 21, 22, 23, 141n. 37, 148n. 10
  see also Humanities One; Humanities Three
Hume, David, 64, 73
Husserl, Edmund, 157n. 54

Implied Reader, The (Iser), 93
In Cold Blood (Capote), 108
In Pursuit of Knowledge (Rhode), 89, 143n. 13
indebted man, x–xi, xiii, xiv, xv, 137n. 4
  see also entrepreneurial man; existential man
Indiana University, 162n. 13
Indiana University Bloomington, 162n. 14
industrialism, 40
Ingarden, Roman, 93
Inside Higher Ed, 2
interdisciplinarity, 35, 37–8
intertextuality, 97
iPad, 84
Iser, Wolfgang, 93

James, Henry, 156–7n. 54
Jameson, Fredric, 31–2, 41
Jealousy (Robbe-Grillet), 91
Jobs, Steve, 152n. 30, 153n. 31, 159n. 25
Johns Hopkins University Press, 153n. 32
Johnson, Phyllis, 90–1
Johnson, Richard, xix
Johnston, Deborah, 106
Journal des Scavans, 81
Journal of French Philosophy, 75, 78
Journal of Philosophy, 74–5, 151n. 8

journals, xix
  branding, 72, 75, 81–2, 85
  business, 72, 150n. 5
  electronic, 81
  philosophy, 73–5, 78;
    heterogeneity of, 73; ranking of, 74
  print vs. digital, 81–7, 152n. 27
  ranking, 72–82, 85–7, 90
  scholarly, 71
  see also individual journals
Joyce, James, 94, 106–8
Julliard, 9
Juneteenth (Ellison), 156n. 53

Kant, Immanuel, 39–40, 41, 64, 134, 149n. 16
Kaufman, Gershen, 145n. 4
Kennedy family, 111
Kindle, 82–3, 84, 152n. 30, 153n. 33
Kirp, David, 4
Kittler, Friedrich, 141n. 41
Klopfer, Donald, 107, 109
Kmart, 113
Knopf, 108
Knowledge Factory, The (Aronowitz), 27, 139n. 3
Kristeva, Julia, 96, 97
Kubler, George, 91

Lakoff, George, 47
Last Professors, The (Donoghue), 5, 27–8
Lazar, Glen, 151n. 9
Leiter Reports, 150n. 3, 150n. 6
Leonard, Andrew, 159n. 28
Letterman, Lynn, 91
Levy, Eugene, 117
Lewis, Sinclair, 107
liberal arts, ix, xviii, xxi, 7–9, 12, 15, 36, 39, 42, 54, 90, 146n. 26
  corporatization of, 12, 13, 54
  curriculum, 9, 12, 54
  distinctiveness of, 7, 9
  fall of, 48
  future of, 7
  model of education, 15
  vs. neoliberal arts, 7, 11, 12, 90
  value of, 12, 36
  see also liberal arts education
liberal arts education, 8, 15, 17
  careerism's impact on, 9
  decreasing value of, 9
  see also liberal arts
Library of Congress, 156n. 53
Lindenberger, Herbert S., 60
literary studies, 3, 60, 61, 65, 72, 79, 147n. 7, 148n. 10
  New Criticism's effect on, 93
Literary Work of Art, The (Ingarden), 93
literature, xix, 2, 19, 21, 91–3, 133, 136, 148n. 10
  corporate, 10, 11, 48, 54, 141n. 37
  curriculum, 10
  rise of prizes in, 157n. 55
  see also Humanities One
Literature as Conduct (Hillis Miller), 156n. 54
Little Brown, 99–100, 101, 102
Lost Soul of Higher Education, The (Schrecker), 33, 139n. 2
Lotman, Juri, 95
Louis Vuitton, 112
Louisiana State University, 117
Lyotard, Jean-François, 29–32, 41, 47, 58

MacGowan, Jack, 91
Macmillan, 152n. 30
Macy's, 113
Madwoman in the Attic, The, 123
managerialism, ix, x, 45, 47, 134
Manteia, 91
Mark Twain and His Circle Series, 115–16
market fundamentalism, 17, 109, 110, 113, 114

Marketplace of Ideas, The (Menand), 35
Mazza, Cris, 113
McDonald's, 112, 114
media studies, 19–20, 21, 22, 148n. 10
  see also Humanities Two
Memoires for Paul de Man (Derrida), 98
Menand, Louis, xx, 22, 29, 35–8, 39, 42, 49, 50, 62, 68, 123, 146n. 26
Merchants of Culture (Thompson), 157n. 1
Metaphysical Club, The (Menand), 35
Middlesex University, 146n. 25
militarization of higher education, 7
military funding, *see under* funding
Miller, Toby, 18–25, 141n. 41, 142, n. 52, 142n. 53, 148n. 10
Missouri Biography Series, 115
Missouri Heritage Readers Series, 115
MLA Handbook, 62, 148n. 13
  see also Modern Language Association (MLA)
Modern Language Association (MLA), 3, 126, 150n. 2
  see also MLA Handbook
Moral Collapse of the University, The (Wilshire), 4
Moraru, Christian, 150n. 4
Murdoch, James, 159n. 25
Murdoch, Rupert, 107, 109, 159n. 25

Nabokov, Dmitri, 156n. 52
Nabokov, Vladimir, 101, 156n. 52
Nadell, Bonnie, 100
National Academies, 116
National Teaching Academy, 41
negative dialogics, 29, 32, 35
  see also positive dialogics
Nelson, Cary, 3, 29, 32–5, 39, 40, 42, 68, 124, 139n. 2

neoliberal academic, *see* neoliberal subjects
neoliberal economy, x
neoliberal subjects, ix, x, xiii, xv, xvii, xviii, 3, 45, 50, 58, 69, 133, 134, 137n. 1, 140n. 7, 147n. 1
neoliberal university, xiii, xv, 2, 10, 27, 28–9, 46, 50, 57, 61, 131, 140n. 1
  academic identity in, 28
  culture of, 50
  fall of, 42, 43
  humanities within, 13–14
  life in, 45
  publication and, 131
  rise of, 45
  study of, 27
  vocational training centers as telos of, ix
  see also corporate university
Netflix, 159n. 28, 162n. 15
New America Foundation, 27, 139n. 3
New Criticism, 93
  effects on literary studies, 93
New Republic, The, 42
New York Times, The, 2, 42, 82, 126, 153n. 33
Newhouse, S. I., 108
News Corporation, 107, 159n. 25
News International, 159n. 25
News of the World, 159n. 25
Nietzsche, Friedrich, 74
9/11 attacks, *see* September 11, 2001, attacks
Nixon, Rob, 147n. 29
No University Is an Island (Nelson), 32–3, 139n. 2
Not for Profit (Nussbaum), 14, 17
nursing, 2, 23
Nussbaum, Martha, xx, 14–18, 19, 22, 24–5, 57, 140n. 7, 147n. 1

O'Doherty, Brian, 91
O'Hara, John, 107

Ohio State University, 5
Online Journal of Current Clinical Trials, 81
Open Humanities Press, 162–3n. 17
Original of Laura, The (Nabokov, V.), 101

Pale King, The (Wallace), 99–103
Palumbo-Liu, David, 150n. 4
Pantheon, 108
paralogy, 29–31, 35, 38, 50
Parliament (British), 159n. 25
pedagogy, 10–12, 13
  corporate, 7–12
  critical, 10–11
  philosophy, 140n. 18, 141n. 37
Peden, William, 115
Peirce, Charles, 63, 73, 74
  studies, 74, 78
Penguin, 108, 110, 152n. 30, 158n. 20, 160n. 35
performance, xii, 45, 71
  measurement of, ix, xv, xvii, 10, 134
phenotext, 97
philosophy, 2, 3, 4, 7, 9, 10, 11, 19, 54, 61, 72, 74, 127, 133, 136, 146n. 25, 148n. 10
  American, 73
  analytic, 75
  critical, 64
  curriculum, 11
  journals, 73–5, 78; ranking of, 74
  pedagogy, 140n. 18, 141n. 37
  reflection on, 52
  see also Humanities One; *individual movements and philosophers*
phobos, 48
Pietsch, Michael, 99, 100–101, 102
Plato, 54
  academy of, 42
  on death of Socrates, 138n. 14
Pleasure of the Text, The (Barthes), 98

poetry, 7
Pool, Gail, 65, 68, 116
positive dialogics, 29
  see also negative dialogics
Postmodern Condition, The (Lyotard), 29
postmodern university, 29, 34, 39, 43, 46, 50, 103
postmodernism, 29
poststructuralism, 90
Pragmatism, American, 6
presses
  large, 105
  small, xix, 105, 109, 110, 111, 149n. 15
  university, xix, 115–18, 161n. 11; impact on academic culture, 115
  see also individual presses
prestige, 18, 30, 71, 75, 89–90, 92, 121, 131, 133, 141n. 30, 145n. 13, 151n. 9, 157n. 55
  of the author, 92, 97–103, 154n. 20
  flawed logic of, 36, 49, 145n. 13
  and journals, 74, 75, 90
  and a university's value, 89
  see also status
Professional Correctness (Fish), 4
Project MUSE, 153n. 32
Project on Student Debt, 139n. 12
Prolegomena (Kant), 149n. 16
Proulx, E. Annie, 82–3
public goods, 16, 17
publishing, 105, 106, 107, 109–11, 114, 115, 118–19, 124, 125–6, 135, 136, 161n. 11
  academic, xix, 4, 115, 116, 118–19, 123, 125, 127, 129, 131, 162–3n. 17; new media and, 128; new models of, 117; sustainable model of, 123, 127, 129
  corporate vs. small press, 110–11, 115
  environmentally responsible, 72, 85, 128–31

and funding, 72, 73, 74
market vs. aesthetics values, 110–11
and neoliberalism, 105, 106, 109, 157n. 55, 157n. 1
print vs. digital, 81–7, 105, 126, 128–31
programs, 54
semiotics of, 84
sustainable model of, 124, 125, 127, 128–31
see also Journals; Presses

Queens College, 1

Random House, 106, 107–8, 109, 110–12, 113, 156n. 3, 158n. 8, 158n. 20, 160n. 35
ranking, 30, 45, 71–87, 134, 148n. 8, 150nn. 1–3, 151n. 9, 151n. 11
and assessment, 71
fever, 71, 75
of journals, 72–82, 85–7, 90, 150n. 3, 150n. 6, 153n. 34
Rawls, John, 18
RCA, 108, 109, 113
Readings, Bill, 4, 27
Rhetoric (Aristotle), 48
Rhode, Deborah, 89, 121–2, 146n. 13
Ricardo, David, 109
Rice University, 117
Rippeteau, Erika Kuebler, 128
Rise of the Creative Class, The (Florida), 20
Roaring Fork Press, 91
Robbe-Grillet, Alain, 91
Romano, Carlin, 67–8
Rorty, Richard, 94
Russell, Bertrand, 73

Saad-Filho, Alfredo, 106
Salon, 159n. 28
Sartre, Jean-Paul, 137n. 5
Saussure, Ferdinand de, 63, 95, 96
scholarly community, 62–4, 65, 124
normative behavior in, 61, 62–5
value of, 122
scholarship, 45, 46, 63, 74, 76, 78, 80, 89, 121–31, 136
corporate, 2–7
digital distribution and, 123, 128–9
humanities, funding for, 7
humanities, material conditions of, 72
impact of, 125, 126–7, 129, 130, 131, 161n. 14
increased emphasis on, 121
metaprofessional, 3
online vs. printed, 81, 85, 86, 128–30
philosophy, 75
for scholarship's sake, 129
traditional, 125
Schrecker, Ellen, 29, 32, 33–5, 39, 42, 139n. 2
sciences, 15, 20, 41, 72, 87, 150n. 5
Scott, Ridley, 11
Scotus, Duns, 52
Second Sex, The (Beauvoir), 11, 140n. 18
semiotics, 142n. 52
Sense of the Past, The (James), 156–7n. 54
September 11, 2001, attacks, 46, 51, 52–3, 55, 146n. 15
impact on humanities, 5, 7
see also terrorism
Shakespeare & Co., 107
Shakespeare, Einstein, and the Bottom Line (Kirp), 4
shame, 145n. 4
shared governance, 1, 33, 34, 45, 47, 48, 55
Simon & Schuster, 107, 152n. 30
Smith, Adam, 109
Snow, C. P., 18
social justice, xiv–xv, 10, 130
Society of Scholarly Publishing, 128

Socrates, xiv, 61
  death of, 138n. 14
Sontag, Susan, 91
Southern Methodist University, 117
Southern Women Series, 116
Specters of Marx (Derrida), 98
Spinoza, Baruch, 63, 135
Stanford University, 60, 89
status, 89–90, 121, 131, 133
  see also prestige
Stein, Gertrude, 107
Stuckey-French, Ned, 116
students, xiv, 1, 10–11, 15, 19, 20, 22, 23, 37, 45–6, 49, 57, 68, 71, 147n. 7
  as active producers of knowledge, 10–11
  as credit hours, xii
  as customers, xvi
  debt of, xi–xii, xiv, xv, 7, 28, 46, 137n. 10, 138n. 15, 139n. 12
  and instructors as collaborators, 11
  vocational aspirations of, 9–10
Subotnik, Dan, 151n. 9
sympathy, 16
symplokē, 63, 72, 79–80, 81–2, 128, 150n. 4, 152n. 32, 153n. 34

Tagore, Rabindranath, 15, 16
target, 112
Taylor, Mark, 29, 38–41, 42, 43, 50, 139n. 8
Taylor, Richard, 100
Tel Quel, 96
Tel Quel group, 96
tenure, 4, 6, 12, 31, 33, 34, 41–2, 43, 129, 131, 144n. 69
  abolishment of, 40, 144n. 69
  book as gold standard for, 162n. 11
  committees, 127, 128, 129
  fate of, 3
  requirements, 123
  value of, 34

terror, 30–1, 46–9, 50, 51, 52, 53–4, 55, 143n. 13
  see also fear
Terror of Neoliberalism, The (Giroux), xv
terrorism, 46, 51, 53, 54, 56, 143n. 13, 146n. 15
  academic, 46, 53, 54–5, 143n. 13, 147n. 29
  classroom, 54
  and coercion, 54–5
  concept of, 51, 52–3, 55
  definition of, 53
  elements of, 54
  neoliberal, 55
  political, 46
  reconceptualization of, 52
  religious, 145n. 5
  and violence, 53, 54–5, 147n. 29
  see also September 11, 2001, attacks
text, 92–7, 98, 102, 155n. 24
  and authorial intent, 93, 96, 101
  birth of, 92–3
  closed, 94
  as écriture, 96
  identity of, 94–5
  open, 94
  as process, 96
  and productivity, 97
  vs. work, 96–7
  world itself as, 95
  see also genotext; phenotext
Thacker, Lloyd, 150n. 1
Thelma and Louise (film), 11, 140n. 18
Thirteen Moons (Frazier), 160n. 32
Thompson, John B., 157n. 1, 162n. 11
Three Days Before the Shooting . . . (Ellison), 156n. 53
Tiffany's, 112
Time-Life, 108
Tompkins, Jane, 60

Index

Transactions of the Charles S. Peirce Society, 73–4, 78
Trouble with Principle, The (Fish), 148n. 9
Twitter, 125, 126, 131

Ulysses (Joyce), 106–8, 158n. 4
Union Theological Seminary, 39
United States National Research Council, 151n. 11
Université de Montréal, 4
Universities in the Marketplace (Bok), 4, 27
University, Inc. (Washburn), 27, 139n. 3
University in Ruins, The (Readings), 4, 27
University of California, Riverside, 19
University of California Press, 117, 118
University of Chicago, 18, 19, 22, 23, 141n. 32
University of Illinois at Urbana-Champaign, 32, 139n. 2
University of Missouri, 116–17
University of Missouri Press, 115–19, 160n. 49
University of Nebraska, 116
University of Nebraska Press, 128
University of Nevada, Las Vegas, 146n. 25
University of Scranton, 117
University of Texas, 102
US News and World Report, 150n. 1, 151n. 11

Veblen, Thorstein, 89, 103, 145n. 13
Velvet Underground, 91
Virginia Tech massacre, 51
vocational training, ix, xviii, xix, 1, 2, 21, 39, 57
vocationalism, 34, 39

Waldenbooks, 113, 114
Wallace, David Foster, 99–103, 156n. 53, 157n. 54
Walmart, 111, 112
Warhol, Andy, 91
Washburn, Jennifer, 27, 139n. 3
Waters, Lindsay, 162n. 11
We Scholars (Damrosch), 4
Wellman, Carl, 53–5
Williams, Jeffrey J., 135n. 7, 135n. 10, 150n. 4
Williams College, 9, 39
Wilshire, Bruce, 4
Wimsatt, W. K., 93
Wolff, Nelson, 153n. 31
women's studies, 38, 115
Women's Wear Daily, 90
Woolf, Virginia, 62–3
Woolsey, John, 107
Work of Mourning, The (Derrida), 98
World War II, 52

Yale University, 22, 49
Yankelovich, Daniel, 8
Yeshiva University, 32, 139n. 2

Ziarek, Ewa, 150n. 4

GPSR Compliance

The European Union's (EU) General Product Safety Regulation (GPSR) is a set of rules that requires consumer products to be safe and our obligations to ensure this.

If you have any concerns about our products, you can contact us on

ProductSafety@springernature.com

In case Publisher is established outside the EU, the EU authorized representative is:

Springer Nature Customer Service Center GmbH
Europaplatz 3
69115 Heidelberg, Germany

www.ingramcontent.com/pod-product-compliance
Lightning Source LLC
LaVergne TN
LVHW051912060526
838200LV00004B/106